A SIMPLE COUNTRY BOY.
BUT WAS HE?

Only in America could an 18-year-old truck driver with a funny sounding name become a worldwide singing sensation, selling millions of records and performing to sold-out crowds wherever he went. On stage Elvis was a man of astounding talent. Abandoning himself to his music and gyrating wildly to its primal beat, he gave everything to his audiences. But what about the private Elvis? What was he like?

In **ELVIS: PORTRAIT OF A FRIEND**, Marty and Patsy Lacker reveal the things that made Elvis' life so exciting and, sometimes, so sad:

- The adoring fans who wanted just a moment with their idol
- The Cadillacs, motorcycles, furs and jewelry he showered on his friends to reward their loyalty
- The wife who divorced him when the pressures of super-stardom began to destroy their marriage
- The doctors who thought they were helping him by prescribing diet pills, sleeping pills and pep-pills to relieve the strain of his fantastic success

Here is the story of Elvis' real life, away from the spotlights and the fame, told by two people who knew and loved the real Elvis.

ABOUT THE AUTHORS

MARTY LACKER was born and raised in New York City. He moved to Memphis in 1952 where he attended Humes High School. After high school, he entered the Army and was stationed in Germany. In 1957, he returned to Memphis where he renewed his acquaintance with Elvis Presley. For several years, Mr. Lacker worked in radio. While living in Knoxville, he met and married PATSY LACKER. They returned to Memphis and in 1961, Marty began working for Elvis fulltime. Marty worked for Elvis from 1961 to 1968 and handled special projects for him until 1977.

LESLIE S. SMITH began his literary career as a war correspondent for *Leatherneck Magazine* during the Korean Conflict. After leaving the Marine Corps, he attended Columbia University in New York City and pursued his interest in writing. Mr. Smith later founded two national magazines in the pet field and one in general aviation and spent many years as editor and publisher of these periodicals.

ELVIS
Portrait of a Friend

by
Marty Lacker, Patsy Lacker
and
Leslie S. Smith

This low-priced Bantam Book has been completely reset in a type face designed for easy reading, and was printed from new plates. It contains the complete text of the original hard-cover edition.
NOT ONE WORD HAS BEEN OMITTED.

ELVIS: PORTRAIT OF A FRIEND
A Bantam Book / published by arrangement with Wimmer Brothers, Inc.

PRINTING HISTORY
Wimmer Brothers edition published June 1979
3 printings through September 1979
Wimmer Brothers deluxe edition published June 1979
Serialized in Ladies Home Journal, *May, 1978 issue; and* Midnight Globe, *August 14, 1979 and August 21, 1979 issues*
Bantam edition / August 1980

Photographs are from author's private collection, Billy and Jo Smith, Mary and Donna Lewis, Sonny and Judy West, Dorise Bearden, Tom Loomis and William N. "Bill" Morris, Jr.

ISBN 0-553-13824-3

Published simultaneously in the United States and Canada

Bantam Books are published by Bantam Books, Inc. Its trademark, consisting of the words "Bantam Books" and the portrayal of a bantam, is Registered in U.S. Patent and Trademark Office and in other countries. Marca Registrada. Bantam Books, Inc., 666 Fifth Avenue, New York, New York 10103.

PRINTED IN THE UNITED STATES OF AMERICA

0 9 8 7 6 5 4 3 2 1

Dedication

To Rose, Henry, Sheri, Marc and Angie Lacker and John Daniels, for their love.
To the guys, for their memories.
And to Crazy, for being.

Marty and Patsy

To all who suffered the pain of reality throughout this soul searching venture.

LSS

Contents

PART THREE View From The Outside

Foreword

Memphis is an interesting city. I was never there in the days of Beale Street fame, but I wish I had been because even the ruins of the once-famous street are exciting. The music of the old-timers can be felt when walking past the deserted buildings. A young boy, dressed too loud for the times and with hair a little too long, can be seen gazing into the window of Lansky Brothers clothing store. The pink shirts and black pants come alive to the sounds which find their way from the now silent pianos hidden behind the boarded doors.

Beale Street is dead, and Elvis Presley is dead. History races forward and replaces the sounds of one era with those of another, but the memories remain. The spirit of the people remains, and the sounds which they created will be a part of our musical heritage for as long as there are those who care.

Prior to arranging to collaborate with Marty Lacker on this book I knew very little about Beale Street, or Elvis Presley. I was never an Elvis fan. His thing was not mine. My part of the project was to organize and arrange the thoughts, and to place properly the periods, commas and question marks.

It was Marty's story and for all I cared the subject could have been the making of cement blocks; but, as the work progressed, I began to see the necessity of learning more about Elvis. When Marty talked I understood the words, but I didn't understand their real meaning. There were also little things which bothered me when we talked, things which were too vague to try to pinpoint and question, but which, nevertheless, seemed to keep the project from coming together in an orderly fashion. I knew that failure would be the end result if I did not become actively involved.

Research was necessary, and it led to months of reading books, magazine articles and newspaper reports about Elvis, watching his motion pictures, listening to his music, watching video tapes of his performances and talking with those who knew Elvis Presley.

The more I learned the more I found I needed to know; and the more I came to know the more certain *facts* failed to make any sense. The former bodyguards, Red West, Sonny West and Dave Hebler, co-authors of *Elvis, What Happened,* described Presley as being so addicted to drugs that restraint in a rehabilitation center was the only solution.

Becky Yancey, co-author of *My Life With Elvis,* said on national television that Elvis did not use drugs. She also said she was Elvis' private secretary and talked about how close she was to him. Ed Parker, author of another book about Elvis, was touted by one of the national weekly newspapers as being Elvis' best friend for sixteen years. He is quoted as having denied the drug reports.

There were wild stories about strange diseases, reports of foul play and talk of Elvis being alive and in seclusion on some distant island. The Shelby County Tennessee Medical Examiner issued a press release which said Elvis' death was not due to drugs, but the newspapers reported that the Chief Pathologist at Baptist Memorial Hospital said the death was drug-related.

There were many versions of the truth but, fortunately, at least some facts were easy to check. There was, for example, no doubt that Red West had worked for Elvis and was close to him from the beginning of Elvis' career. Sonny West had also been close to Elvis for years, and Dave Hebler was what he claimed to be. However, they had all been fired only months before work began on their book and some of the extremes contained therein could be attributed to resentment, or a desire to sell a sensational book about a famous man who was no longer a friend.

Becky Yancey was far from being a private secretary. She worked for Elvis' father in an office on the Graceland estate. Her salary, of course, came from Elvis' earnings and since a book by a private secretary is surely going to sell more copies than one by an office worker, she can be forgiven the stretching of the truth. The fact is, however, she had little way of knowing if Elvis was popping pills or eating chocolate ice cream.

Ed Parker was a karate instructor who began working for Elvis as a sometimes bodyguard after the firing of Red, Sonny and Dave. Parker, who is not to be confused with Elvis' manager, Colonel Tom Parker, had known Elvis for some years, but certainly had no claim to the title of *best friend,* a title which rightfully belonged to George Klein if one doesn't count any of the group of men who worked for Elvis. If, however, they are included, then there is little doubt that Billy Smith was Elvis' best friend as well as being his cousin and trusted companion. After Billy, came a whole list of the men who were close to Elvis, including Marty Lacker who was close enough to be Elvis' best man at his wedding.

Jerry Schilling, a close friend and associate of Elvis, tells a story about being approached by a reporter during a recent visit to Las Vegas. The reporter said, "Mr. Schilling, I understand you were Elvis' best friend."

"No," Jerry replied, "I was second best, but I tried harder."

The point is simply that being touted as *best friend* may help to sell books or newspapers, but it does not put the author in a position to know the truth, if the claim is mere advertising propaganda.

If the truth was the truth as told by Red, Sonny and Dave, then why didn't they do something about it before tragedy occurred? If they couldn't do anything, then why didn't Elvis' father or Colonel Tom Parker or Doctor George Nichopoulos, Elvis' personal physician and close friend, do something before it was too late? What about all the other friends and associates? Was no one concerned? If there were drugs, how were they acquired?

None of it made a lot of sense at the beginning, and even after the tentative completion of Marty's manuscript, I realized there were still many unanswered questions. The picture was not finished. The missing pieces had to be found to, quite frankly, make this book a commercial success, but also to make it something more valuable than just a portrait of a friend.

Marty and I decided to include the views of Patsy Lacker, Marty's wife, as well as information gathered during days of discussions with friends, relatives and associates of Elvis Presley.

There are those whose absence is conspicuous. Some we were not able to reach and others, for their own reasons, decided not to participate. The two women who were closest to Elvis, Priscilla Presley and Linda Thompson, both felt they did not want to say anything for publication in the book. Priscilla said it was because she was involved in contracts for a television special about Elvis, and Linda said she was simply tired of talking about him.

Joe Esposito felt he may someday want to write about Elvis and, therefore, he didn't think it would be wise to have anything published at this time. Charlie Hodge told Marty he would be willing to meet with me, but when I called for an appointment he told me I would have to call his business manager. Charlie's business manager is Dick Grob, a former Elvis employee, and Dick had told Marty he did not want to say anything.

To all of those who did agree to discuss their relationship with Elvis we are indebted. Their cooperation has helped remove many of the feelings of uncertainty which surrounded the life and death of Elvis Presley. Each had his or her own story to tell and each expressed a view of Elvis which was his alone. All contributed to this book.

Marty Lacker is an honest man. There is not a single doubt in my mind that everything he has told is absolute truth, but Marty is also a compassionate man who feels strongly about his friends and the memory of Elvis. His truth is often a gentle truth which reflects concern over the feelings and reputations of those with whom he lived and worked for so many years.

Patsy Lacker has been married to Marty for twenty years. She has lived through the good and the bad times. Sometimes bitter, sometimes sad, Patsy tells a story of unhappiness in the midst of wealth and glamour, but she also tells a story of love for her husband and for their friend, Elvis Presley.

I have learned a lot from this project. I've met many people who were associated with Elvis, and I've liked most of those I've come to know. I've laughed with them at the funny stories and been sad about those which were unhappy. I have not become an Elvis *fan* but I've grown to understand something about the man, and I've seen a little of what the true fan has seen for years.

Being an outsider has its advantages as well as its disadvantages. It is necessary to work to learn what others already know, but an outsider is not impaired with emotional ties which often cause others to avoid following a path when it begins to lead into a painful area. And there were painful areas. Elvis Presley was an uncommonly talented young man who brought many hours of joy to millions of people. That he died at an early age is a tragedy.

I have no reason, or desire, to praise or condemn Elvis Presley or any of the people who were a part of his life. My task, in fact, would have been easier had it been possible to simply write a book glorifying Elvis and categorically denying all reports which may make him less than superhuman to his fans. The truth, however, is the only thing of value with which we have to work. The seeking of the truth has brought to light many facts which may help to better understand those dangers which confront us all, and which may ultimately lead to an accounting for the death of Elvis Presley. The cards were dealt long before I came on the scene, my place is to report how they were played.

LESLIE S. SMITH

PART ONE

Portrait of a Friend

Marty Lacker

Chapter One

The Early Years

When we moved to Memphis in 1952, I wasn't too pleased with the idea of living in what I thought would be a small Southern town. New York was home and, for a fifteen-year-old boy, this was a big change. Economics, however, dictated the move and, if I remember correctly, my opinion wasn't considered anyway.

Once there, I soon grew to accept the city and have, over the years, come to consider Memphis as my home. It has changed since 1952, but then all places have. In those days it had a charm which was centered in its black music culture. Now, it's more an electronic culture than the down-home type which gave birth to so much of today's good music and to Elvis Presley.

Elvis and I first met at Humes High School. We were never what I would consider good friends, in those days, but we had something in common which made us as close to each other as either of us was to anyone else. The main thing that drew us together was our distinctive clothing. My habits and most of my clothes came with me from New York and I'm sure I looked like an outsider. Elvis dressed in mod clothing which was bought in Memphis but looked more New York than Memphis.

Sometimes the other guys would kid us about our dress but, contrary to many reports, it wasn't a big thing. The most I remember was the kids occasionally asking, "Hey, are you going to outdo Presley tomorrow?" I guess they said the same thing to him about me.

As time went by, George Klein, Red West and I became fairly close. Red and I played football, which was a big thing in the South, and George was involved in school politics. Red and I played for Humes and we often saw Elvis at games. He was always alone and usually just walking around the stands. Elvis was a loner and a dreamer, but, to my knowledge, his dreams never revolved around music. As with most of us, they were probably the dreams of poor boys who somehow knew their dreams were not likely to come true.

For a short time, Elvis worked for a tool company in Memphis but the job ended when he got into a fight with his foreman. Elvis has said the fight began over the length of his hair. From there he went to work for Crown Electric, driving a truck. In later years, he often spoke of those days and of being fairly certain he would become an electrician.

While Elvis was still in school he often sang and played the guitar at school activities and at parties in friends' homes, but it never seemed as though music was his entire life. It appeared that he liked to perform, when asked, but he never pushed himself or his music. If anything, he was somewhat shy. Most of the music he did in those days was country, gospel or blues.

The steps to success, for Elvis, took a soaring leap one night in July, 1954, when Dewey Phillips, Memphis' best-known disc jockey, played a record called, *That's All Right Mama*. The recording was an instant success. I was listening to the car radio while driving down Vollentine Street and heard Dewey predict that Elvis would be a star.

While working for Crown Electric, Elvis had begun his own career by paying four dollars to make a record as a gift for his mother. There were, however, others who helped. Elvis possibly would have become an electrician had it not been for Sam Phillips, who owned Sun Records, and especially for Marion Keisker who worked for Sam and recognized the talent of this unusual young man. Elvis never forgot her as long as he lived.

Elvis and I had gone our separate ways. We were out of school and I was working in a new shopping center in Memphis; this was several months after the night *That's All Right Mama* was first played. I saw Elvis again when he entertained at the grand opening of the center. He was sensational.

Two months later I went into the army and shortly thereafter was sent to Germany. While I was there, Elvis became a star, as Dewey Phillips had predicted.

During the following years of our association, Elvis would often spend hours talking about the early days, the days when he worked for Crown and performed at night. The four-dollar record began the career, but it was a tough beginning. He was scared to death when he went into Sun to make the recording. Marion Keisker, who was in the office alone that day, asked him who he sounded like and he told her "I don't sound like nobody," more because he couldn't think of anything else to say than because it was true. He had a number of idols in those days and tried to sing like several of them.

Marion, as we all know, was impressed and made a tape of part of the first side of the recording, *My Happiness,* and all of the second side, *That's When Your Heartaches Begin.* She has said she did this because Sam often talked about wanting to find a white singer who had the sound of a black, and she thought Elvis did.

Sam Phillips, a trim, good-looking man, was known as one of the pioneers in recording black music. His background and early years were immersed in country and black music. To this day, his musical preference is the same. His recording studio and production company are now operated by his oldest son, Knox, but Sam still keeps an eye on the business. In addition, he also owns and operates some radio stations in the south. It is a pleasure talking to this distinguished gentleman who is capable of giving a complete history lesson of music along with some definite ideas for the present and future of the industry.

When Sam first heard the tape recorded by Elvis back in the fifties, it seems he liked what he heard but not enough to contact Elvis, and it was several months before they actually met. One day Elvis returned to the studio to cut a second four-dollar record and Sam was there. He and Elvis talked some and Elvis recorded *Casual Love* and *I'll Never Stand in Your Way*. Sam was impressed, Marion has said, but according to Elvis, he didn't show it. "There was some talk about trying to arrange work but he didn't really encourage me."

"I'd hang around the radio station a lot in those days and watch the gospel groups. I really liked the Blackwood Brothers and sang with them sometimes," Elvis said. "I almost got a real job with them once when one of the guys was going to leave, but he changed his mind."

The Blackwood Brothers Quartet had, for years, been a favorite of the entire Presley family, particularly Elvis' mother, Gladys. When she died, the Blackwood Brothers were asked to sing at her funeral. The Quartet still makes its home in Memphis.

Elvis told us that even without Sam Phillips' encouragement, he was sure, at the time, that he would be a singer but he wasn't sure he would be able to make a living at it, so he continued to work for Crown. He liked driving the old Ford truck, but music was the thing, and he sang wherever and whenever he could.

About eight months after Elvis cut the first record at Sun, Marion says she reminded Sam of the "young man with the long hair" when he was trying to think of someone to record a song he thought was good. With Sam's approval she called Elvis, and, according to Elvis, he ran all the way to the studio. "I was so excited. I could hardly believe they really wanted me. Nervous, God! I don't know how we managed to record anything that day."

In fact, they didn't record much that day. The one record they made, *Without You,* which was the one Sam wanted to record, was awful. Elvis tried some other songs but none were very good. Sam, however, still thought Elvis had talent, but he needed to find the right style and he needed one hell of a lot of help.

Elvis has often said, "The day was a complete wreck. I couldn't do anything right. Probably because I kept trying to do what I thought they wanted and not what I wanted."

Sam and Marion liked Elvis, he was very polite and he did have an air of excitement about him. "He was never still for a moment," they have said. "Just full of life. You almost knew he had to do something."

Sam arranged a meeting between Elvis and Scotty Moore who was then a young, enthusiastic boy who played the guitar with a local group. Elvis, Scotty and Bill Black, who played bass, began rehearsing almost everyday after work. They would meet at Sun and try to sing and play all the songs they had ever heard, but it was months before Sam made a recording. They were trying to find a style but it just didn't come off. When Sam finally did begin to record they were at best fair, certainly not good.

They were taking a break when, as Elvis said, "We started clowning around. I was banging on my guitar and singing *That's All Right Mama,* just goofing around. Bill was doing the same thing with his bass and Scotty started on his guitar. We were jumping around, acting like a bunch of kids and just having a good time, Sam ran in and said we should do it again. We thought he was crazy."

Sam was anything but crazy. He had heard the real Elvis Presley sound and that was what he was looking for. They spent several days trying to find the right song for the flip side and finally settled on *Blue Moon of Kentucky*. It, too, got the Elvis treatment but it was more a country song than the blues rhythm of *That's All Right Mama.*

When they listened to the record they were all excited by the sound and Sam took it to Dewey Phillips at WHBQ radio station. Dewey was Memphis' best-known disc jockey. His show, *Red Hot and Blue,* concentrated on blues music by black artists. He was what is known as a personality disc jockey, saying very loudly any crazy thing that came into his head. Although he and Sam Phillips were not related, they had black, or what was then called "race," music in common. Sam made the records and Dewey played them. A typical Deweyism was one he used the night he played Elvis' record for the first time, "Get ya a wheel barrow full of goober dust, run it through the front door of Poplar Tunes Record Shop and tell Papa Joe Joe Coughi 'Daddy, Ol' Dewey sent me from *Red Hot and Blue!*' " Dewey was a personality all right. For years before he died, Dewey would call everybody associated wth Elvis by the name of Elvis.

When he played Elvis' *That's All Right Mama* the phone began to ring and did not stop for the rest of the show. Dewey played the record many times that night because people kept wanting to hear it again and again. He called the Presleys to get Elvis down to the studio for an interview. Elvis was at the movies. He told us, "I wasn't going to stay home and have to listen to people on the radio laughing at me. No sir, I was nervous enough about the whole thing. I figured Mama would tell me about it later and I'd rather hear it from her than the radio."

His mother went to the theater and told Elvis to go down to see Mr. Phillips who wanted an interview. Elvis told us, "I ran all the way. Man, was I excited. When I got there we just talked some. I didn't know we were on the air because I saw some records going and I thought he would start the interview later. After a few minutes' talk he said, 'Okay, Elvis. Thanks.' I said, 'When do you want to do the interview?' and he said, 'We just did.' Boy, at least it was painless."

The record sold about seven thousand copies and was number three on the Memphis country charts for some time. Elvis made some money from it but he continued to work for Crown until his nightly performances made it impossible for him to hold a full-time day job.

Sam arranged bookings on *The Grand Ole Opry* and *Louisiana Hayride* on the strength of the record's success, but the *Opry* didn't go well. Elvis sang *That's All Right Mama* and *Blue Moon of Kentucky*, with Scotty and Bill. Elvis said, "When we finished singing, Denny, he was head of the talent office, told me he thought I should try driving a truck again. I was so upset all the way back to Memphis that night. Denny later said he knew from the first I would be a star."

The *Louisiana Hayride* booking was a success. Elvis said, "It went right. Everything about it went right. We did the same songs and everybody loved them. They asked us to come back on the show and we later got a contract to be on every week for a year."

It was during the first show at the *Hayride* that Elvis met D.J. Fontana who soon joined Elvis' group as drummer. Elvis, Scotty and Bill continued to do as many shows as they could book. Some were great but others didn't go over at all. Mostly the failures were when they played to an older audience or when Elvis would do nothing but country ballads. When he let himself go with his own style and there were younger people in the audience it was always a madhouse. They loved him and never failed to let him know with their reactions. Elvis has said that Scotty was a great influence on him in those days. He helped create the Elvis Presley style.

Scotty, in fact, was Elvis' manager for a short time before they met Bob Neal.

Bob Neal was a disc jockey on WMPS in Memphis, with a country music show. He and Elvis had known each other for several years and they seemed to fit together well at the time. By then Elvis had recorded *Good Rockin' Tonight* and *I Don't Care if the Sun Don't Shine* for Sun. The record didn't do as well as his first but it received good comments in *Billboard*, which was worth a lot even then.

When Bob Neal became their manager he changed the name of the group, which by this time included D.J. Fontana, to the *Blue Moon Boys*. They began to do more and more shows and they had a good following on the radio stations. The shows were just about always within driving distance of Memphis in what was called the schoolhouse circuit because they performed in small country schoolhouses. Very little advertising was ever done but they would pack the places and the audiences grew more and more excited about the show. Elvis was well on his way to success.

With success, however limited, came the third record, *Milkcow Blues Boogie* and *You're a Heartbreaker,* and more distance between gigs. The boys would drive everywhere; Texas, Tennessee, Mississippi, wherever they could get a spot between the weekly trips to the *Hayride*. They would perform, get in the car and start driving again and sleep when they could. Elvis said, "It was wild, man, but it was fun. Bill, Scotty and D.J. would get real upset with me because I wanted to stop at every road-side fruit stand and load-up the car. Sometimes I would stay at the stands a little longer than I should and then be late for the next show. There were times they threatened to take me to the nearest airport to catch a plane to the next show. We could go on and on without even thinking about a real night's sleep. Drive and perform, drive and perform and drive some more. It was wild."

A few years later, on one of those driving occasions, Elvis did rent a small private plane in order to make a show in Oklahoma. It was foggy and the plane lost its power in mid-air while attempting to make an emergency landing. The landing gear wouldn't go down because of the power failure and the manual handle was frozen. Elvis had to work to free the manual handle while the pilot looked for a place to land.

It scared the hell out of Elvis and caused him to stay away from flying for years.

An earlier near-disaster occurred once when the group was driving to a show date and they smelled something burning; they threw the instruments out of the car and then jumped after them only seconds before the car went up in flames.

Yes, it was wild. And Elvis' lifestyle was to become even wilder with the appearance of the Colonel.

Many people have said that Colonel Tom Parker and Elvis Presley were made for each other and I believe that's true. I'm sure Elvis would have become a superstar without the Colonel, he just had it in him, but would not have done it as fast, and he may never have become as big, and he probably wouldn't have earned as much money had they not joined forces. I didn't know the Colonel then, of course, but I have often heard Elvis talk of the days when they began.

Colonel Parker is probably one of the greatest promoters in show business. He had years of experience, prior to meeting Elvis, as the manager of Eddy Arnold, Hank Snow and Gene Austin, three of the nation's top country singers. He had grown up in a traveling carnival and show business was his life. His association with Elvis began when he helped Bob Neal organize a show for Elvis in New Mexico in 1955.

After the New Mexico show, Elvis and the group toured with Hank Snow through the Southwestern states and then made a trip to Cleveland with Bob Neal for a gig at the Circle Theater. Things were going well. *Billboard* wrote that Elvis was "the hottest thing today."

When, however, they traveled to the big city, New York, to audition for Arthur Godfrey's *Talent Scouts* they met rejection. It was Elvis' first airplane ride and his first trip to New York but it all went sour when the *Talent Scouts* turned him down. Elvis often said to us, "I didn't like New York and they didn't like me. The whole thing was a bad scene. Sure, I was unhappy when they turned me down, but it didn't bother me nearly as much as the *Opry* thing did. Maybe I was just a little older."

Shortly thereafter Sun released another Elvis record, *Baby Let's Play House* and *I'm Left, You're Right, She's*

Gone. These received good ratings in *Billboard* and *Cash Box*. Elvis, Scotty, Bill and D.J. Fontana continued to tour the Southwest.

During this period Elvis experienced a lot of *firsts* for a young man not long out of high school. In Jacksonville, Florida his fans actually caused a riot and tore off his clothes. There was, of course, some physical danger but Elvis laughed about it. He loved the attention and he loved to see an audience warm-up. He was at his best when an audience would be semi-quiet, they were seldom really quiet, but if he wasn't getting the reaction he expected he would work and work until he had them turned-on.

Baby Let's Play House was Elvis' first record to appear on a *national* chart of best-selling records. *Mystery Train* and *I Forgot to Remember to Forget* was released by Sun, the last record Elvis did for Sam Phillips. RCA, with some prodding from the Colonel, purchased Elvis' contract from Sun Records for $35,000 and gave Elvis a $5,000 bonus for signing. This was a lot of money in 1955. The Colonel also negotiated an agreement with Hill and Range Music, Inc. which gave them the rights to publish the first Elvis Presley song folio with the words and music to Elvis' recorded songs. They would also administer Elvis Presley Music, Inc. and Gladys Music, Inc. which would publish all the words and music to Elvis' future records. Elvis was to receive fifty percent of the royalties.

Colonel Parker did the negotiating with RCA and Hill and Range, but Bob Neal was still Elvis' manager and continued to be until, by mutual agreement, the Colonel took over the job. The Colonel eased Elvis off the *Louisiana Hayride* so he would not be committed to weekly appearances on that show. RCA released all the recordings, which Elvis had made for Sun, under the Victor label which, of course, increased sales due to their better distribution and promotion. Elvis recorded *Heartbreak Hotel* and *I Want You, I Need You, I Love You* for RCA with Scotty, Bill, D.J. and the Jordanaires, a group which was to stay with him for a long time.

About the same time the Colonel booked Elvis on the Tommy and Jimmy Dorsey *Stage Show*, on CBS-TV, for six Saturday night shows at $1,250 per appearance. With the television exposure and the promotion of *Heartbreak Hotel*,

Elvis began to gain recognition throughout the country. In fact, he was a smash-hit on the West Coast which seemed to adapt more readily than did the East. Elvis recorded his first album in New York and continued the frantic traveling from city to city for personal appearances.

Heartbreak Hotel exploded like a bombshell and sold over two million copies, becoming the number one record in the United States and the Dorsey television shows were a tremendous success. Red West, a school friend, and Elvis' cousin, Gene Smith, joined the tours. Red did most of the driving and generally helped the group keep up the grueling pace. Elvis said, "When we were doing *Stage Show* the schedule was so wild there were times when we would leave Red in one town, where we had been doing a show, and fly to New York to go on television. Red would drive the car to the next city where we were going to perform and we would fly there after the television show was over.

"Once we drove from New York to Los Angeles, then down to San Diego, then back to Denver. I got sick for a couple of days from that trip. I don't know how any of the guys kept it up, but as hard as it was we had a lot of fun. We were moving so fast I think we never knew how good everything was going."

Elvis and the Colonel went to Hollywood in April of 1955 where Hal Wallis arranged a screen test with Paramount Studios. The test apparently was satisfactory and the Colonel was offered a contract for Elvis to do three films. The first to be made within a few months. The price was right, $100,000 for the first, $150,000 for the second, $200,000 for the third.

Hal Wallis made a shrewd move after signing Elvis. Instead of putting Elvis in one of his own pictures immediately, he allowed 20th Century Fox to star Elvis in *Love Me Tender*. In this way, Mr. Wallis was able to recoup the money he had paid Elvis for his contract and it afforded him the opportunity to gauge the public reaction to Elvis, the movie star, before investing any more of his own money. This paid off even further in later years when Elvis' movie price was a million dollars and Hal Wallis still had Elvis under contract for a couple of pictures at the lower price. Needless to say, Wallis made a bundle.

Elvis made another appearance on the Milton Berle

show while he was in Hollywood and this too was successful.

Failure came for Elvis and the Colonel a few weeks later when Elvis began a two-week schedule at the Frontier Hotel in Las Vegas. Vegas was not ready for Elvis. He didn't play to an empty house but he did not fill it either and, as he said, "The audience sat on their hands. They just would not respond. Oh, they were polite, but that was about all. It didn't work, that's all. It was a bomb."

The Colonel and the management of the Frontier agreed to tear up the contract and forget the whole bad experience. Elvis did some more appearances in several cities, including Memphis where he was headlined over Hank Snow for the first time. Then it was back to New York for the new Steve Allen show. The Steve Allen show was opposite Ed Sullivan, which was interesting because Sullivan had said he would never have Presley on his show. When the Steve Allen show, with Elvis on it, received over fifty-five percent of the television audience, Sullivan suddenly had a change of heart. The fifteen percent of the audience that Ed kept may not have been enough to convince him to stick with his moral values.

The media had a field day with Elvis. Every editor who could not think of anything else to moralize about harped on the evils of rock 'n' roll, and, especially, Elvis Presley. There were movements to ban teenage dances, begin a national curfew for anyone under twenty-one, make everyone wear a short haircut and God only remembers what other foolishness. The Russians even joined the hue and cry by banning Elvis' records. Moscow said that Elvis Presley was a new form of American propaganda and the possession of one of his records was absolutely forbidden. They would not have their youth corrupted.

Jack Gould of the New York *Times* and Jack O'Brien of the New York *Journal-American* seemed to have a contest going to see who could heap the most abuse upon Elvis. Elvis later went on the Sullivan show and even though he was shown on camera, while singing, only from the waist up, he helped Ed garner over eighty-two percent of the audience. RCA began to release records, by Elvis, by the stack and all of them did extremely well. The recordings were done in Hollywood and New York and Elvis ran the sessions. He would decide what songs he wanted to record and which takes were good. There was very little rehearsing, everything was spontaneous. This early in Elvis' career, his recordings accounted for ten percent of the company's business.

The Colonel continued to promote Elvis. The price for a concert was raised to $25,000 or a percent of the box office, whichever was greater, and this was a hell of a price in those years. The promotion boggled the mind and everything worked. There were Elvis Presley shoes, sweaters, bracelets, bobbysocks, purses, shorts, pants, jeans, pens, magazines, pictures and probably fifty other things. Elvis and the Colonel received a percentage of every item that was sold. Money came so fast it's doubtful Elvis ever knew just how much he was making.

Elvis' first movie, *Love Me Tender,* was a dramatic failure but a box-office success. Actually, this was true with each of the thirty-one Hollywood-type films he made. None was ever considered good by the critics and yet they all made money. The money was great, of course, but the poor quality of the scripts and the songs bothered Elvis for as long as he lived. He wanted to be a good actor and there were many who believed he had the talent, but he never once had the material. There were many times when he would talk about Hollywood and the films he did and he never said too much good about either.

It was when he was making *Love Me Tender* that he went back to the town where he was born, Tupelo, Mississippi, for an appearance at the Mississippi-Alabama Fair. It was a royal homecoming for Tupelo's favorite son. He earned $10,000 for the appearance, which he donated to the town of Tupelo.

Chapter Two

Entertainer to Army Private

After returning from the army, I began radio school with the hope of becoming a disc jockey. I again became good friends with George Klein, who had remained close to Elvis. George was a disc jockey in Memphis and it was, at least partly, due to his influence that I decided to pursue the same career. After I'd been home about a month, George asked me to go with him one night to see Elvis. Needless to say, I was delighted as I had wanted to see Elvis again but was reluctant to just go knock on his door. He was, after all, famous and busy.

We went to the house that evening and George, who was completely at home there, was showing me around the grounds when Elvis and Anita Wood joined us. "Hi," George said, "Elvis, you remember Marty, don't you?"

"Yeah, man," Elvis said. "How you doing? I heard you were back from the Army."

After he had introduced me to Anita, I remember saying to Elvis, "You have sure come a long way!"

In his usual quiet, polite way, Elvis answered, "Yeah, God has been good to me."

As was his habit even in those days, Elvis stayed up most of the night talking or playing pool, and that night, which was the first of many to come, I stayed up with him. Elvis loved to talk and tell stories. We would talk about everything you could possibly think of. Things we knew nothing about, but we would talk about them, ask each other questions, listen to what each one had to say and talk on and on into the night.

I began to see Elvis often after that first night and shortly came to feel completely at home at Graceland. It is a beautiful place and so far beyond anything I had seen before that I never ceased to enjoy being there.

Roller skating was a big thing for us in those days. Elvis would rent the Rainbow, a skating rink in Memphis, after it was closed for the night and a whole gang of us would go skating. We had special games we played on the skates and some of them could be rough. The first time I went to the Rainbow with the guys I didn't know what was going on when they brought boxes of protective padding from the car. I quickly learned, however.

One of the games we all liked was choosing-up sides and having each team go the opposite end of the rink and skate head-on into each other. The winning team was the one with the most people standing after the crash. Billy Smith, Elvis' cousin, was one of the best. He was just a kid but, boy, was he fast. Elvis was good too. He often let outsiders into the rink and sometimes there would be one or two guys who wanted to show their girls how they could knock Presley down. Elvis could take care of himself but Billy, Red West and all of us, in fact, were determined that the games would not turn into a "let's get Elvis" show.

We also played "whip" a lot. There was one girl, always with us at the rink, who was a pretty, feminine, young thing but man, was she tough. She always situated herself to be next-to-the-last person on the "whip." Her timing was perfect and she would let go at just the right moment so the end guy would crash into a wall or something else equally substantial. We were always banged-up, but, fortunately, no one was seriously hurt.

The Fairgrounds Amusement Park was also a part of our lives. Elvis would rent it after closing hours and we stayed on the rides until we were sick of them. It was a ball. We usually started off on the roller coaster which Elvis loved. He would stand up in the damn thing and just have a great time, but everyone's favorite was the dodgems, the little bumper cars. We made up teams and played a game called "war." This would go on for hours at a time, banging into each other until we were unable to continue. We put a lot of those cars out of commission until they told us we couldn't use them anymore if we continued the rough stuff.

Elvis was so taken with the dodgems that one night he decided to have a track built behind Graceland, complete with cars. It was 2:30 in the morning when this decision was made and nothing would do except for me to call Bernie, my brother-in-law, who had been doing a lot of design and remodeling at Graceland, and ask him to come over and work out the plans. Needless to say, Bernie thought we were all crazy but agreed to meet us at Graceland the following morning.

The three of us met and discussed what Elvis wanted, which was a complete track with the best cars available. Bernie, who was not an expert on dodgem cars, agreed to find out what he could and get back to us. I learned later that he met with the head of the amusement park and was given a complete education in the building and operation of a dodgem track.

The estimate to build the track and buy the cars was $115,000, which we thought would be enough to make Elvis say forget it. The price, however, didn't bother him, and all he wanted to know was when it would be finished. The more Bernie got into the plans the more he began to think it was a terrible idea. He and I again met with Elvis and Bernie told him the track would be an ugly monster outside the area where Elvis' grandmother lived and would ruin the beauty of Graceland.

Elvis asked Bernie, "Are you saying you don't want to build it?"

"That's right," Bernie answered, "you are going to regret doing it and I don't want to do something that's not going to be right."

The project ended there and we continued to use the dodgem track at the Fairgrounds.

Elvis was great with his fans. He never refused an autograph to anyone and he would let some, who happened to see us, into the Fairgrounds. As long as they were polite to him, he was the same to them and he always seemed to enjoy seeing them have a good time. He paid for everything at the park, Pronto Pups, hamburgers, whatever anybody wanted.

It was the same thing at the house or wherever we might go. Elvis would be great with the fans. He spent hours at the gates of Graceland signing autographs or just talking with the people and there was seldom a time when we drove in or out that he didn't stop for at least a few words. He liked them just about as much as they liked him.

I remember once when someone asked, "Doesn't it bother you always having people trying to get to see you?"

He answered, "It would bother me a lot more if they didn't want to see me."

By then he had completed *Love Me Tender, Loving You* and *Jailhouse Rock.* We continued to party whenever he was home. The days, or I should say nights, were filled with fun at the Fairgrounds or the roller rink or just staying home talking. Alan Fortas, Lamar Fike, Louis Harris, Cliff Gleaves and Arthur Hooten had joined the group. I think those days were some of the best of Elvis' life. They certainly were of mine.

Then the army got into the act.

On December 20, 1957, Milton Bowers, chairman of the draft board in Memphis, delivered Elvis' draft notice to Graceland. Elvis was ordered to report to the Memphis draft board on January 20, 1958, but he was also scheduled to return to Hollywood in January to film *King Creole.* Paramount sent a letter to the draft board asking for an eight-week delay but the draft board answered that any request would have to come from Elvis. Paramount had committed over $300,000 to the film and they would lose most of it if the film was not completed before Elvis went into the army, so Elvis wrote to the draft board and requested the delay.

Mr. Bowers and the other two men who made up the Memphis draft board couldn't do anything right. Either the pro-Elvis or anti-Elvis people were going to be up-in-arms over the decision they made; but, to their credit, they granted the delay which was certainly no big thing. The average draftee had little difficulty obtaining a deferment during that time.

Sure enough there was a storm of protest from those who thought the deferment was preferential treatment. Elvis' fans were just about as vocal in their protest against his being drafted in the first place. It was Christmas, but there was probably little cheer in the Bowers' home that year. Mr.

Bowers had been quoted as saying, "I eat, sleep and drink Elvis Presley. I've got the whole thing up to my teeth."

In the meantime, the Pentagon was also up to its teeth with Elvis Presley. Special conferences were called to discuss the problems inherent in drafting the United States' foremost teenage idol.

Elvis thought it was all very funny. He was, in a way, looking forward to going into the army.

In January, Elvis and some of the guys returned to Hollywood. They went on a train and whenever the train passed through a town the station would be packed with Elvis fans. Elvis always went out back to wave or sign autographs when the train stopped. It was an exciting trip which they all enjoyed.

King Creole was one of the best pictures Elvis made. It was probably his favorite from an acting point of view. Again, the critics didn't think it was all that good but it made a lot of money. When they finished working in Hollywood they went, again by train, to New Orleans where the location work was being done. The crowds, at the stations along the way, were just as large this time. Everybody wanted a glimpse of Elvis. That was true in New Orleans also. Elvis told us it would take half-an-hour just to cross the street, the mass of people was so great.

On March 24, 1958, Elvis was sworn into the United States Army, becoming serial number U.S. 53310761 and many said that would be the end of his career. They didn't take the Colonel into account. Two years was not going to be all that long and he had the ability to keep Elvis' name, music and motion pictures before the fans for ten times that, if necessary.

After a few days at Fort Chaffee, Elvis was sent to Fort Hood in Texas for basic training. The trip was made by bus but the army would not release the names of the towns where the bus would stop. There had been enough problems getting Elvis from Memphis to Fort Chaffee. Fans were everywhere. There was, he has told us, a lot of good-natured kidding with his fellow recruits but most of the guys just accepted him as another G.I.

There was a lot of speculation about Elvis going into the army's Special Services branch and spending his two years entertaining the other troops. The Colonel, however, made an announcement that Elvis did not want any special treatment, he would not go into Special Services. There are many reports that Colonel Parker felt the army should pay the same price for Elvis' talent as anyone else and if it wasn't prepared to do that then Elvis would not spend two years singing for free. Knowing the Colonel, I'm sure these reports are true.

It has also been widely reported that it cost the United States government $500,000 a year in lost taxes for Elvis to be in the army. In view of his earnings and tax bracket, there is little doubt that the reports are accurate.

The eight weeks in boot camp passed rapidly for Elvis. He always said he enjoyed the training but didn't care too much for Fort Hood. His two weeks at home after boot camp were spent recording some new songs and relaxing at the Fairgrounds and roller rink with Anita Wood, who was then his best girl. *King Creole* opened when he was home, and some critics even said it was good. So it was a happy homecoming and leave for Elvis.

When his leave was over Elvis returned to Fort Hood for another three months or so of advanced training. Elvis didn't like snakes and Fort Hood was loaded with them. There were many times in later years when he told us about waking at night and finding a snake in bed with him; when they were not there he would often dream that they were. As a matter of fact, he became something of an expert on snakes even though he didn't like them. Maybe it was a kind of fascination. He had grown up in a snake-infested area, Tupelo, and he told of times when his father would kill a snake which had managed to get into the house. Hours were devoted to the discussion of snakes, the deadly ones, the good ones, all kinds. I often thought he made up names as he went along, but he knew a heck of a lot more about them than any of the rest of us.

In August of that year, Elvis' mother died. He was in Memphis on emergency leave at the time. Elvis loved his mother to the point of worship and he really suffered at her death. Things, however, somehow managed to go on and he returned to Fort Hood about a week after the funeral.

Elvis expressed his feelings for his mother once at a press conference when he said, "She was very close, more than a mother. She was a friend and I could talk with her anytime of the day or night if I had a problem. I would get mad sometimes when she wouldn't let me do something, but I found out she was right almost every time."

When he finished training in Fort Hood, Elvis was sent to Germany where he became a scout for the army. When he arrived in Germany he was greeted by hundreds of screaming teenagers who acted the same as his American fans always did.

Elvis' father and grandmother traveled to Germany in a few weeks to join him and they took Red and Lamar with them. There are many stories told of the days in Germany. Elvis became friends with Charlie Hodge and Joe Esposito, both of whom would later work for him and remain close friends until his death. The Colonel continued to say no whenever the army tried to get Elvis to entertain or do something as Elvis the rock 'n' roll star rather than Elvis the scout, and Elvis continued to be a good soldier.

There were, during this time, reports of Elvis being killed in automobile accidents and all sorts of other *facts* which the newspapers somehow knew but which, fortunately, never happened. Elvis, and the guys who were in Germany with him, managed to find ways to have a good time in the house they rented. Their pranks resulted in their being asked to leave their first German home, which was a resort for older people. It seems the management didn't think the older guests appreciated some of the fun and games the guys would get into.

After moving from the hotel, the group found a house on Goethestrasse which was owned by a huge German woman. They wanted her to move out but when she saw Vernon, her eyes lit up and she refused to leave. For most of Mr. Presley's life he has been a handsome man and the Frau took a liking to him, but Vernon did not feel the same way. She was nosey and bugged the hell out of Grandma Presley. Grandma is a tough old lady with a great sense of humor who doesn't mind saying exactly what is on her mind. Elvis told us of the time the Frau kept coming into Grandma's kitchen causing problems. Grandma warned her a few times to stay out but when that didn't work, Grandma finally decked her. Elvis laughed about it. In spite of all this, there were never any serious problems in Germany.

Meanwhile, the Colonel kept things going at home.

Records which had been held back were released every few months and the Colonel held regular press conferences to let the newspaper boys know what the future offered. There were times when he told of the welcome home party they would have on closed-circuit television in hundreds of cities for Elvis when he was discharged. This, the Colonel said, was the best way to have all Elvis' fans share his return. The Nashville papers reported that Elvis had signed with ABC for a series of television specials for great sums of money.

Elvis met Priscilla Beaulieu, who was later to become his wife, and began to spend a lot of time with her. Priscilla was the daughter of an Air Force Captain who was then stationed in Germany. They saw each other for four or five months in Germany before Elvis was discharged, which finally came in March, 1960. His last days in Germany were hectic with press conferences being held everytime he had a free minute. Everybody wanted to know when he was going to get married, how he liked army life, how his superiors had treated him, what he would do first when he arrived home, was he going to record again, was he going back into the movies, when would he be on television, was he going to grow his sideburns again, how many public relations men had been assigned to him while he was in the army, what would he do if rock 'n' roll ceased to be popular and a hundred or so other questions which Elvis answered as best he could in his still polite manner.

And then he was a civilian again.

Chapter Three

Khaki to Gold

After his return from the army Elvis began a schedule of recording sessions and movies mixed with lots of nights of parties at the Fairgrounds or the roller rink. Football was also a big thing. We played at the high school stadium, which Elvis would rent, and had make-up games at Graceland. The games were always rough-and-ready with lots of cuts, bruises and bangs but the guys, including Elvis, were a tough lot who enjoyed the activity.

The first show Elvis did after his discharge was as a guest on Frank Sinatra's television special, for which Elvis was paid $125,000. The show was videotaped in Miami, Florida and Elvis traveled there by train. The Colonel made sure the trip was well-publicized and every town on the route was filled with Elvis fans. The show was taped at the rather famous Fountainebleau Hotel where Sinatra was performing. Dean Martin, Sammy Davis, Jr., Joey Bishop and Peter Lawford were in town at the same time so there was more than enough talent to fill the area. Elvis did a fine show with Sinatra which got a rating of over forty-one percent of the television audience. *Billboard* was something less than kind to Elvis in their review of the show, but his fans thought he was great.

In 1960, Elvis did *G.I. Blues* for Paramount and then *Flaming Star* for 20th Century-Fox. Both were financial successes but again they were dramatically less than rewarding. *Wild in the Country* was also made for 20th Century-Fox for the following year. Once more the pattern was the same, financial success and dramatic failure.

Elvis did a smash-hit benefit performance in Memphis and then went to Nashville for an appearance before the Tennessee State Legislature. The senators had passed a resolution which payed tribute to Elvis for the fame he had brought to Memphis and all of Tennessee. This was the time he said, "When asked if I'm going to eventually move to Hollywood to live, I say, I like to play there but Memphis is my home."

Elvis then flew to Hawaii to begin production on *Blue Hawaii* for Paramount. On his arrival, the airport was teeming with throngs of people. Hawaii is noted for its gracious welcome to visitors and the peoples' natural hospitality; this, coupled with their genuine admiration for Elvis, created the biggest, noisiest and most extravagant welcome Hawaii had ever experienced. Tears came to Elvis' eyes as the emotion of the crowd became his own and a mutual love affair began and remained with him all his life.

Prior to leaving the mainland, Elvis and the Colonel had heard that the people of Hawaii were trying to raise funds to build a memorial to the U.S.S. *Arizona,* the battleship which was sunk by the Japanese during the attack on Pearl Harbor. There were more than eleven-hundred men killed when the *Arizona* was destroyed and they were still entombed in the ship. The people of Hawaii wanted a memorial over the spot where the ship rests but they needed about $52,000 to begin the project.

After talking it over with the Colonel, Elvis decided that he would do a concert and pay all the expenses, including buying their own $100 tickets to the show, and donate the gross receipts to the building fund. The only condition they stipulated was that all the proceeds would go direct to the building fund with absolutely nothing taken out for anything else.

The show was a great success. Over $60,000 was raised through the sale of tickets. It was also one of the longest shows Elvis ever did. He sang nineteen songs to an audience which responded with all the enthusiasm expected from true Elvis fans. There are those who say the audience responded with *so much* enthusiasm that few people heard the songs, but it was a great show. Elvis really put himself into it as though he had already decided it would be his last public appearance for many years.

The benefit performance led to a touching incident which occurred almost five years later when we were in Hawaii to film *Paradise, Hawaiian Style* for Paramount. It began one evening when we were talking and someone brought up the subject of the memorial. Elvis said, "You know, I've never seen it. I wonder if we could get over there while we're here."

The Colonel picked-up on the idea and arranged to have the Admiral at Pearl Harbor send his launch to the pier to take Elvis and a group of us to see the memorial. When we arrived, Elvis was to place a wreath on the memorial where there is engraved a list of the names of the men who died with their ship. As he started to go to the designated place some of the photographers and others began to follow until he stopped and indicated with a wave of his hand that he wanted to be alone. He went to the marble wall, where the names are engraved into the wall in gold, placed the wreath in the proper place and remained standing there for several minutes. I never asked, but I'm sure he was saying a prayer for those who had given their lives for their country.

Blue Hawaii was about like the previous motion pictures Elvis had made, a financial success only. Elvis grew to love Hawaii and would return as often as possible in later years. The filming of *Blue Hawaii* was about as relaxed as any motion picture can be and Elvis, the Colonel and all the guys who were there with them seem to have enjoyed the visit.

After *Blue Hawaii* Elvis returned to Memphis but soon left again to begin *Follow the Dream* for United Artists. This film was no better than the others but it did give Elvis a chance to do a little comedy for which he had a natural talent.

The records continued to sell. An album made from the songs in *Blue Hawaii* reached the five-million-dollar mark and many of the others were doing about as well, if not better.

The parties resumed in Memphis when Elvis returned after finishing *Follow That Dream.* The parties were games, or talking or watching television or movies. There was very little alcohol consumed at Graceland. Elvis had some in the house but he seldom had a drink and didn't too much like those around him to take more than an occasional cocktail. Considering some of the violent physical activity of the games at the amusement park or the roller rink this is probably just as well. There was enough danger with everyone being cold sober, God only knows what would have happened had we been drinking.

There was one character, named Scatter, who didn't care too much what Elvis thought about drinking, and he would consume everything alcoholic he could find in the house. Scatter was a chimpanzee. Elvis had bought him from some man after he saw the chimp perform on television. We all loved Scatter and probably should have kept him off the booze, but in those days it seemed funny to see him drink somebody's cocktail when they were not looking. Scatter came to every party dressed in his own suits and had a great time stealing drinks or terrorizing the girls, and there were always lots of girls to terrorize.

When Scatter was being good he was a lot of fun to have around, but there were times when he drove everybody right up the wall. He would leap on the pool table in the middle of a game and either grab one or two of the balls and run away with them or he would start throwing them at anyone who happened to be in the room. Once he grabbed a cue stick and began to use it as a club against the guys who were playing at the time.

He never wanted to go to his cage at the end of an evening, and would get into the most inaccessible places in the house, to defend it against anyone who tried to get him out. One of his favorite spots was under the grand piano where he could avoid capture for hours at a time.

One night Scatter was particularly difficult. In the basement den of the Bel-Air house, a full-sized movie screen had been built into the wall and was hidden behind curtains. Billy Smith and I were trying to get Scatter into his room for the night. We began running after him across couches and chairs. To avoid us, he began climbing the curtains which hid the movie screen. We started yelling at him and he suddenly used the curtains as though they were a swinging vine. He went right into the huge screen leaving a big, gaping hole. As he swung out, he dropped to the floor and walked to his room as though he knew he had really exceeded even himself. Scatter could make life miserable when he wanted.

There was another time when Scatter was locked in the basement of one of the houses in California for the night and he found and tore every telephone line out where they came through the wall. Now this was a nice basement, it wasn't like he was being punished or anything, he just wanted to stay up with the people and was mad at all of us. It took the telephone company two days to fix the phone lines. I think those guys would have killed Scatter had they been given half a chance.

The man who lived next door was bitten by Scatter and he got mad and threatened to shoot the chimp. That made Elvis mad and there were a few minutes when we thought the whole neighborhood was going to be involved. We liked to dress Scatter in his best clothes and take him for a ride in one of the Cadillacs just to watch peoples' faces when they saw him sitting in the car as though he owned it. We tried to find a trick car which could be driven from the back seat but had a regular steering wheel in front. We thought it would be a great gag for Scatter to drive his own car but we never could find one.

The chimp became very difficult to control in his later years and had to be confined to a large cage in the rear of Graceland. He was well-cared for and visited constantly by Elvis or one of the guys until Scatter died.

One evening in 1961, we were playing pool. It was my turn to shoot and when I began to take aim I noticed a football helmet near the table. Elvis was talking with me but doing something else at the same time and turned away for a minute. For some reason, I reached over and picked up the helmet, put it on my head, and began again to shoot. About that time Elvis turned around, saw the helmet and started to laugh so hard he doubled-up. It wasn't really *that* funny, but he thought it was. When he finally could talk without laughing he said to me, "Take that damn thing off, there's something I want to talk to you about."

"Okay," I said.

"Why don't you come with us tomorrow when we leave for Hollywood?"

I had just left my job at the radio station and knew he

was offering me a chance to work for him. He was leaving the following day to begin to film *Kid Galahad* for United Artists.

"Man," I said, "I'd love to, but I'm going to have to think about it a little."

His attitude changed completely. He put down the cue stick, picked up the newspaper, held it in front of his face as though he were reading and said, "Well, don't think about it too damn long."

"Hey," I said, "I've got to think about my family. I'll talk it over with my wife and let you know tomorrow, if that's okay. You know I'd like to go."

"Okay," he answered. "But you know we're leaving tomorrow night."

I was, at the time, the only member of the group who was married and I also had a child. Elvis and the others were single with few responsibilities and he couldn't quite understand why anyone would need time to decide to leave the next night and travel two thousand miles from home for an indeterminate period of time. He actually seemed hurt that I didn't say yes immediately.

After talking with my wife we decided I should go, and the next morning I went to Graceland and said to Elvis, "Okay, I'm ready to go. What's my job going to be?"

Elvis said, "Don't worry about it. There's plenty to be done."

I was on the payroll.

The group of friends around Elvis became known as the Memphis Mafia. An astute newspaper reporter tagged us with this name during the time Elvis required that we wear dark, mohair suits to give a respectable appearance. We never objected to the name and Elvis thought it was funny. Among ourselves, however, we referred to the group as the guys. Through the years, new men would become a part of the operation and some of those who had been around would leave to do something else. Often someone would leave for one reason or another only to return again in a month or a year. It was a changing group but for the most part it was a group which remained loyal to Elvis all his life.

These men were a very important part of his life and my story about Elvis would not be complete without a brief description of those who spent a portion of their lives as employees and friends of Elvis Presley.

Gene Smith was Elvis' cousin, they grew up together and were close friends. It was natural for Elvis to turn to Gene when the need arose for a traveling companion. Gene went everywhere with Elvis and was probably the closest person to Elvis for the first few years. They had a misunderstanding in 1962 and parted company. From time to time, in later years, Gene visited Elvis at Graceland.

Elvis had another cousin, Junior Smith, who was disabled during the Korean war. One morning Elvis received a call to learn that Junior had died. Elvis took the news quite badly as he was extremely fond of Junior.

Billy Smith, another cousin, was the youngest of the boys and was Elvis' favorite. His concern and affection were always apparent and it was obvious that Billy had the same love and loyalty for Elvis. No one was allowed to take advantage of Billy and many times Elvis would say that he wanted to be sure that Billy grew up to be a good man. He was not disappointed. Billy was a constant companion to Elvis up until the day Elvis died. Billy now lives in Mississippi with his wife Jo and their two sons, Danny and Joey, and works for the railroad in Memphis.

George Klein was president of the senior class at Humes High School in 1953, the year he and Elvis graduated. George is one of the nicest men I've ever met. I have never heard anyone say anything bad about him. He is nice to everyone, and he was to Elvis in high school. Elvis never forgot a friend and very early in his career he asked George to travel with him. Later George went into radio and became a program director and one of Memphis' most popular disc jockeys. He remained close to Elvis until the end. Elvis once told me, "George will be my friend forever, I'll never forget how friendly and kind he was to me at Humes."

Bobby "Red" West was a schoolmate at Humes where he was an All-Memphis football player. Red helped Elvis out of a few jams with so-called tough guys while in high school and Elvis, never forgetting a kindness, asked Red to travel with him. Red went along as a friend, driver and security man. As the years went by Red worked as stuntman and actor in Elvis' pictures. At one point Red worked in the television series *The Wild, Wild West* as a regular. He also developed a talent for songwriting and wrote songs which Elvis and other artists recorded. Red married Elvis' former secretary Pat Boyd in 1961 and they have two sons, Brent and John.

Lamar Fike left Texas and showed up at Graceland one day in 1957. He followed Elvis and the guys to Los Angeles and he's been around ever since. Lamar and Elvis got along well with each other, they joked a lot and got mad a lot but the mad would last at most a day-and-a-half and they would be back joking again. Lamar left Elvis in 1962 and became road manager for Brenda Lee for awhile, then later became manager of the Nashville office of Hill and Range Music. He returned to work for Elvis at the same time he became manager of two country singers. Until Elvis died, Lamar was with him and he is now managing the two country artists. Nora, his former wife, and Lamar have a son, Jamie, and a daughter, Leslie.

Elvis was a high school football fan and was keenly aware of Alan Fortas, who was an all-Memphis lineman for arch-rival Central High. He was introduced to Elvis in 1957 by George Klein. Alan began working for Elvis just before he went into the army and went back with him after his discharge. Alan was in charge of transportation before he became foreman of the ranch in Mississippi and remained there until the ranch was sold. Alan left Elvis in 1968 but remained a close friend. Alan has a son, Budin.

Joe Esposito is from Chicago and he met Elvis while they were in the army. Elvis asked Joe to come to work for him after they were discharged. Joe soon became foreman of the guys. He worked with the books, paid the personal bills and coordinated activities between Elvis and the Colonel's office. He was Elvis' right-hand-man until he left for a brief time in 1964. At that time I assumed Joe's duties and when he returned we shared the responsibilities. We also shared the honor and the joy of being Elvis' best man when he was married. Joe has two daughters, Debbie and Cindy.

Charlie Hodge also met Elvis when they were in the army. Charlie had been one of the *Foggy River Boys* with Red Foley and their common interest in music brought Elvis and him together. Charlie worked with Elvis on stage and remained with him all of his life.

Sonny West, Red's cousin, met Elvis in 1958 and joined the group in 1960 as part of the security force. Sonny is a big man and could always take care of himself. He also became a stuntman in Elvis' movies and, along with Red, did fight scenes with Elvis. Sonny was an aspiring actor for awhile and has starred in two pictures of his own. He did advance work with the Colonel on Elvis' tours, going into each city a day ahead to set-up security. Sonny and his actress wife Judy have a son named Bryan.

Ray "Chief" Sitton was part of the group for a few years. He often came to the gate at Graceland before he was hired by Elvis. Ray is a huge man and not one to be missed in a crowd of people. Elvis, when he drove in or out of the gate, often stopped and talked for a few minutes with the fans who were there. He became accustomed to seeing Ray at the gate and would say "Hi, Chief, how's it going today?" or something similar. Ray had no way of knowing about Elvis' habit of calling everyone he didn't know "Chief." One night we were in the den when one of the guys came in and said to Elvis, "I just came through the gate and Chief stopped me and asked if he could come up to the house to see you."

"Chief?" Elvis said. "Who the hell is Chief?"

"I don't know," was the answer. "He said you knew him and always called him Chief."

"Man, you know I call everybody Chief. Okay, bring him on up." That's how Ray got a job and from then on he was called Chief by all the guys.

Richard Davis played touch football with us in Memphis. In 1962, he went from California to Seattle where Elvis was filming *It Happened at the World's Fair*. Elvis liked Richard and asked him to stay on. During the time he was with us he was in charge of Elvis' wardrobe. From time to time he would leave and come back. In the early seventies he left and went into promotion in the music business. Richard still lives in Memphis and has a son, Ronnie.

Mike Keeton began working for Elvis briefly in 1964. Elvis always retained a strong feeling for the Assembly of God church and Mike attended the same church. Mike's wife is Gladys and they have a son, John.

Jerry Schilling is a young man who first met Elvis in 1964 while playing touch football in Memphis. Jerry began working for Elvis that year and soon became a good friend. While filming a movie in Hawaii in 1965, Jerry met his now ex-wife, Sandy. Jerry had a manner which Elvis liked but sometimes Jerry's liberal views and his inability to keep those views to himself got him into minor disagreements with Elvis. It was good for all concerned however and they remained close friends until the end. Jerry left Elvis' payroll to become an actor but soon became road manager for various recording artists, including Billy Joel. He is currently road manager for the Beach Boys.

Marvin "Gee Gee" Gambill began working for Elvis about a year after he married Elvis' favorite female cousin, Patsy Presley. "Gee Gee" is a happy-go-lucky guy and easily made friends with Elvis. He was in charge of Elvis' wardrobe while he worked with the group. After a few more years on the road he settled down in Memphis with Patsy and their two children, Jimmy and Deena.

Dick Grob was a sergeant in the Palm Springs police force. Dick began accompanying Elvis as a member of the security force in 1969 and three years later quit the police force to work full time for Elvis. Dick was with Elvis until the end. Dick lives in Memphis with his wife, Marilyn, and their three children.

Ricky, David and Bill Stanley are the sons of Dee Presley, former wife of Vernon Presley. They arrived at Graceland in 1960 when they were little children. As they grew older, Elvis took them on tours as personal aides. Ricky and David were with Elvis until he died.

Al Strada came on the scene in 1972 in California. He was hired to guard the house at night while Priscilla and Lisa were there and Elvis and the guys were on the road. Elvis liked Al and put him in charge of wardrobe while on tours.

Dave Hebler was an expert in karate and a teacher when he first met Elvis in California in 1972. Soon after, Dave, a quiet unassuming guy, joined Elvis' payroll as a part of the security force.

Sam Thompson met Elvis through his sister Linda, Elvis' longtime girlfriend. Sam was a former sheriff's deputy in Memphis when he went to work for Elvis in the security force. He remained with Elvis until the end and is now with the Shelby County Sheriff's Department.

Throughout the years, for brief periods of time, Elvis had a personal hairdresser travel with him and Larry Geller and Sal Orifice filled that role. However, when Elvis was in Los Angeles, Pat Parry Gerson, a longtime friend and talented hair stylist, was usually called to do the job. She was a frequent guest at Graceland and a good friend to Elvis and the guys. Pat remains a hair stylist in Beverly Hills, living with her doctor husband, Jerry.

Other people who briefly worked for Elvis were Arthur Hooten, Cliff Gleaves, Louis Harris, Bobby Smith, Jimmy Kingsley, Dean Nichopolous, Steve Smith and James Caughley.

It still seems incredible to me that a large group of guys can work together, eat together, live together and play together without someone being killed.

We did, in fact, have our arguments and gripes, but living that close to each other, we would often keep things to ourselves in order to avoid an argument or a fight. But then, when one or two people were out of the room, we would talk about them. Maybe five or six guys would be sitting around, Elvis included, and the conversation would soon shift to whoever wasn't there and they would be literally ripped apart. I know, because I took part in those sessions and I sure as hell know for a fact what was said about me when I wasn't there. When Elvis wasn't present we talked about him and he talked about us when we weren't around. If the problem was serious, most of us weren't bashful about confronting the unhappy party face-to-face.

I can honestly say that of the more than twenty men who worked for Elvis, at one time or another, only three or four were genuinely disliked. In his infinite weird wisdom, Elvis would purposely keep someone on the payroll simply because he knew the group wanted to get rid of him. Even though Elvis was just another one of the guys, he liked to remind us who was boss.

One thing he wouldn't tolerate was a troublemaker, someone who would cause fights and then pretend that he was the one being picked on. We once had a guy like that and Elvis got rid of him fast. He equally could not stand, and even hated, anyone who would lie or steal.

There have been many things written about our group but one that particularly annoys me is the accusation that the group would not allow Elvis' old friends and acquaintances to visit him after Elvis himself had invited them. Often, Elvis would run into someone and, to be polite, say, "Why don't you come down to Memphis and visit me?" or "When you're in Memphis, come by the house." He was sincere at the time he said it but time passed before that person called or came down to the gate asking for entrance to the house. By then Elvis had forgotten the invitation or he would be in a different frame of mind. Usually, these people showed up or called during the day and that is the time when Elvis slept. There were always permanent instructions that he was not to be awakened except in emergencies.

We told visitors the situation but felt that most of the time they didn't believe us. In most cases we would later tell Elvis that certain visitors had either called or come to the gate and, for whatever reasons of his own, he would say sometimes, "I don't want anyone up here tonight and I don't want to talk on the phone." He really disliked talking on the telephone. It was his house and his life and we respected that.

There has also been speculation as to the amount of salary the group received. Up until a few years ago, the salaries were not as much as was generally believed. During the first few years, no one was paid a salary. All expenses were paid while traveling, including room and board, and the thrill of going to different places and the excitement of being involved in show business was enough for the guys. But even this wears off when there is not a penny in the wallet and nothing for necessities such as toothpaste.

When I first went to work for Elvis, I was paid $45.00 a week. My expenses were paid while we were in California and I lived in Elvis' house in Bel-Air. Meanwhile, the $45.00 had to cover my expenses back in Memphis for my wife and daughter. Within two years, I was drawing $75.00 a week and when I assumed the duties of personal bookkeeper and foreman, I was raised to $150.00. Shortly after Joe returned we were each given a raise to $205.00 a week. During those years, Joe and I made the highest salaries because of the nature of our work.

The money was probably sufficient for the single men, in view of the fact that all expenses were paid. Even when we were not on the road their expenses were covered as they either lived at Graceland or in a motel nearby and Elvis paid the bill.

Joe, a few of the guys, and I were married and, in order to be with our families while Elvis was in Memphis, we had to pay our own expenses in addition to the existing expense of our families.

During the last few years the salaries were raised to meet the cost of living.

This information is given simply to set the record straight. None of us were slaves and we always had the alternative of seeking other employment. However, we, as individuals, were not fabulously wealthy even though we lived with the king who very generously shared his food, home and lifestyle.

Elvis' penchant for gift-giving relieved the strain considerably in the form of Christmas bonuses, cars, jewelry and cash. All of his lavish gifts were greatly appreciated and helpful but most of the married guys agreed that it would have been better to receive a larger, more realistic salary so we would know what could be counted on every week to cover the cost of raising a family.

But then, Elvis was Elvis, and while he had no concept of the cost of a loaf of bread, he knew the pride of ownership and joy that only a gleaming white Cadillac could bring to a poor southern boy. His gifts were from the heart and he gave them because it was what he wanted to do.

There were many outside the group, of course, who were an important part of Elvis' life, such as Scotty Moore, Bill Black and D.J. Fontana, who worked for him in recording sessions and live performances in the earlier part of Elvis' career. Many writers have wondered why the team broke up. When the concerts stopped and the concentration was on making movies, there was a lot of idle time for Scotty, Bill and D.J.; it also meant a big cut in the money they made. The movie companies were paying the good money only for Elvis. The three of them asked for a salary comparable to what they felt they could be making on the road and they were refused. Bill Black went on to become a recording star in his own right, Scotty Moore went into record production and engineering and D.J. Fontana became a popular session musician in Nashville.

Dr. George Nichopoulos came into Elvis' life one day in 1966. We were riding the horses at the ranch when Elvis became ill with one of his customary colds. We tried to locate his regular doctor, but failing, we called George Klein's former wife Barbara, who worked for Dr. Nichopoulos. He agreed to a house call and has been Elvis' personal physician ever since.

He began coming to Graceland every day and made himself available to Elvis whenever necessary. If Elvis needed to go to the doctor's office, it was arranged for him to do so after normal office hours. Dr. Nick, as we called him, became, more or less, one of the boys and was a good friend. In addition, he became family doctor to most of us and his wife, Edna, became friendly with the wives of the guys in the group.

When Elvis began performing in Las Vegas and throughout the country, Dr. Nick traveled with him. He was a superb racquetball player and winner of many tournaments and he interested Elvis in the sport. Dr. Nick felt it would be a great addition to the exercise fitness program he prescribed for Elvis. Soon Elvis and the guys were playing every night, all night. Elvis liked the game so much he spent thousands of dollars building a beautiful place behind Graceland to house his own glass-walled court, private locker rooms for men and women and a beautiful plush lounge complete with bar and game room. Elvis spent many a night in that building, including his final one.

Dr. David Meyer was called in to treat Elvis when it was learned that he had a mild case of glaucoma. It was due to Dr. Meyer's quick action and expert skills that Elvis' eyesight was saved. A young man, living in Memphis, David is a top specialist and his services are sought throughout the world. He lectures at many of the leading medical schools. With his likeable personality, he soon became a favorite of Elvis' and the guys', visiting in Las Vegas and other cities. David treated and helped some of the members of our families and saved the eyesight of a group member's son.

Dr. Lester Hofman was Elvis' dentist and a friend for years. Dr. Hofman was another who was accommodating to Elvis when needed. He and his wife, Sterling, became friends with most of the guys and he treated our families.

This is a fairly good representation of those in the group and some others who were close to Elvis; of course, my most intimate knowledge is of Elvis and the Memphis Mafia.

Everyone of the guys had a nickname. We called Elvis "Crazy" because of some of the far-out things he would do. Lamar was known as the "Great Speckled Bird." My nickname was "Moon." That came to me when we were driving from Memphis to Los Angeles to make a film; as usual it was night and we were in the Dodge mobile home. Elvis was driving and Joe and I were in front with him. The other guys were in the cars. We were talking and joking around in our usual crazy mood. Andy Williams was singing *Moon River* on the radio and all of a sudden Joe starts singing to the music: "Moon Lacker, wider than the sea." Well, we started cracking up, especially Elvis. My face is kind of round and I don't have much hair on top of my head and this prompted Elvis to look at me while we were all still laughing and say, "Moon Lacker, you poor old bald-headed sonofabitch." From then on I was "Moon."

All of us laughed when we read some of the newspaper accounts of the duties of the Memphis Mafia. Often the papers made us sound like a bunch of flunkies who would be sad when Elvis was sad and laugh only if he laughed, but never louder. These stories may have been good copy for the press but they were just not true. When we were on the payroll we each had jobs to do and we did them; I think we did them well. Elvis, at those times, was our employer and if he wanted something done in a special way, of course, we did it that way.

Elvis Presley was a multi-million-dollar business and we were a part of that business. Had any of us worked for General Motors we would have been loyal to that company and when we worked for Elvis Presley we were loyal to him and did everything possible to perform our assigned tasks to the best of our ability. When, on the other hand, we played, we played hard and had a great time doing it. The friendship which existed was more important than the employer-employee relationship. To a man, we cared for Elvis and he cared for us. We laughed when something was funny and cried when something was sad; and, we did either one according to our own feelings and not because of the mood Elvis was in at the time.

We all knew, though we were never told, that part of our jobs was to maintain the Elvis Presley public image, one of politeness and good manners. We always tried to do exactly that. The Presley image was probably easier for Elvis to maintain than it was for most of the group. Elvis was a naturally polite, well-mannered person; except on those occasions when he, like all of us, became angry about something. Elvis had a real temper and when something happened to upset him, he could react with great verbal violence, but so could we all.

We argued within the group, got mad at each other, felt hurt, offended and jealous. There were times, I'm sure, when each of us hated Elvis and times when he hated each of us. We also loved each other as true friends, in the same way that we all loved Elvis and he loved all of us. I suppose what I'm trying to say is that we may not have been saints, but we sure as hell were not sinners either.

Chapter Four

The Movies

There were twenty-two movies made after *Kid Galahad* was finished, but that was the first for me as a paid member of the group. We went on location to Idlewild, California, where Elvis did all the boxing scenes. It was a beautiful place with lots of snow and trees. Elvis loved it and we stayed about three weeks before going to Hollywood where the picture was finished. During the filming, Elvis briefly dated numerous girls, including Connie Stevens. But it was none of these girls who caused a problem for me while we were in Idlewild, it was a girl from out-of-town.

Sonny was on location with us working on the film as stunt man. He was not working for Elvis at the time. Sonny had invited a good-looking girl to come for a visit and she made the trip with a girl whom Elvis had invited. Elvis saw Sonny's girl, liked her looks and began turning on the charm.

The following weekend we went to Palm Springs and when Elvis asked Sonny's girl to go with him, she quickly accepted. Needless to say, when Sonny learned of the week-end tryst he was furious and refused to talk to Elvis for days.

In the dressing room one morning Elvis asked, "What's Sonny so damn bugged about, how come he doesn't come around and talk to me?" Either Elvis didn't remember the week-end with Sonny's girl or he was putting on a good act.

He looked at those of us in the room but we were reluctant to tell him what was wrong. Receiving no answer, he turned to me and said, "Go talk to Sonny and see what he's pissed off about."

As a new member of the paid employee group, I had not yet assessed the nature of the changes, if any, my new status would require. This whole scene took me completely by surprise, and without thinking, I went to Sonny and asked why he wasn't talking to Elvis and assured him that the reason would not be repeated to Elvis.

Of course, Sonny confirmed that he was angry because Elvis had taken his girl to Palm Springs. Like a dope, I went back and told Elvis, who then went to Sonny and explained that he didn't know the girl had come to Idlewild to see him and assured him it wouldn't happen again. Sonny wasn't too happy with me and I wasn't too happy with myself.

After that, the only time I told Elvis anything about the guys was when they were in need. Sometimes they asked me to talk to Elvis for them but most of the time they didn't need to ask, I just did it. I knew Elvis would always want to help.

Almost from the beginning I was Joe Esposito's assistant. He was foreman of the guys and rather a personal secretary to Elvis. He handled Elvis' money, paid the bills and such as that.

After *Kid Galahad* came *Girls, Girls, Girls* for Paramount. Then there was *It Happened at the World's Fair* for Metro-Goldwyn-Mayer. Next there was *Fun In Acapulco* which received greater coverage in the press from an untrue incident than did the finished movie.

Someone said that Elvis didn't like the Mexican people, the press reported the story as gospel truth and the Mexican government said Elvis would not be welcome. So Elvis missed Mexico and Mexico missed Elvis and neither one probably cared very much, but the story just wasn't true. Elvis had nothing against Mexico or the Mexicans. There were a lot of individuals he didn't like and when he became angry with them he would sometimes make reference to their religion or race, but then many people are guilty of this shortcoming. But, Elvis wasn't the type of person who disliked an entire nation or race of people.

Viva Las Vegas was one of his best musicals and grossed almost six-million dollars. It was during the filming of *Viva Las Vegas* that Elvis met Ann-Margret, or Rusty Ammo or Ann Margrock, as some of us used to call her. She is a beautiful person, not just a physical beauty but a genuinely nice person. She was a lot of fun, always laughing and singing. We loved being around her as she was super nice to the guys. Elvis cared a lot for her and I truly believed they loved each other, but, for some unexplained reason, they abruptly stopped seeing each other. They continued to care and think about each other long after that, I know Elvis did. The ironic thing is that they were so much alike.

Kissin' Cousins, with Yvonne Craig, came next and this was the first film in which almost every one of the guys had speaking parts. In the earlier films some were extras but this was a new experience for all of us. Elvis was paid three-quarters of a million dollars, plus fifty percent of the profits, for starring in this movie.

In *Roustabout,* Elvis acted with Barbara Stanwyck, for whom he had great respect. He commented, "Working in scenes with a great actress like Barbara Stanwyck made me a better actor. She gave me a lot of encouragement." We quickly learned that the crew called Miss Stanwyck "Missy," out of affection, and since we shared that feeling, we called her "Missy" also. One thing we learned and respected was the film crew's opinion of people, if the crew liked them, they were all right. Even with Missy's help, *Roustabout* was still not much of a movie. In that film, Racquel Welch made her debut in a bit part.

The set for Metro-Goldwyn-Mayer's *Girl Happy* was Fort Lauderdale but that was another location we didn't see. Shelley Fabares was in the film and she and Elvis became good friends. We all became close to Shelley and remained so for many years. Elvis and I began to refer to her as "our girl" and when one of us would talk with her, we would always tell the other, "I talked with our girl today." This was the time we also met Mary Ann Mobley.

Tickle Me was made for Allied Artists and as bad as it was, it helped that company get out of a financial hole. *Harum Scarum* was terrible, but it earned Elvis a million dollars, plus fifty percent of the profits. It required only eighteen days to complete. The co-star was Mary Ann Mobley. The Colonel, I hear, suggested adding a talking camel to the cast but that never happened.

Frankie and Johnny, with Donna Douglas, was next for United Artists and then came *Paradise, Hawaiian Style.* Many of the scenes in it were filmed at the Polynesian Culture Center on the island of Oahu and Elvis loved it there. His dressing room was beautiful, a replica of an ancient Hawaiian palace. The center is operated as a school and as an embodiment of Hawaiian culture by the Mormon Church. They have young people from all the islands who study there. At night they perform an extravagant show using the costumes of the different islands. We came to know and love the kids who lived and went to school at the center. Elvis even wanted all of us to move into the area where they lived, but it wasn't possible.

By the end of the picture there was a great feeling of warmth with the kids and on the final night, they invited us to a special farewell ceremony in our honor. We met on the grounds of the center in front of the Maori tribe assembly hut. We were told to walk in a straight line toward the Maoris. Elvis chose me to be the spokesman for our group. When we reached the Maoris, their leader threw down a leaf in front of me. This was their custom, their challenge. If I retrieved the leaf, we were friends, if not, we were enemies. I picked up the leaf.

We were ushered into the big hut and were told to sit against the wall on the floor. One by one, the young people from each island told us how much they cared for us and then, as part of the ceremony, each one put a lei around the neck of the person who was their favorite. Elvis, of course, had more leis than anyone else but it made me feel good to be the one they liked most, next to Elvis. The leis came to the top of my head. Then it was my turn to speak for Elvis and the group. It was an emotional experience I will never forget. We later learned that this was the first time the young people from the islands had ever honored any celebrity or visitor.

One of the guys, Jerry Schilling, fell in love while we were in Hawaii. After returning to the mainland, I told Elvis that Jerry wanted to get married. Elvis not only paid for the wedding but also paid for Jerry's plane fare back to Hawaii and the return trip for the bride and groom.

Spinout for Metro-Goldwyn-Mayer came next. Shelley Fabares worked with Elvis again and that was about the only bright spot in the movie. Then there was *Double Trouble* with Annette Day and Yvonne Romain for Metro-Goldwyn-Mayer and *Easy Come, Easy Go* for Paramount when Elvis played a frogman in the Navy. Elsa Lanchester was in it and she was really funny to work with. *Clambake,* again with Shelley Fabares, was made for United Artists shortly before Elvis was married.

It was at this time that I learned how much Shelley really meant to Elvis. Elvis had told only me, Joe, and Billy and a few of the guys, that he was going to marry Priscilla and that the date was set. This was one thing he didn't tell anyone outside the group. One day, on the set, Elvis and Shelley were in his trailer dressing room when they called him to do a shot. Shelley came out and I went in. Elvis hesitated a moment and said, "I just told her."

"Told her what?" I questioned.

"That Priscilla and I are getting married, I wanted her to know. I trust her not to tell anyone."

Shelley was the only person outside the inner-circle to learn of the upcoming wedding and this, to me, was proof of Elvis' deep affection for her.

Stay Away, Joe was released by Metro-Goldwyn-Mayer in March of 1968 and was followed in May with the same studio's *Speedway,* even though *Speedway* was filmed first. Nancy Sinatra was co-star.

Live a Little, Love a Little came in October of 1968, again for Metro-Goldwyn-Mayer. *Charro* for National General Corporation was released in March 1969 and *The Trouble With Girls,* for Metro-Goldwyn-Mayer, in May of the same year. *Change of Habit* with Mary Tyler Moore, for NBC Universal came out in October 1969, and *Elvis: That's The Way It Is* was released by Metro-Goldwyn-Mayer in November of 1970. *Elvis: On Tour,* ended the age of Elvis Presley movies.

Elvis got along with most of the directors for whom he worked, but Norman Taurog was his favorite. He had a great flair for comedy and so did Elvis. As a matter of fact, Mr. Taurog, among his many credits, directed most of the Dean Martin-Jerry Lewis movies. He is one of the kindest and most considerate men we met and he understood and cared about

Elvis as a person. Long after he stopped making movies, Elvis continued to see and stay in contact with Mr. Taurog.

When Sony first introduced their video home recorders Elvis bought one and brought it to the studio. These were the original reel-to-reel sets before the cassettes were perfected. He showed it to Mr. Taurog and just casually mentioned that it would be a great asset to a director or an actor. You could video-tape a scene and immediately play it back to see if it was good. Mr. Taurog agreed and then, without thinking anymore about it, went out of the dressing room to set-up the next scene. Well, Elvis was not going to let the idea die.

He turned to me and said, "Go out to Sony and buy another video recorder, I want to give one to Mr. Taurog."

I answered, "These things are new and scarce, we had to wait three months for this one, I don't think they will have another one in stock."

"I know you can do it, Moon, but if you can't I'll give him this one and the next one Sony gets will be mine."

When I contacted them, Sony said they wouldn't have another for a few weeks, so Elvis called Mr. Taurog back to the dressing room and presented him with the recorder. He was really moved by the gift and asked if I would bring it to his house that night and show him the mechanics of operation. I liked Mr. Taurog very much and was most happy to accommodate.

In later years, Mr. Taurog became ill and Elvis saw or telephoned him as much as possible. He later presented Mr. Taurog with an automobile and other gifts and, for a very short period, he hired Mr. Taurog's son Jon to work for him. Mr. Taurog directed nine of Elvis' pictures.

Elvis greatly respected Fred De Cordova, who directed *Frankie and Johnny*. De Cordova is now producer of the *Tonight Show*. During filming, Mr. De Cordova's mother died and all of us admired the courage he displayed during this very difficult period.

Another director we liked and, I believe, the feeling was mutual, was Arthur Nadel, the director of *Clambake*. He was an easy-going, talented director with a great sense of humor. We, as usual, during most of Elvis' pictures, would cut up and play pranks on each other and some of the people in the cast and crew, Elvis joined in. It was a way of breaking tension and monotony. However, we never did these things while rehearsal or shooting was in process because moviemaking is expensive and each minute wasted costs thousands of dollars. We were well aware of that fact, but if we forgot, the Colonel reminded us.

We played pranks on everybody during *Clambake* except Mr. Nadel. Well, he liked us so much that he felt hurt that he was left out. We waited until the end-of-the-movie party, which happened to be given on his birthday. It was a happy party and there had been prepared a large cake for Mr. Nadel's birthday. Red, Richard, Sonny, Billy and I were sitting at the table which held the cake and all at once, we each had the same idea. Hardly able to contain our mischievousness, we carried the cake to Mr. Nadel's table, pretending it was for the purpose of blowing out candles. As we reached his table, we tipped the cake very slowly, so he would know what was coming, and then dumped the cake on his head. Everybody laughed, especially Mr. Nadel, and, at last, he felt like one of the guys. All of this may sound childish, but it was an essential part of the lifestyle of a group of guys who were doing the same things day-in and day-out. We had to let off steam. It was always done in good humor and in the spirit of friendship. We never imposed our brand of fun on anyone who could not understand and enjoy these things as much as we did. A strange way of letting people know we liked them perhaps, but nonetheless, it was our way.

One of those we neglected was a director whom Elvis came to dislike as much as the rest of us. He was an arrogant man, who felt his intelligence and humor were far superior to those of anyone around him. The poor man was wrong. We did our best to ignore him, but Elvis had to work with him. He began to be unusually demanding and got on Elvis' nerves but Elvis would just smile and do the scene. It seemed that he kept pushing Elvis just to see how far he could go.

One day Elvis was feeling rotten and had a temperature of around 104 degrees; he was sweating and could hardly breathe. He should have been home in bed but he kept doing this scene over and over again for the director. Elvis would not quit and go home. He always had a determination that wouldn't allow him to give in, and also, he felt he had made a commitment when he signed the contract and, no matter what, he was going to live up to it. I think he acquired that trait from the Colonel. Once the Colonel made a deal, he lived up to every part of it. You got no more than was agreed but you definitely got no less, and he expected the same in return. He never let any one of us, including Elvis, forget it.

As for Elvis' co-stars, he had one sort of romance or another going with them while making each movie, in addition to other girls he knew. There were, however, a couple of co-stars who didn't turn him on at all but he was pleasant with them.

During the years of frantic film-making a lot of other things also happened. Between making the movies Elvis liked to vacation in Las Vegas and we made many trips there.

Just as Elvis liked to see peoples' faces when he gave them gifts, he also enjoyed watching reactions when he shared something he found exciting. This he tried to do on my first trip to Las Vegas in 1963. We were going there first and then on to Los Angeles to make a film. Elvis, Billy, Joe and I were in the Dodge mobile home and the rest of the group were in the cars. Throughout the entire trip from Memphis, Elvis kept telling me how much I would enjoy Vegas and that the greatest thrill was to see the city, for the first time, all lit up at night.

We were about thirty miles outside Boulder City, Nevada when the mobile home broke down. It was daytime and Elvis kept insisting that we would wait in the mobile home until it got dark because he didn't want me to see Vegas for the first time in the daylight. Twenty minutes later he said, "Let's get in the damn car and go to the nearest motel and wait 'till it's dark and then go into Vegas."

Elvis, Billy, Joe and I checked into a little motel on the highway and the others stayed in the mobile home to guard our luggage until a tow truck arrived. We weren't in the motel more than a minute when we discovered they had no television.

That blew the whole thing and Elvis said, "Moon, I'm really sorry, but let's get out of here and get to the comforts of Vegas." It made not the slightest bit of difference to me, but he was really disappointed that his plan didn't work.

After 1969, when Elvis began performing there, we stayed at the International Hotel, later renamed the Las

Vegas Hilton, but in those days we always stayed at the Sahara Hotel because Elvis liked it and Milton Prell, a good friend of Colonel Parker and president of the hotel, usually arranged space for us.

Generally we had half a floor where we could control security, which was an ever-present problem. We kept one security man at the elevator and one just down the hall. It was mainly a daytime sleeping and nighttime playing life, but that's what Las Vegas is all about anyway. We usually got up about four or five in the afternoon, had a leisurely breakfast and took our time getting ready for the evening.

Sometimes we went to dinner shows, like those at the Lido, where they had big productions. They almost always stopped the show to introduce Elvis to the audience. This was common practice in Las Vegas during a regular show, but it seldom happens during production shows. Of course, Elvis was always popular with other entertainers and they seemed to be genuinely pleased that he was in the audience.

I remember once when we went to the Flamingo to see Jack Carter and Julie London. Jack introduced Elvis to the audience. We were sitting in a booth and, after the introduction, it was obvious that people in the audience were trying to get a better look at Elvis. They were nice enough not to bother him during the show, but when it ended a good portion of the room came over to get his autograph and shake hands. He stayed there for an hour and a half after the show signing autographs and talking with the people. He appreciated the way they had allowed him to enjoy the show. It was always great to see the way people reacted to Elvis, even in a place like Las Vegas where big stars are seen all the time.

Sometimes we went to a second show if someone we wanted to see was appearing or we would just fool around at the hotel for awhile and then go to a lounge late at night. Elvis was a great fan, as far as the lounge shows were concerned, of Fats Domino and Della Reese. He liked the way both of them sang and was particularly impressed with the way Della Reese did some of her songs.

Elvis thoroughly enjoyed the craziness of Don Rickles when he first started working the Sahara lounge. Elvis never forgot something Don said the first time he attended the Rickles' show. Everyone knows that Rickles cuts-up everyone who comes to see him perform, especially celebrities. When

Elvis walked into the lounge Rickles introduced him to the audience and said, "Normally I would be making fun of him, as part of my act, but this man is an exception to me. I know how much he cared for his mother and how he took care of her. Ladies and gentlemen, I have nothing but respect for a man like that, that's all I can say."

Then, looking at Elvis, he spat out, "Now sit down, Presley, you're making a fool of yourself."

Rickles' love for his own mother is well-known and he meant what he said about Elvis.

In later years Elvis went to the same lounge to see Chuck Berry perform.

A late night special for all of us was to go to the New Frontier and see Clara Ward, the gospel singer. This was the younger Clara Ward, her mother was also a famous gospel singer. She was from Memphis and she had a really fantastic gospel group with her. We would go there at maybe four o'clock in the morning and sometimes we would be the only ones in the lounge. We enjoyed the show and Clara did a lot of special things for us, singing all the songs she knew we liked.

We never went to bed before daylight. After the late show we often had some people come to the hotel or our own group would just sit and talk until the night was gone. Then we would sleep all day, get up and do it again. Once, we continued this routine for six weeks.

Elvis really never had any close relationships with celebrities other than Nick Adams. Nick visited Graceland often and was with us in Hollywood. It hit Elvis hard when Nick died.

There were casual meetings from time to time, with Tom Jones, Marty Allen, Joan Rivers, Buddy Hackett, Bobby Darin and Jack Lord. The celebrity he had known and whose company he enjoyed from the beginning was Sammy Davis, Jr. Sammy came around in the early days at the Beverly Wilshire Hotel and in later years he and his wife would visit in Los Angeles and Las Vegas.

We were in Las Vegas once during the winter for four or five weeks before we decided to leave and return to Hollywood. There was one fellow at the Sahara, Johnny Joseph, who was then a senior bell captain, who took care of all our luggage. There were probably ten of us and there were tons of it. We called Johnny and he helped us load everything into the station wagons and we left. About a third of the way to Hollywood, we found the roads were blocked by snow. So Elvis said, "Okay, let's go back."

Back at the Sahara Johnny had to help unload all the luggage and get it back up to the rooms. We stayed for a few more days and called Johnny again to help. The weather reports had said all the roads were open, but it turned out not to be true. Back to the Sahara and more work for Johnny. He was ready to quit the following week when it happened the third time.

Las Vegas was always a ball. The service and food were great and it was one of the few places where we could relax. Security was necessary but, because of the atmosphere in the city where there were so many people to be seen, it was less of a problem than in many other places.

Elvis' eating habits were weird. There was a period in Los Angeles when he ate meat loaf, mashed potatoes, gravy and sliced tomatoes for dinner every single night. This was when we were there for all the movies and he kept it up for two solid years. Every single night, meat loaf, mashed potatoes with gravy and sliced tomatoes. In Vegas once, he started to like Italian food and had the same chef come to the hotel suite every night to fix an Italian dinner for us. He just never tired of it. His hamburgers had to be extra, extra, well-done, almost burned, with onions, pickles and mustard. If they were not, he would throw them away.

We had fun. We were in Las Vegas so often over the years that we grew close to many of the people who worked at the Sahara and Hilton Hotels. The security force, of course, had to know all the group in order to know who could be allowed into our area. All the guys rough-housed with them. Once, at the Hilton, the security guards had taken some huge cardboard boxes, cut slits in them, pushed broom handles through one of the slits in each box, gotten inside and when we came out of our rooms into the hall they began charging at us as though they were tanks. It was a riot, those damn boxes lumbering along with their broom cannons weaving back and forth. About four of us plowed into them as if they were tackling dummies and we had boxes and brooms and people from one end of the hall to the other.

Elvis always joined in the play and enjoyed it as much or

more than the rest of us. It did a lot to break the tension which would build from the really tough schedule we all had when the movies were being made or when there were a lot of personal appearances. Once, the security guards handcuffed Red to a pipe and it was a long time before we could get him loose. Another time we handcuffed one of the security guard's hands behind his back, tied his feet together and left him lying on the floor in the hall.

We did something real crazy at yet another time. Bill Medley of the Righteous Brothers was doing a solo act at the lounge of the Hilton. We all knew and liked Bill, and Elvis had known him for a long time. On this night we were returning to the suite by our usual back-hall route and were passing the stage door of the lounge where Bill was singing. Elvis opened the door and we all followed him through, straight across the stage! The audience became unglued when they saw Elvis Presley walk across the stage and Bill dropped the microphone. He later told us that when he saw these figures coming at him from the dark of the wings he thought kooks had decided to wipe him out. When he saw who it was, he was so taken aback he just froze.

The next night when we were going by the same stage door, Elvis and I looked at each other with the same silly grins on our faces. I opened the door and across the stage we went again, but this time I hesitated long enough to tweak Bill on the cheek as we went past. The audience just fell apart and Bill began to laugh so hard it must have been ten minutes before he could continue singing. We did that once more before we left town and again the audience and Bill just roared.

It was a fast, crazy life but it also had its serious side. Once in 1964, when we were in Los Angeles there was an incident involving two English girls, which was quite serious and sad. I've recently, by the way, read an account of this event which placed it in Memphis but then went on to say it was just a story and never really happened. I can tell you it did happen. I wrote the checks and was a party to the whole episode. We were living in a house on Perugia Way in Bel-Air where there was always a party going on at night. Elvis would often let some of the fans in to join us and several times twin girls from England had been to the house. We all knew and liked them but none of the guys had any romantic interest. They were just a couple of kids who enjoyed being at the house and were good company.

One Sunday morning Joe Esposito, who did not live at the house, called and told me the girls had called him wanting to come to the house. He said they sounded almost hysterical and had told him it was an emergency. They did not have the house phone number, which was unlisted, but had managed to find Joe's number. Anyway, I said okay and they came to the house about an hour later. They were crying and so upset it was some time before I could find out that the previous night they had returned to their apartment and found their mother dead.

The two girls and their mother had been in the United States only a short time. They had no relatives or friends in this country and were living in a small apartment in one of the beach cities south of Los Angeles. Instead of going to church that morning with their mother as had been planned, they had to call the pastor of the church and ask him to help arrange to have their mother's body taken to a funeral home. They tried, with his help, to arrange to have the body sent back to England but found the cost was staggering. The girls had very little money and they didn't know what to do.

Joe and I decided that Elvis would want to know about this so I took them into the den where he was. We were fortunate that he had not yet gone to bed. When the girls saw him they began crying again.

"What happened?" Elvis asked.

"Our mother's dead! Our mother's dead!" both of the girls sobbed at the same time. He put his arms around them and led them to the sofa where he tried to get them calmed down enough to tell him what had happened.

They were just too upset to talk so he turned to me and asked, "What happened, Marty? How did it happen?"

I told him the story and explained that the girls had very little money and that the funeral home would not do anything unless payment was guaranteed. The girls had come to us as they had no one else.

He looked at me and said, "Handle it for them."

I knew he was giving me authorization to pay the expenses and that I should help them make the necessary arrangements. Elvis paid for their mother's body to be sent back to England and, after learning that the girls wanted to return to the United States after the funeral, asked me to buy round-trip tickets for them. So they would not be concerned about expenses during their time of sadness, he instructed me to give them adequate money. Elvis knew what it was to loose a mother.

It was just the kind of thing he would do, and, in fact, he did do. I was there.

There haven been many *facts* written about Elvis and all too often they are not true. It must be terribly difficult for anyone truly interested in his life to sort the whole thing out. In this regard, I have restricted my stories to only those of which I have personal knowledge, those which Elvis told me and information which is public knowledge.

The English girls were fans and fans were important to Elvis. He appreciated their loyalty and the way they worked to promote his records and movies. Colonel Parker was also aware of the importance of fans and fan clubs and did everything possible to see that every fan letter was answered.

The mail was astronomical. Ten thousand letters in one week were not at all unusual but somehow they were all answered. I worked in the office behind Graceland for a short period once when I was unable to go with Elvis on a trip. I kept busy part of the time reading the fan mail and sorting it for answering and believe me, some of it was wild.

Most of the fans were great and simply wrote to tell Elvis how much they enjoyed his performances but there were also the others. There were girls who sent pictures, often nude pictures, and offered themselves if they could just get to see him for a few minutes. There was one woman named Presley who was convinced she was Elvis' long, lost cousin and she would write every week and begin her letters *Dear Cousin Elvis.*

There were tales of woe from people who, according to their letters, were suffering from every disease listed in a medical dictionary and some others which the doctors have not yet named. All could be cured if Elvis would just see them or, at least, send money. Get rich schemes came in every mail delivery. The writer could guarantee Elvis a million-dollar return if he would finance their business, invention, screen test or whatever idea seemed best at the time. These were the weird ones and, I guess, they attach themselves to all famous people. Elvis sure had his share.

There were also fans who were really impossible. Once in the northwest, Elvis had to quit in the middle of a song and leave the stage because of the fans. I was still in the army at the time, but Elvis told me the story. "The stage," he said, "was in this big stadium. I was set-up near one end and a lot of people who didn't have seats were allowed on the field but they were supposed to stay at the far end. No way! When we started the show they began to move toward the stage and there was no stopping them. Some of the guys turned all the lights on and warned the crowd over the microphone that we would stop the show if they didn't stay where they were. They kept on coming and somebody said, 'Get the hell out of here!' and I took off."

"It turned into a real riot and some of the guys were caught in it. Those people ruined the stage and a lot of the instruments. They were screaming and carrying on so you would have thought it was a lynch mob."

There were times when we were in Hollywood doing the movies and the filming always began early in the morning so all of us would go to bed before too late at night. Fans would come to the door at two, three or four o'clock in the morning and ring the bell. I often answered and they would be standing there on the doorstep and one would say, "Can we see Elvis?"

"I'm sorry," I would answer, "but he is asleep." It was tough to be polite but we always began by being that way and if the unwanted guests just left that would be the end of it. More often than not however, they would say, "We just want to see him for a few minutes."

"I'm sorry," in a firmer voice, "but he's asleep. We're working a very hard schedule and he needs his rest."

"Can't we just go to his door and look in at him? We won't wake him up."

And so it would go on and on, until we would have to end it by telling them to get off the property and get off right now.

The Colonel has estimated that there are more than a quarter million members of Elvis Presley Fan Clubs. This is the true hard core of the Elvis fans. They are the ones who buy every record, see every movie, travel across the country to see a personal appearance and exchange newsletters, photographs and souvenirs with each other.

The great majority, of course, are the millions of fans who just like Elvis and his voice, buy his records and see an occasional movie or appearance when they can.

Chapter Five

Changes

After the first taste of being constantly on the road, I found I didn't want to be away from my family all that much and, even though the excitement was fun, I decided to leave the payroll and go back into radio in Memphis. I worked for a station there for a few months, but it didn't go well and I left to look for something else. About the same time our son was born and the expenses really left me flat broke.

One morning I opened a letter from Elvis and there was a note in it which said George Klein had told him I was short of money. There was also a check for $300.00 in the envelope. I really appreciated it, and wrote him a thank-you note and told him I would repay the loan as quickly as I could. Most of the time everybody had good intentions of repaying anything they would get from Elvis, but it just never happened and he didn't expect it.

Every week I set aside a few dollars until I had about fifty dollars saved. My wife, Patsy, and I were the only two at Graceland with Elvis one afternoon and he was getting ready to go upstairs when I said, "Elvis, can I talk with you for a minute?"

This was usually the way somebody would begin when they wanted to borrow something from him, and he could tell. He didn't really like to be asked a lot for money unless it was important. He looked at me and said, "Yeah, what is it?"

From my back pocket, I pulled out the envelope with the fifty dollars in it and said, "Here, it's not all of it, but it's as much as I have saved to pay you back. I'll get the rest as soon as I can save it."

He opened the envelope and looked at the money and at me. He was so surprised. I went into the other room and sat down to read the paper. It was about five minutes before he came out and started to go up the stairs when he stopped and said, "Man, you don't know what this does to me. You are the first person, the very first person who has ever paid me back. I don't believe this."

He had the biggest smile on his face I've ever seen when he ran upstairs.

About twenty minutes later he came out into the back yard where Patsy and I had gone. He was still grinning and holding the envelope in his hand. He said, "Here, I don't want it. You need it more than I do."

"No, I'm not going to take it back," I said, "I owe you the money."

"No," he answered, "I don't want your money. Just the thought of wanting to pay me back is enough."

"No, I owe you the money, now keep it."

He put it down on the table and said, "Damn it. Take the damn money. I don't want it."

I was beginning to be irritated. "If you don't take it, I'll burn it now. It's your money."

He said, "No, I'm serious, man. Just the thought is enough. Take it." He left it on the table and walked away. I put the envelope back in my pocket.

Shortly thereafter Alan called me in Knoxville and said Elvis had told him to ask if I wanted to come back to work. I did, and began again to work for Elvis. After a few days I went to Elvis' father and told him to take $25.00 a week out of my pay check until the $300.00 was paid back and asked that he not tell Elvis. The deductions were made as I requested.

We began the trips again to Hollywood, and the world of movie making. Elvis didn't like to fly then and we had a Dodge mobile home which we would drive from Memphis to Hollywood and back. It was a lot of fun. We would drive all night and sleep in a motel during the day. Security was always a problem. If anyone found out we were in a motel there was no way we could get any rest.

When we checked into a motel usually Joe Esposito or I would go in and get the rooms, which wasn't easy. I don't know why but we never used credit cards then, it was either cash or check. When we would ask for eight rooms, but wouldn't tell the desk clerk who they were for, there was often concern on their part about being paid. Eventually, I called on Kemmons Wilson, founder and board chairman of Holiday Inns, Inc. Mr. Wilson started Holiday Inns in Memphis and the headquarters remained there. I explained our predicament while we were on the road and the position we were in when we asked for so many rooms. He in turn gave me a letter of credit, good at any Holiday Inn, in which he personally guaranteed payment of the bill. We never had any more trouble.

Prior to making the arrangement with Kemmons however, we once stopped at a Holiday Inn in Texas on the way back to Memphis. Joe had arranged for the rooms and somehow the news got out that Elvis was there. Well, there were a dozen photographers, and television people, and I don't know how many fans in front of the place when we went to leave. Elvis called everybody into his room and really got mad. He was screaming at all of us but especially at Joe, who was foreman at the time. Joe kept saying, "Hey, Elvis, it's not my fault. I didn't tell anybody."

"It's not anybody's fault. It . . ." I began, but he looked at me and said, "Shut up! I don't want to hear it." He was really mad.

We managed to get out without too much trouble but he wouldn't talk with any of us from the motel to Graceland. When we did reach home he got out of the mobile home and went to his room and didn't come back down. When we had left the motel rooms, Joe had hung back to talk with Elvis, but of course, I didn't know what was said. Joe was upset over the whole thing, his family was in Los Angeles and I guess he decided he had had enough of it all.

A week went by and one day Joe said to me, "If he's not going to come down here and talk about this I'm going to leave. I'm going to quit."

I tried to talk him out of it because I knew how much he

and Elvis cared about each other. He wouldn't listen though, and said, "No, I'm leaving. There's no reason for me to stay here."

He gathered the checkbooks together, some checks which were made out and waiting for Elvis to sign, and some bills which had to be paid. He gave them to me and said, "When he comes down try to get him to sign these checks, and send them out and give him the rest of the stuff."

I said, "Okay, but I wish you would stay."

"I'm going to call his room but if he won't come down and talk with me I'm leaving."

He called Elvis and, of course, I heard only one side of the conversation. Joe said to Elvis, "Well, if you are not going to come down I'm leaving. I'm going back to California to work."

When he hung up the phone he came over, we shook hands and he left. Well, Joe was no more than outside the gate when Elvis came down. He said, "Did he leave?"

"Yes," I answered.

"Okay, I want some breakfast."

Elvis never liked to fire anybody and this just may have been his way of doing it. I don't really know. I didn't say anything until he finished eating but then I brought the checkbooks and checks which had to be signed to him and said, "Joe asked me to give these to you. He said to tell you these checks should be signed and mailed."

"Well," he said, "looks like I got me a new bookkeeper and foreman."

"No," I answered, "Joe just wanted me to give these to you."

"I said it looks like I've got me a new bookkeeper and foreman and the raise goes with the job."

That's how I became foreman of the Memphis Mafia.

In 1964, when I assumed Joe's duties as personal bookkeeper and foreman, the job necessitated my being close at hand virtually twenty-four hours a day. After about a week of going back and forth to Patsy and the children, Elvis suggested that I move into Graceland with my family. My wife, Patsy, my daughter, Sheri, and my son, Marc, and I moved into two downstairs rooms. My youngest daughter Angie was born while we were living there. There were advantages and disadvantages in living at Graceland. The surroundings were nice and it cut our expenses down, but privacy was at a minimum and it just wasn't like living in our own home. After almost a year, a new apartment complex was built near Graceland and we moved there, along with Mike Keeton and Larry Geller and their families.

A long time after Joe resigned and returned to California, we were in Hollywood and I called him to see how he was doing. He had been working as an extra in the movies but wasn't doing very well. He was also hurt that none of the other guys had called him or been in touch. I would have felt the same, if it had happened to me.

I said, "Man, why don't you come on up to the house? This whole thing is really crazy."

Joe said, "Well, find out if it would be okay for me to come up, and let me know. I'm not going to go there if he's still mad."

That night Elvis and I were alone in the den and I said, "By the way, I talked to Joe today."

"Oh really," he said, not even looking up from his newspaper.

"Yeah," I answered, "I invited him to come up to the house."

He blew up. He said, "Damn it, why did you do that?" He was furious.

"Wait a minute," I said, "Elvis, you don't understand."

"No, it's you who doesn't understand." He threw down the newspaper and charged to his room.

I called Joe and told him I was sorry but that it didn't seem like a good idea for him to come to the house. Later that same year, when we were back in Memphis, we had just come home from some all-night movies and the phone rang, it was Joe. We talked some and then he said, "Man, do you think Elvis will talk to me?"

"Why, what's wrong?" I asked him because I knew Elvis would ask what Joe wanted.

"Things are just not doing too well out here. I get tired of having to stay by the phone all the time and wait for a call about work as an extra. I'd like to come back to work. Do you think he will talk with me?"

"I think he will, but I'm not sure. I'll ask."

"Is he still up?"

"Yeah," I answered. "Hold on. I'll call his room."

I buzzed Elvis on the intercom and said, "Joe's on the phone."

"What does he want?"

"I think he wants to come back."

"Do we need him?" He was leaving it to me to decide.

Without hesitation, I answered, "Yeah, we need him."

That may not have been completely true insofar as the workload we had at the time was concerned, but Joe was a valuable man and I wanted him and Elvis together again.

"Let me talk to him," Elvis said. So I went back on the line with Joe and told him Elvis was on the phone and then I hung up.

A few minutes later Elvis buzzed me back and said, "Get on the line." When I did he hung up.

Joe said, "I'm going to need some money to get back there. He said to come back." I was happy that he would be with us again.

When Joe returned we shared the responsibilities. I continued to keep the checkbooks and pay the bills and Joe coordinated a lot of the work with Colonel Parker. We really worked well together and things seemed to be much better after that. Joe and his family moved into the apartment complex near Graceland where Larry, Mike and I were living.

There were other times when Elvis would get mad beyond all reason. He was usually very polite and seldom used bad language or did anything to upset anyone, but when he did become angry about something, he would really blow.

Elvis hated to be called a son of a bitch. One time he told me, "I get a little angry when arguing with people, but if anyone ever called me a son of a bitch, I'd deck him. It makes me think they're calling my mother that name."

All well and good, most people don't like to be called that either, but when he got mad he would call anyone a son of a bitch and anything else he could think of. He disliked having others curse around any girl he was with, but he would do it. He would use profanity around his girlfriends and around our wives or girlfriends without thinking of it. There was a time when I used bad language a lot and Elvis said to me, "How about watching your language around Priscilla, she doesn't need to hear talk like that."

Well, I was half-angry and half-amused at the contradiction because of the language he used, not only around my wife, but also around Priscilla. I looked at him and said, "I don't complain when you talk that way in front of Patsy, and you wouldn't stop if I did."

He thought about that for a second, smiled and said, "You're damn right, you bastard." We laughed. One thing I seldom saw him do was use profanity when strangers were around although when he really got mad, he didn't care who heard him.

Elvis became angry once about the slot-car track he had built at Graceland. Everybody had cars on the huge track. He had spent thousands of dollars to have a special room built and the slot-car track installed. We all raced the little cars, and nobody paid too much attention which car they used at any given time. This one afternoon we were racing the cars and some of the guys started complaining that they didn't have their regular cars. At first it was all in fun but they kept it up, just bickering back and forth. Elvis listened to this for awhile and then blew up. He called every one of the guys everything he could think of, he threw a couple of the cars against the wall and walked out of the room. We were all pretty ashamed of our childish display but the track was given to a local orphanage and the room converted to a trophy room.

Elvis was very religious, He never went to church because he was afraid of what might happen to the service if he walked in and fans were in the congregation. He felt, however, that he could reach God wherever he happened to be, church was not necessary. There were certain feelings he had about some preachers who were only interested in money and he didn't want to be associated with them. Others, he thought were hypocritical. One thing he really disliked was to have someone try to push religion on him, or preach to him. An exception, at times, was his Aunt Nash, Vernon's sister, who was an ordained minister. He would often sit and talk with her about the teachings of the Bible.

He became fascinated by many of the oriental religions and spent days reading and studying every book he could find on the subject. I often brought these books to him when I would find them in stores. He appreciated the thought and, after reading the books, would always tell me how much he enjoyed them.

There was a time when he became interested in the Self-Realization Park in California and spent many hours talking with one of the women in charge. Elvis put great stock in what this woman had to say and he would call her from all over the country. I never knew how, but when he wanted to talk with her, he always managed to reach her regardless of where she happened to be.

Elvis was deeply moved by gospel and spiritual music, and he loved the people who sang it. He spent hours listening to groups like the Harmonizing Four and their great bass singer Jimmy Jones. He liked the Golden Gate Quartet and the Statesmen Quartet. All of his male backup vocal groups, the Jordanaires, The Imperials and J.D. Sumner and the Stamps, were gospel groups.

Life after death was one of Elvis' beliefs and he often talked about it. He believed he had been put on this earth for a special reason but he didn't know what the reason was, or at least he never expressed it. But he talked about everything else. He talked and talked and talked.

Elvis was a delightful person to be with. He would dart from subject to subject like a butterfly trying to taste every flower. He had a child's enthusiasm, curiosity and imagination. If his interpretation of events didn't quite fit the facts, he would alter them to fit his whims. He told stories over and over and often would say things like, "Joe will tell you that's true, he was there." And Joe, or whoever he picked at that time, had not been within a thousand miles of where the event about which he was talking had taken place.

There was no way he could keep a secret. He would come to me and say, "Now don't tell anybody else, I don't want anybody else to know," and then go on to tell me something we were going to do or someplace we were going to go.

Within an hour every one of the guys or someone outside the group, would know and he would say, "There's a leak in this damn organization." He was the leak, he had told everybody.

Elvis explained everything. He would be talking to one or all of us and would explain why something worked, how it worked, who made it, where it was made, what materials were used to make it and everything else he could think of about it, even if we already knew. He loved words and once had me buy each one of the guys a dictionary and notebook, and we all sat around at night and learned new words and how to use them. He really enjoyed doing it. Each guy would pick a word from the dictionary and we would all discuss it, pronounce it, write it with its meaning in our notebooks and learn it.

Elvis respected all religions and his generosity was overwhelming. I once mentioned to Elvis that the Jewish congregation in Memphis was having a drive to raise funds to build a million-dollar community center and asked if he would help. He responded by donating $12,500 to build three music rooms in memory of his mother and in honor of his father and Colonel Parker. In addition, a donation was given in memory of Alan's father.

Another time he told me he wanted to create a symbol of brotherhood and together we designed a watch on whose face appeared every twenty seconds a cross and a star of David. These were made by Harry Levitch and we distributed them to friends. Elvis asked me to arrange, at a later time, to have a footstone placed at his mother's grave with a cross on one side and a star of David on the other, with the inscription, *Not mine, but thy will be done.*

He was a great fan of General Patton and General MacArthur. He learned General MacArthur's farewell speech by heart and often quoted parts of it to us. Elvis liked George C. Scott in the movie *Patton* so much that he would see it over and over until he knew every word and action in the script. He liked military things and military people. Once when we were living in California he decided we should all visit General Omar Bradley and, without even calling first, we all went to the General's home. General Bradley was a real gentleman and welcomed us and we spent several hours talking with him and looking at the trophies from his years of military service. Elvis was proud of his friends and he would not even have considered going there without the whole gang going along, but the General seemed to enjoy the visit also.

Comedy was another love. I'll bet we saw every Peter Sellers' movie a dozen times and I know we watched *Doctor*

Strangelove at least fifty times. I'm not exaggerating, at least fifty times. Elvis also liked Woody Allen and would watch his movies whenever possible. He loved things which were funny and would find funny things in almost any situation. There were times when it was embarrassing. He often laughed in the middle of the most serious event and nobody knew what he was laughing about. At other times he would lean over and whisper something funny to one of the guys who would break-up in the midst of a serious situation, looking like a fool and nobody knew it was Elvis who had started it.

Elvis liked big voices and big sounds. He loved to watch symphony orchestras on television and very often would get up and conduct the orchestra while standing in front of the television set.

Boxing and football were favorites on television. He liked Rocky Marciano and later Muhammad Ali. He met Ali once and gave him a custom robe as a gift and was pleased to see Ali wear it at one of his fights. Jim Brown, Bobby Mitchell and Rosie Grier were his favorite football stars and he liked the Cleveland Browns as a team. Elvis and Jim Brown hit it off great when they met. They seemed to have a lot of respect for each other and Jim once visited Elvis at Graceland.

Talent, more than anything else, seemed to be the thing which attracted Elvis. He respected real talent and had an appreciation of it. This is a trait not often seen in people as talented as Elvis.

Chapter Six

Elvis Meets Some Greats

Elvis had a great influence on all pop music, of course, and the Beatles were no exception. When they made their first trip to the United States they, through their manager, tried to arrange with Colonel Parker a meeting with Elvis, but because of a conflict of dates and locations it was just never possible for them to get together. When they came back the following year, 1965, they were going to be in Hollywood at the same time Elvis was making a film, so a meeting was arranged.

We were living on Perugia Way in Bel-Air at the time and Elvis had asked them to come to the house. Well, the news of the meeting had leaked out and it was impossible to move on the street that night. It was packed with the Beatles' fans, as well as the usual crowd which was always there to see Elvis. When the Beatles arrived they had their security, we had ours, and the neighborhood was covered with local policemen trying to keep the crowd in control. The fans came close to breaking down the gates.

Colonel Parker was present, as was the Beatles' manager, Brian Epstein. Some of our wives and children, who wanted to meet the Beatles, had been invited too, so there was a fair-sized group inside, but nothing compared to the army of fans who waited just beyond the fence. When the Beatles came they were in awe of Elvis. Elvis knew what the Beatles had accomplished and had a great appreciation for their talent, but Elvis was one who treated the janitor and the company president exactly the same. He didn't want the meeting to have the flavor of the subjects being granted an audience with the king. He just wanted to know the Beatles as people, to have a down-to-earth relationship with them.

There was one area in the den where we usually sat down and talked at night. It had a long sofa and Elvis sat in the center and the Beatles were on each side. They just sat there and stared at him. No one said a word for an awkward length of time. Finally Elvis broke the silence by saying, "Look, if you guys are just going to sit there and stare at me all night, I'm going to bed."

That broke the ice and he continued, "I thought we would get together and talk and exchange experiences, and maybe sing and play a little."

When he said, "sing and play a little," they almost flipped. This was what they had hoped would happen, a fun evening. We all began to talk and have a good time and later they got around the piano with the guitars and had a hot jam session. They worked well together and some of the songs and music that were done that night should have been recorded it was so fantastic.

There was a small coffee table that opened to become a full-size roulette table and, later in the evening, everyone began playing and had a really good time, particularly Joe and the Colonel who were the bankers and did quite well.

As the Beatles were leaving, one of them invited us to the house where they were staying. The following evening, Elvis was not able to go but three or four of us went to their house and the Beatles told us that before they came to the United States that they had told their manager that the only person they wanted to meet was Elvis.

It was about that time we all got motorcycles, all except me. Elvis had a Harley Davidson which he would ride whenever he could and sometimes we all rented motorcycles and went along. The neighbors, in quiet Bel-Air, complained when there was too much noise but we didn't do it often enough to cause any real problem. One afternoon, however, we were in the den talking when Elvis said, "The weather is so beautiful out here, I want everybody to be able to go motorcycle riding. Alan, call the motorcycle place and tell them I want thirteen Triumph Bonneville motorcycles."

Alan said, "You going to buy them?"

"Yeah, I want everybody to have a motorcycle."

"Wait a minute," I said, "if you're buying one for me don't do it. You know I don't like riding that much."

"I want everyone to have one, get thirteen."

"Elvis," I said, "don't waste your money. I'm not going to ride it, so don't buy it."

We had a short argument but he kept saying, "Damn it, I want you to have one," and I kept saying, "I don't want it."

When Alan went to the phone I went with him and said, "Don't get one for me."

Alan called and found a place that had twelve and came back and told Elvis he had located them, and they would be delivered. Elvis didn't like to wait for anything and he said to Alan, "Call them back and tell them I want them here in an hour."

Alan answered, "I don't think they can have them here that fast. They are probably in crates and they have to put them together."

"I don't care. Tell them if they can't have them here in an hour we'll get them at another place."

"Okay," Alan said and went back to the phone.

The motorcycles were delivered in just a little over an hour. When they arrived Elvis saw there were only twelve and he said to me, "I thought I told you to get one."

"No," I answered, "I told you I don't want one."

They all went riding and, of course, the Bel-Air Association was up-in-arms about the noise. They wrote a letter and made it very clear that if we were going to live there we would have to stop the motorcycle riding. Elvis, however, figured he would outfox them so he hired a truck which would come to the house every Saturday morning, which was the time he wanted to ride, and load on all the bikes and take them to the Bel-Air gate. Elvis and the guys would go down to the gate, get on the bikes and go riding ouside Bel-Air. The truck would be there when they returned and bring the motorcycles back to the house.

Elvis continued to keep after me. Everytime a motorcycle was mentioned or they would get ready to go riding he would say, "Moon, get a damn bike. I want to give you one."

This went on and on with me always saying, "I don't want one."

A day came when he started about it again and I said, "Elvis, I told you I don't want one. I don't like the damn things and I don't want it."

"Then go out and find something else you want and buy it," he said and walked out of the house.

Now, we had a new routine started. Everyday he would ask, "Did you find something you want yet?"

I finally said, "You don't have to buy me something just because I didn't want a bike. Everybody else likes riding and appreciates the motorcycles and that's cool with me, I don't want anything, man."

"Well, I want to buy you something."

One afternoon, I had been waiting several hours to see Elvis. His father had arrived for a visit and I assumed Elvis would get to me the first chance he had as there were several checks needing his signature before being mailed. Through a window I saw him go out and get into the Rolls with his father. Now, he knew I had been waiting for him but when I went to the front door to ask how long he would be gone, the car raced out of the driveway and Elvis just gave me a little wave and a smile.

I said to myself, "To hell with it," and left the house and went back to my apartment to have dinner with my wife. No sooner had we sat down and started to eat than the phone rang. Sonny West was on the line when I answered and he said, "Elvis wants you up here right now."

"Man," I said, "I just got home."

"I'm just telling you. He said he wants you to come here now."

"What the hell for?" I asked.

"He needs a couple of checks, and he wants to sign the ones you have," he answered.

"Damn it, Sonny," I was mad, "I've been waiting there to see him for hours, now I'm just sitting down to eat."

"He said he wants you now, and I think you'd better come."

I was really mad. I threw my briefcase into the old Ford

and cursed all the way to Bel-Air about the inconsiderate bastard. When I drove in the gate he was in a new white Cadillac and backed it up until he had blocked the driveway. I slammed the door of my car as I got out and walked toward him. He got out of the Cadillac and I said, "Man, your timing is great. I've been waiting here all afternoon for you to sign the damn checks."

"Well, I had to go do something."

"You could have at least told me."

"Here," he said and held the Cadillac keys up in front of my face.

"Here, what?" I wasn't to be placated with his charm.

"Move that car back into a parking space and then put the keys in your pocket. The car is yours."

He caught me completely by surprise. No one had ever given me anything like that before and I said, "Wait a minute, Elvis."

"Damn it," he said, "I told you to go out and buy something but since you wouldn't do it, I had to. I don't want any arguments, the car is yours."

I was stunned and completely overwhelmed. I couldn't keep the tears from coming to my eyes. Billy was standing right next to me and, after I hugged and thanked Elvis, I reached into my pocket and gave the keys to the Ford to Billy and said, "Here, I got something today, now I want you to have something. You have been talking about getting a car for your wife to drive, now you have one."

Elvis thought he had gotten rid of the noisy old Ford, but he was happy to see me give it to Billy and Billy was pleased to receive it. Later he sold the Ford and gave me half the money.

That wasn't the end of the story. Elvis got such a kick out of seeing my reaction to the gift of a Cadillac that within a week he had bought one for each of the guys in the group.

Elvis enjoyed giving gifts, but once he had a hard time giving something away. This was when he heard the yacht *Potomac,* which had been used by President Roosevelt, was going to be sold at auction or scrapped. Elvis was a great admirer of President Roosevelt and the work he had done with the March of Dimes. He decided to buy the *Potomac* and give it to the March of Dimes to be used as a floating museum. Elvis and Colonel Parker thought the March of Dimes would be delighted to have it to use as a fund-raising museum. It was, of course, a very historic ship with a lot of mementos of the Roosevelt years.

The Colonel bought it at the auction for about $50,000 and announced they were going to give it to the March of Dimes. When, however, they approached that organization, the March of Dimes people were polite but refused to accept the gift. It upset Elvis quite a bit because he couldn't understand why they didn't want it. As a matter of fact, I never did understand why they didn't accept, but I guess it had to do with the cost of maintaining the ship. Elvis never really got over it. He said once, "They could have accepted it and then sold it themselves and kept the money. I didn't care what they did with it, it just seemed that it would have made a good museum."

Anyway, they refused to accept the ship so he went to several other charities but none of them wanted it. I think they all said that the maintenance costs would be too much. He finally went to Danny Thomas, who was doing so much for St. Jude Children's Hospital in Memphis and asked him if St. Jude would like to have the *Potomac*. Danny Thomas said yes and arrangements were made for a meeting between Elvis and Danny in Long Beach, California, where the papers would be transferred aboard the ship.

We had been in Las Vegas for weeks before the transfer was to take place. The day before we were to be in Long Beach, we drove to Los Angeles from Las Vegas and then on to Long Beach the following morning. We all looked like ghosts from the Vegas weeks of being up all night and sleeping all day.

We arrived in Long Beach, California, looking very much like the real Mafia. All the guys were wearing sunglasses and were dressed in dark business suits, which, when contrasted with our funeral-room pallor, made us appear to be midnight gangsters who were seeing daylight for the first time.

The docks were lined with reporters and photographers ready to record the transfer of a famous ship from one star to another. We had the opportunity to inspect the ship before the ceremony began, and it was eerie seeing all those mementos from history. The ship was in a run-down condition. As a matter of fact, the bed sheets looked like they had not been changed since President Roosevelt slept on them. The only part that looked good was the side of the hull which faced the dock and, therefore, the cameras. Colonel Parker, in his infinite way, had had that side painted.

The ceremony took place at a long table on the top deck where Elvis and Danny were seated. After the signing of the transfer papers both made a short speech about their mutual interest in children and the work being done at St. Jude's Hospital.

Elvis had hoped the ship would become a museum to President Roosevelt and there were plans to do that on the Mississippi River at Memphis, but, apparently, the cost was more than the hospital could hope to recover. The ship was later sold by the hospital to, I believe, a salvage company which used it in their work. The hospital, of course, received all of the money from the sale which, I think, was $65,000, so they were very happy.

There's another presidential story which was rather funny, the way it turned out. We were in Hollywood making *Girl Happy* for Metro-Goldwyn-Mayer and doing some filming on the back lot near the swimming pool. We heard from Colonel Parker's office that President Johnson's daughter, Linda Bird, wanted to meet Elvis and would be over about one o'clock in the afternoon. She was dating George Hamilton at the time and was interested in the motion picture industry, in addition to being an Elvis fan.

There is a vast green field just behind the pool area and when one o'clock arrived we saw Linda Bird Johnson approaching from the far end of the field with George Hamilton at her side and several Secret Service men on each side of them. It is almost necessary to have a mental picture of the situation in order to see the humor in the way it came off. When Elvis saw them coming toward us in what looked like a skirmish line, he said, "Okay, you guys are my security so let's meet them halfway. Flank me on both sides just as they are. Keep your eyes on them and stare them down."

We were all laughing but managed to pull ourselves together and assume a tough appearance as we lined up on each side of Elvis and marched across the field to meet the other group. As we drew near, they stopped and we stopped. Elvis went forward to meet Linda Bird and George. We stood there without the hint of a smile on our faces, with our hands behind us or clasped in front staring at the Secret Service men. It was like a formal ceremony with Elvis, Linda Bird and George between these two lines of bodyguards. The Secret Service men didn't seem to know what to do with themselves, it was obvious that we stood ready to protect Elvis from Linda Bird, George and them! We stayed like that until the center group finished talking and Elvis returned to us. Then we marched back to the pool area, trying hard not to break-up before we were out of earshot. I think we made the Secret Service men self-conscious or else they thought we were a bunch of nuts. We never did find out what they really thought, but we loved it.

Elvis' crazy antics never ceased. He would do things on the spur of the moment like riding in his $50,000 Mercedes limousine and all of a sudden open the sun roof, stand up, hold up a flashlight or walking stick and yell at the top of his voice, "Woe, ye mothers."

There were times when he would do the same thing at the house when watching something on television he didn't like. He was warning those he thought were doing wrong to beware of the wrath of God. It was his version of the Biblical passage, *Woe ye scribes and pharisees.*

As much as his antics were crazy, his concern for other people was genuine. Graceland is located on a main thoroughfare in Memphis, formerly a highway to Mississippi. The traffic is heavy on the boulevard and there have been many accidents in front of the gates of Graceland. When fans visited the house they had to park on the street or in a parking lot at a shopping center across the street.

One day, a couple with a small child stopped to see Elvis' home. They parked across the street and as they were crossing to the gate of Graceland a car hit the mother and child. The woman was only slightly injured but the child was killed.

Sonny heard about the accident a few hours later and after investigating learned that the couple, from out-of-town, had nowhere to stay and very little money. He asked Elvis if it would be all right to put them in a motel while they made arrangements for their baby. Elvis told Sonny, "Hell, yes, and let me know what else they need and what we can do."

For years the Gospel Music Dove awards were held in Memphis and each year Elvis would do his best to attend. He never sat in the audience, because of the security problems, but in a private section behind the stage. There were often five thousand or more people who came from all over the country to see and hear every major gospel group and artist.

Elvis was in his glory listening to the Statesmen, Stamps, Oak Ridge Boys, The Imperials and many others, including the Blackwood Brothers Quartet. Just before the end of the program Elvis would be introduced to the audience and he would go out onto the stage, make a bow and then leave the auditorium without singing. It was their time, not his.

Elvis would make up his mind to do something and do it. I remember one evening I was at Graceland with Elvis, Priscilla, Joe and Joanie Esposito when Elvis decided he wanted to play water polo and we played. That, of course, would not be unusual except that Elvis never liked to go into the deep end of a pool. He couldn't swim, but that night he decided he was going to do it and he seemed to completely lose any fear he had of the water and swam as well as the rest of us. From then on he spent a lot of time at the pool where he either swam or practiced diving with scuba tanks. He also spent many hours sunbathing.

His mood could change in a minute and we learned one of the quickest ways to make it change for the worst was to let him hear us ask about it. There was a time when we heard one of the guys ask, "What kind of a mood is he in today?"

He exploded and yelled, "You just put him in a rotten-ass mood! I'm sick and tired of everybody wondering what kind of a mood I'm in. If you would all do your damn jobs right I wouldn't be in a bad mood."

That used to bug the hell out of us when he would get mad and say someone wasn't doing his job.

There was a time in the sixties when we were doing a recording session in Nashville and were joined by an RCA Artists and Repertoire man, Felton Jarvis. Felton had previously produced some big hits with Tommy Roe, Fats Domino and other artists. Felton was a great Elvis fan and they soon became good friends. One of the reasons Elvis took to Felton so quickly was because of Felton's sense of humor. It was crazy, very much like Elvis', and he was just as weird, in many ways.

Felton's office was decorated like a jungle and to add some authenticity he kept his pet there, a fifteen-foot live boa constrictor. He kept it in a burlap sack on the floor and he loved to watch people's eyes bulge when the sack started to move.

Felton kept things lively and Elvis moving at the recording sessions. While Elvis sang, Felton would get up and lip synch to Elvis' voice and imitate Elvis' wild stage movements. Elvis loved it and soon insisted on having Felton at all of his sessions.

When Elvis began performing in Las Vegas, Felton was in charge of the sound system and he went on all the tours.

One day we learned that Felton had a kidney disease. He had to undergo dialysis and would not be able to continue on the tours for awhile. He became very thin and lost a lot of his stamina, but Felton was a fighter and he wasn't going to let the disease defeat him. It was several months before he could resume his duties with Elvis.

When he did return he brought a new song, *Burning Love*. It was obvious while Elvis was recording that Felton wanted to do his imitation but his condition kept him from it. After the session Felton went to Elvis and apologized for not providing his usual enthusiasm. Elvis looked at him in amazement and said, "Hey man, here you are trying to fight this problem you have and you're worried about providing me with enthusiasm. You are something else!"

Elvis knew that getting a kidney transplant was difficult because of the cost and the scarcity of kidney donors. He asked Felton, "Look man, do you mind if I help you get a kidney?"

Needless to say, Felton was greatly touched by the offer. Weeks later, after Felton had given him all the information necessary, Elvis called the head of the hospital where the kidney bank was located. Elvis told him about Felton's need and then said, "Doctor, this man means a great deal to me and many other people. He has brought a lot of joy to others and it would really mean a lot to me if he could receive a kidney. In return, if there's anything I can do for the hospital I'll be glad to do it."

The doctor had received Felton's records from his Nashville doctor and, without hesitating, he told Elvis that if Felton meant that much to so many people he would get the needed kidney. The only thing the doctor asked in return was that Elvis visit the hospital and kidney bank and see the work they were doing. Elvis agreed.

Felton got his kidney transplant and has been his crazy, weird self ever since. Elvis would have it no other way.

Chapter Seven

Cowboys and Country Gentlemen

Early in his career, while doing one-night stands in the south, Elvis often took a few days of rest in Biloxi, Mississippi, where he had the use of riding horses. He enjoyed telling the story of a time when he, Red West, Arthur Hooten and Gene Smith were riding. Arthur, a big heavy-set man, was on a horse that bolted and started to run fast, he couldn't stop it. Red and Elvis started riding hard after him but before they could catch the horse, Arthur leaped off and grabbed a big tree limb, holding on for dear life. This was just one of the horse stories Elvis used to tell. He liked riding horses and did all his own riding in the movies.

One day, in 1966, we were sitting around and Elvis mentioned that Priscilla wanted a horse so she could ride around Graceland. After thinking about it for awhile, he suggested that we go find out what horses were available. He bought Priscilla a beautiful black horse and she named it Domino.

After seeing Priscilla riding her horse, he decided he wanted one also. A Palomino was what he really had in mind. We heard about a beautiful one in Mississippi and went to see it. Elvis fell in love and bought the Palomino on the spot for $3,500. It was a quarter horse and Elvis named it Rising Sun. Next, came a horse for Vernon called Midnight and then more horses for others to ride. This necessitated the cleaning of the little-used barn located in the back of Graceland's fourteen acres. We repaired and scrubbed the inside of the barn and even managed to create a little lounge area. This became the center of considerable activity and we began spending a lot of time there.

Tennessee is known for its walking horses and the suburb of Collierville was the home of one of the all-time champions, Carbon Copy. Elvis wanted to see the famous horse and the luxurious Lenox Farms where Carbon Copy's owner lived. We went there almost every night and Elvis rode some of their Tennessee walkers. He tried to buy Carbon Copy but the price was incredibly high, even for Elvis. Instead, he purchased another walker called Bear.

There were horses all over Graceland, including a little Shetland pony called Boogaloo. The little pony would kick, all over the place, anyone unfortunate enough to have gotten behind it. Pretty soon the fourteen acres had more horses than it could hold.

Elvis began talking about the advantages of having a ranch near Graceland, with large open spaces for riding the horses. There would be room for everybody to get together and ride. We started driving frequently into Mississippi and kept passing a beautifully-kept ranch on Goodman Road, near Bull Frog Corner. It had a barn, cattle house and crossings. In the middle was a lake with a white arched bridge and a tall white cross behind that. Elvis was impressed and it seemed that everything else looked shabby in comparison. The only problem was that the ranch was not for sale.

We kept looking and looking, as Elvis had his heart set on finding just the right place. Weeks went by, and one day Alan came up to the house and told Elvis there was a "For Sale" sign in front of the beautiful place on Goodman Road we had passed so many times. We jumped in the car and rode down there quickly. Elvis was happier than I had seen him in a long time. We learned the name of the owner and made arrangements to meet with him at the ranch the next day.

After driving over the one-hundred-and-sixty-three acres, we went to the ranch house with the owner. He suggested to Elvis that he stay there for a few days so he could determine if the ranch was what he wanted. Elvis, however, was never one to wait when he wanted something and he said,

"Well, thanks, but if I wanted to buy the ranch, how much are you asking?"

"$375,000," the owner answered. His back was to me and I shook my head to indicate to Elvis that I thought it was too high. Elvis said, "Will you take any less?"

"I don't see how I could," the owner answered.

"Well," Elvis said, "let me think about it. I would like to have it."

We stayed there for a few days and before leaving Elvis told the owner he would like to buy the ranch but would need a few days to think it over. We went back to Graceland and Elvis talked about the ranch and the horses we could have. It still seemed like a lot of money to me and I felt certain we could get the price down if the owner kept the herd of cattle. They were a rare, expensive breed, and all Elvis really needed was the land. When I suggested this, Elvis said, "Good idea, what the hell do I want with cattle anyway. Why don't you and Alan go down tomorrow and see what you can work out with him?"

The next day Alan and I went to talk with the owner of the ranch. We began the conversation by telling him that Elvis wanted us to determine the value of various items on the ranch. We asked about some of the farm equipment and then I said, "What are the cattle worth?"

"Oh, about $70,000 to $75,000," he said.

"Well, I'll tell you what," I said, "why don't you keep the cattle and sell Elvis the ranch for an even $300,000?"

"What would I do with them?"

"Sell them."

"Yeah," he said, "I could do that but it's about three months before the auction and that's where you get the best prices."

"Well, what if we kept them for you until then?"

"I think that might be okay, then," he said.

About the time he finished agreeing, the phone rang and when he answered, I heard him say, "Well, yeah, that's the way I thought you felt about it. Okay, here I'll put him on."

He called me to the phone and when I answered, Elvis said, "Don't try to do anymore. I told him I want the ranch and we'll pay the price."

"But, Elvis," I said.

"No, I don't want to talk about it." He cut me off, "Come on back here."

Alan and I were annoyed at his sudden change, which we thought made us look ridiculous, but we thanked the owner for his time and went back to Graceland. Elvis never told us why he changed his mind, but we thought it was because his father had expressed some interest in the cattle and Elvis decided to keep them for him.

After the deal was closed and Elvis became the new owner of the ranch, he changed the name to Circle G, G for Graceland. We then went through the process of moving all the horses from Graceland to the ranch. Elvis wanted everyone to spend the first night in the ranch house. Good trick, since there were over twenty guys and their wives and only one bedroom. But everybody was excited about the new place so we slept on the floor in the various rooms.

Elvis then went on a spending spree. It was time to paint-up, fix-up and change some of the furnishings in the ranch house. The first thing was to buy a new king-size bed for Elvis and televisions for each room. Next on the agenda was a truck for Elvis. He bought a big double-cab pickup for himself and when he saw some new Rancheros and El Caminos he bought one for Priscilla, one for himself, then one for one guy, and then another and another until he bought thirty-three, giving each away.

He gave them to strangers, to carpenters who were building a fence around the front of the house and most anyone who happened to wander by. The funniest thing he did was trying to give a truck to a truck salesman, but Alan stopped that just in the nick of time.

I set up a little office at the dining-room table, filling out the new truck papers in each person's name and prayed I gave the right papers for the right truck to the right person. He bought a big six-horse moving van and stake-bed truck and they were never used. To sort them all, I had a sign-painter friend emblazon Circle G on the doors of each truck and then paint inside the door the initials of the person to whom it belonged. In a period of three weeks he had spent $98,000 on trucks and had given most of them away. The magnitude of that figure still remains in my mind because of an incident which happened one rainy night.

About two in the morning, we were all standing in the mud outside the office of the ranch barn when Vernon came to me and, showing me an adding machine tape with totaled figures, said, "Marty, what are we going to do? Look at this figure! $98,000 for trucks?" Vernon was shocked.

It came as no surprise to me however, as we had all cautioned Elvis that he was going overboard on trucks, but he didn't want to hear it, he was happy. The only thing I could say to Vernon was, "I don't know what to tell you to do, Mr. Presley. He's your son."

Elvis gave me a truck after a strange incident. One day he told me to fly to Las Vegas to take care of some business and that I should fly right back, so off I went to Vegas. The business took two hours and I boarded the plane for Memphis. I no sooner returned than Elvis told me I had to go back, so off I went again, stayed a couple of hours and returned. When he again told me to go to Las Vegas, I argued, but he won, so I left for the third time in two days.

I returned to Memphis at 6 a.m. and made up my mind that I was going to get some sleep. I was in bed about two hours when I heard someone banging loudly on my front door. It was impossible to ignore, so I finally went to answer while yelling for whoever was banging to quit. I was half asleep and mad as hell.

I jerked the door open and there stood Elvis and Red. I took one look at Elvis and said, "Oh no, I'm not going back there again."

He laughed and said, "Come on outside, I want to show you something."

It was freezing and snowing, I had on nothing but my shorts and here's damn fool Elvis telling me to come outside. I grabbed a coat and followed him to a Ranchero. He handed me a set of keys and said, "Here, this is yours, you earned it in the last two days." He and Red got into another car and sped away before I could say a word. I opened the door of the Ranchero and saw Priscilla's initials inside. He had given me her truck! The next day he bought her another.

There were more horses, cattle, trucks, farm equipment and trailers arriving every day. It was truly a fun time. We were at the ranch almost every day and often at night, except for the few times when we returned to Graceland. Everyone liked the ranch and the relaxed atmosphere and we all became cowboys.

Elvis bought each of the guys his own horse and riding together was great fun, leisurely rides and spirited ones. Elvis, Priscilla, Sonny, Billy and Red enjoyed racing the horses at full speed. As for myself, I'm not that great a rider. As a matter of fact, a fast crawl is my speed.

One day I was on Red's big, red horse, whose name, for some reason, was Big Red. Elvis, Priscilla, Billy, Lamar, Richard and I went riding. To start things off, Lamar's horse brushed against a tree and knocked him off. That should have been an omen to me. Big Red was the type of horse which would not walk if another horse was running near him. Alongside Big Red and me came Priscilla, who liked for her horse to gallop. I reminded her of Big Red's habit of running if another horse ran and asked her not to gallop her horse. Had I not been so stupid, she might have just walked on by.

With a gleam in her eye, it was "Hi-ho, Domino," and they were off! Naturally, Big Red, with me on board, took off after them. I was scared as hell and yelled for Big Red to stop and for Priscilla to stop, and neither one did. I finally mustered enough nerve to look up just as Big Red headed straight for a barbed-wire fence. Well, I panicked and knew it was time to leave. Closing my eyes, I lifted my leg over the saddle and, as Big Red picked up speed, jumped. I was certain my time had come. The wind was knocked out of me as I landed on my back but luckily there were only a few bruised ribs. That was when I gave up horses and turned in my boots.

Just before Christmas 1966, Elvis, Joe and Joan Esposito and I were driving around the ranch when we reached the northeast corner where there was a gate and a long driveway. Elvis was talking about how great it would be if all the guys and their families lived on the ranch, forming our own commune.

I said to him, "You've been wondering what to give the guys for Christmas, I have an idea. On the left side of this driveway, your land goes all the way to the fence at the back. Why don't you deed one acre of land to each of the guys and let them build their own house on it? Most of them have always had the dream of owning their own house someday and you could make their dream come true, and yours, by having them all together."

He was excited with the idea, as were Joe and Joan. I continued, "You should stipulate that should they stop working for you or if they were fired, you would have the option of buying their house and land at current market value. That way, you wouldn't have anyone living here if you didn't want them."

"Moon, you've got it, man, that's what I want to do."

I had just moved into my new house over the line in Memphis. It had been designed and built for me by my brother-in-law, Bernie, so I was not asking for any land at the ranch for myself. I knew, however, that the guys also had their dreams and I was delighted with myself for having thought of the idea.

Before he went to tell his father what he wanted to do, Elvis told me, "I want to build a big, new beautiful house for Priscilla and me on the ranch. Moon, you and Bernie fly to Los Angeles, show him the house in Trousdale Estates that I liked, tell him I want something similar, only better." Bernie and I left immediately for Los Angeles and were gone two days. When we returned, Bernie began working on tentative house plans. Meanwhile, the group had to return to Hollywood with Elvis for another movie. While there, Elvis told me that he couldn't deed the land to the guys as his father was opposed, thinking it unwise.

Upon our return to Memphis, we went to the ranch. I called Bernie one day to ask about the house plans. It sounded as though there was something he wanted to tell me but simply said, "You'd better talk to Elvis, it looks like the house isn't going to be built."

That evening Elvis seemed unhappy and disturbed. For some time he didn't say what was wrong until I mentioned that I had spoken to Bernie about the house plans. He looked at me and said, "The house isn't going to be built and I don't want to talk about it."

He never did discuss it either, but later I learned that, even though Elvis wanted it, Vernon had dissuaded him.

It was still in Elvis' mind, however, that all the guys who wanted to live on the ranch should be allowed to do so. He first bought a trailer home for Billy and moved it onto the ranch. Then he bought a big, luxurious one for Vernon to use when he wanted. That was it, we started taking daily trips to trailer display parks and, one by one, he bought trailers for each of the guys. I continued to stay in my home in Memphis.

Some of the neighbors complained to the Mississippi Building and Health Departments that Elvis was starting a trailer park. We were refused permits for installation of electricity, septic tanks and other utilities to the trailers. Bernie and his friend, the chief plumbing inspector, met with the city officials and convinced them that the ranch was not a trailer park. The permits were issued that night and the utilities were connected. Elvis liked Vernon's trailer so much he bought one for himself and he and Priscilla stayed there instead of the ranch house.

Elvis was despondent over the neighbors' complaints. He asked his father, Red, Bernie and me to come into his bedroom. We sat on the floor and he was close to tears when he said, "All I want in life is to give my friends the fun and luxury they've never had. Why do people want to stop me? It's a joy for me to see my friends happy. All I want is to see people happy to be alive."

The next day he had gone from despondency to anger when he called Alan and me in and said, "Screw those damn neighbors, to hell with the sons of bitches. Moon, find out how much their properties are appraised for and you and Alan see if you can't get them to sell to me."

Alan and I were able to interest a few neighbors but they wanted to talk to Elvis. He went back with us and offered more than the appraised worth of their properties. They must have been thinking, "Well, here's super-rich Elvis Presley, so we're going to become wealthy too," and they upped their prices. The preacher, who lived across the road, asked for more than double what his property was worth. Elvis kept his cool until we returned to the ranch, then he started yelling, calling everyone of the neighbors all the names he could think of, and those were considerable. He was hurt and he was mad.

He continued, "I want a high, damn fence built around this place so those bastards can't see what's going on and I want the guard at the gate to know that neighbors are not welcome!" That was that, no more was said about or to the neighbors and we never heard from them again. Elvis spent $10,000 for phone communications to the house and trailers and about $140,000 for the trailer homes. Alan Fortas became ranch manager and did a marvelous job. Even when we went to Hollywood, Alan stayed at the ranch. He seemed a natural for the job and said he really liked it.

After Elvis and Priscilla were married, the ranch seemed to become less important to him. We went there occasionally but most of the time was spent at Graceland. Elvis then asked his father to sell the equipment and the trucks which still belonged to him. He also wanted most of the horses returned to Graceland. Then, he finally told his father to sell the ranch. A disastrous sale was arranged with a man who planned to convert it into a gun club. A big club house was built on the land but never used, as the gun club was ruled illegal in the state of Mississippi. The ranch was returned to Elvis and finally sold again. Elvis lost a ton of money on that ranch.

My sister and brother-in-law, Anne and Bernie Grenadier, worked on several projects at Graceland between 1964 and 1966. They began by designing and building a waterfall in the den. Before they began the project, Bernie told Elvis that he would build it only if Elvis agreed not to see that portion of the den until the waterfall was completed. When Bernie said that, I thought he had lost the job before it ever began, but, to everyone's surprise, Elvis said, "Michelangelo, you are something else. Go ahead and do what you think best and I won't look."

Bernie covered half the den and windows with sheets so his working area was blocked from view. During the days that followed, we played football just outside the window where Bernie was working inside. Elvis always told us jokingly to throw the ball over his head near the windows so he could have an excuse to peek in past the sheets.

It was great for everyone the night Bernie gave the den back to Elvis. He loved art and was really pleased with the new waterfall which Bernie and Anne had created.

Shortly after this project was completed Elvis asked Bernie and Anne to design and build a meditation rose garden next to Graceland. The area where he wanted the garden placed was next to the house and was not visible from the road. It would afford the privacy he sometimes needed, a place where he could sit and think. At that time, Elvis had no way of knowing that it was to become a garden he would love and visit often during the remainder of his life, a lovely area which is now his final resting place.

The site had originally been designed around a bird bath which had crumbled and was in pieces. The ground was covered with broken cement and the whole place was a shambles. This is how it had been when Elvis moved there. Just beyond the bird bath were some colonial columns which looked as though they were about to fall.

Once again, the same bargain was reached between Elvis and Bernie. Elvis agreed not to go near the area until it was finished, but being as large as it was, and open toward the house, he probably saw some of the work as it progressed.

The project required a considerable length of time and while it was being completed Elvis and the group returned to Hollywood. About two weeks after our return to Graceland, Bernie asked me to tell Elvis his yard would be returned to him that night. After we went to the movies early in the evening and returned home, Elvis and Priscilla made a grand entrance into the garden.

Bernie had transformed the miserable location into a spiritually-beautiful sanctuary. The four columns were reworked and made to look as though they were ancient Roman and an arch was placed on top. He then built a curved wall six feet behind the columns, with steps leading to it. The wall was built with aged, imported bricks from Mexico. Set into the wall were three large stained-glass windows which were purchased in Italy. The windows were back-lighted so that the beauty of the stained glass could be seen at night. Bushes, hedges and flowers were planted and life-size statues of ancient Roman soldiers were brought from Italy and placed around the garden. In the center of the garden a magnificent water fountain was built. It automatically changed sprays fourteen times and was coordinated with underwater colored lights which changed at the same time as the spray. At four sides of the fountain were torch pots to be lit at night. It was a work of art.

There were tears of joy in Elvis' eyes as he looked at the work which had been done. As was his way, he avoided Bernie for the rest of the evening. It was never easy for Elvis to express his appreciation.

Within a few days Bernie began a new project for Elvis.

This time the job consisted of building a room to house a slot car track. The room was later used to display trophies.

The last project Bernie and Anne contracted to do for Elvis was redecorating his private quarters on the top floor of Graceland. Again, Elvis and some of the guys were in Hollywood during most of the project.

Anne became good friends with Elvis' grandmother and they spent at least a few minutes visiting each day. Grandma, as she was called by almost everyone, was the keeper of the keys to Elvis' quarters while he was away from Graceland. As a result, there was considerable contact between her and Anne during this time. Anne continues to have the utmost respect and affection for Grandma as she is truly a remarkable woman.

Elvis' bedroom was redecorated in a Spanish motif. The walls were upholstered in red and black velvet and the ceiling in leather with two television sets installed in such a way that the viewer could watch them while in bed. It was a beautiful room and when Elvis saw it on his return from Hollywood, the tears came to his eyes again. He commented that he had never seen anything as beautiful.

Unfortunately, as successful as the project had been, the work had created certain problems within the Presley household. Elvis' father, Vernon, resented any non-family member being in the home. The resentment often came to the surface when Elvis was not there to see it. Problems had begun during the period when Bernie and Anne were working in the house, and had led to a confrontation and bitter words prior to our return from Hollywood.

The day after Elvis had expressed his joy at seeing his newly remodeled quarters, he changed completely. When I went to the house he met me and, without any warning, started ranting about my sister and brother-in-law. He was in a rage and was screaming that Anne and Bernie had upset his family. I tried to remain calm to learn why he was so upset. I couldn't understand as he had been so pleased when he had seen the work, but when he began to call Anne, Bernie and the rest of my family obscene names, I lost my temper also.

When I had finished telling him what I thought of him and his father who had started the whole thing, I walked out of the house.

I stayed away about five days. I was angry and hurt by

his behavior, but Elvis meant a great deal to me, too much to just forget.

I had to know if our friendship had ended so I drove to Graceland. There I met some of the guys who told me Elvis was downstairs in the den watching some movies with his father.

I went down to the den and a couple of the guys saw me first and said, "Hi, Marty."

Elvis said, "Turn the lights on."

He got up, looked at me and started smiling. I just stood there with as little expression on my face as I could manage and waited to hear what he had to say. He said, "I'm sorry about what happened the other day. I'm under a lot of pressure." It was the first time I had ever heard Elvis say, "I'm sorry."

I looked at him and said, "Man, I hope you don't ever do that again. I just can't take it when you call my family things like that."

"Come here," he said, "I want to talk to you some."

We went into the other room where we sat down and he said, "I'm sorry, man, but there's a lot of pressure and a lot of problems but I want to tell you something I haven't told anybody else. Priscilla and I are going to be married and we want you to be best man at the wedding."

I almost fell over. Of all the guys and friends around, he was asking me to be his best man. I couldn't believe it. Well, to me, he had just wiped out all the unpleasant things that had happened, especially when he continued, "Priscilla and I talked about it and decided you were the one we wanted." Then he added, "Don't tell anybody, we don't want to announce it yet."

Later that night I had dinner with Elvis and Priscilla and while we were eating I leaned over to her and said, "Thank you."

She said, "Oh, he told you."

All was right again.

Elvis seemed to like my taste and would usually ask me to pick out clothing for him when he didn't want to go shopping himself. Once, I helped design the wardrobe for two of his movies. It began at Graceland where we were talking one evening shortly before leaving for Hollywood to film

Double Trouble. Elvis said, "I sure would like to have something different to wear in this movie. You know, something really sharp. I wonder if we could design something."

"We sure can try," I said.

He and I went to the table and I began making a few sketches from some of his ideas and some of my own. Before the evening was over we had developed a style which he liked and I worked up rough sketches for several outfits. They did look sharp and the following day I called the Colonel's office and asked if he would try to get the studio to use our designs.

The Colonel would do just about anything for Elvis, and the Colonel could do just about anything he decided to do. It wasn't long before we heard from him that the studio said they would let us do it. I began working with the wardrobe man, Lambert Marks, and with Elvis' approval we designed most of his clothing for the film.

Later, we did the same thing for the film *Spinout.*

Elvis liked to design things, or think up ideas which someone else would design. This was the origin of the TCB necklaces which we all wore. We would often say to each other, "TCB, man, TCB." The TCB was, I think, originally a black saying which meant "take care of business." It was just one of the things we all began to say, and Elvis came up with the idea of making the charm with TCB and a lightning bolt on it. This meant take care of business, fast. The fast part came from his way of always wanting something done yesterday, or as he would say, "Quickness is what I dig."

One of the charms was made for each of the guys who was close to him. As Elvis wanted, they were a symbol for all of us, something with which we could identify as a group. When these were finished, he decided the wives or girlfriends should also have something. He came up with the same basic design but used the letters TLC for *tender, loving care,* rather than the TCB. Everyone was proud to have them and they were worn constantly.

Elvis, being Elvis, had more than enough made for everyone and he began to give them to other people, sometimes even taking them from one of us to give to someone else. I remember the time when we were in his room with a new man Elvis wanted to hire. He was telling this guy that he would enjoy working with the group when he said, "Even though you're new, I'll get you a TCB." He turned to me and said, "Moon, let me have your TCB and I'll get you another."

"Now wait a minute, man," I said, because we all treasured them and I didn't like the idea of mine getting away.

"I'll get you another, Moon," Elvis said, "just let me give it to him now."

About three months elapsed since Elvis took my TCB and we happened to be in Las Vegas, but I was scheduled to go to Los Angeles. The charms were made by a jeweler in Beverly Hills, near Los Angeles, so I asked Elvis, "Do you mind if I stop by Beverly Hills and pick up a new TCB?"

"What for?" he asked.

"You remember taking mine about three months ago, don't you?" I said.

"Oh hell, didn't I get you another one, Moon?"

"No."

"Well sure, stop and order a few TCB's and TLC's so we'll have some extras."

Actually, there were not too many people who got a TCB or TLC who didn't deserve them. Elvis was a good judge of character and I remember only three guys out of all those who worked for him who turned out to be really bad apples. That was a pretty good average considering the number of guys who came and went over the years.

Elvis always had to approve the TCB and TLC order because he didn't want them to be given to just anyone, though he gave some to people he later wished didn't have them. Once, Becky Yancey, a girl who worked in the office for Vernon, told some of the guys that she was hurt because she didn't have a TLC and when Elvis heard about it he told us to give her one if she felt that badly about it.

He didn't like it though. As a matter of fact, he was angry. He felt that had he wanted her to have one, he would have given it to her. She later let it be known that since he gave automobiles to his cousin Patsy and some of the wives, that she felt she should also be given one. She didn't get the car. Actually, only two girls who worked in that office were close to Elvis. His cousin, Patsy, and Pat Boyd.

Our TLC and TCB charms are now being cheaply imitated by promoters. Even though imitation is a sincere form of flattery, those of us who own the expensive originals, given to us personally by Elvis, can't help but slightly resent the intrusion into a very personal camaraderie which these charms represent.

Things did not always run smoothly. There was trouble off and on which usually came from the outside. Once, for example, when we were in Las Vegas, Elvis invited a crowd of people to the hotel. We were all having a good time, all that is, except one girl. She kept trying to come on with Elvis and he wasn't paying any attention to her. She really thought she was something else.

She finally became angry and began talking in a very loud voice. Well, one of the guys asked her to hold it down and she started calling him a stooge and flunky for Elvis. She was being plain obnoxious. Elvis heard it and became angry, he thoroughly resented the implication and he said to her, "If you don't like it here, why don't you get the hell out?"

She started screaming at him so I took her by the arm and began to lead her to the door when she turned on me. I just tightened my grip on her arm and continued to walk toward the door. When Elvis saw what I was doing, he said, "She's going to leave by herself, Marty. Just let her go on out."

By that time we were at the door, so I opened it, sort of eased her out and very politely said, "Good night. It was nice meeting you," and slammed the door.

Incidents like that happened occasionally but we never took them seriously. If the people didn't behave too badly, the incidents were quickly forgotten. The only time we became really concerned was if we sensed an element of danger. There was always the chance of some kook managing to gain entrance and taking a shot at Elvis, just to make a name for himself.

Tours, and the travel arrangements for them, were the times when we were most careful. There were times when we would travel by commercial airline and they allowed us to drive the car onto the tarmac and get into the plane without going through the terminal. We were allowed to wait in the car until the other passengers were on the plane and then board before takeoff without causing too much commotion. Sometimes there would be a problem on the airplane when a fan saw Elvis and wanted to talk to him for the entire trip.

When that happened we never said anything to the person involved. Instead, we took one of the airline personnel aside and asked that the problem be resolved by them. The fan was usually escorted back to his or her seat.

Elvis was an impulsive man. There were many times when he would suddenly say, "Let's go to Palm Springs." Sometimes it would be Las Vegas or some other place and we would simply go away for four or five days. There were often times when I thought he had been thinking of doing something for a long time, but wanted us to think it was a spur-of-the-moment decision. It almost seemed that he enjoyed keeping people off balance. If he thought someone was getting too sure of himself or his job, he would do something to make the person doubt the security of his place. None of us ever really understood Elvis. He was a complex man, a man of many moods.

We were driving in the scenic cruiser to Memphis from Hollywood and, as we were passing through a small town in Arkansas, we were listening to George Klein broadcasting on the radio from Memphis. Elvis was driving, as he usually did, when George played a new record by Tom Jones called, *Green, Green Grass of Home*. It was a beautiful record and Elvis wanted to hear it again.

He stopped the cruiser at the nearest pay phone and said, "Moon, go on out there and call George, tell him to play that again."

"Elvis," I said, "he can't play them back-to-back. You know that." Most of the top stations do not allow their disc jockeys to play a record more than one time during an hour and some even have rules which forbid the playing of any record more than once in a three-hour period.

"I don't care," Elvis said. "Tell him I want to hear it again."

"Okay," I answered, got out and went to the phone and called George.

When he answered the phone, George asked, "Man, where are you guys?"

"We're on our way home. Right now we're in Arkansas. You know that record by Tom Jones?"

"Yeah, *Green, Green Grass of Home*. It's great, why? I'll bet Elvis likes it."

"He likes it so much he wants you to play it again."

"Man, I can't do that," he said.

"George, I know. I told him that but he still says he wants to hear it again."

"Okay," George said.

"Give me about two minutes to get back in the bus, George."

I went back to the cruiser and Elvis drove away without even asking the results of the conversation. About that time George's voice came on the radio, "Here's for all the guys out on Highway Sixty-four, coming into Memphis." He played the song again.

Well, for some reason the song brought tears to Elvis' eyes, as well as those of several of the guys. Maybe we were just in that kind of mood or something, but it sure made us feel blue.

Elvis stopped at the next pay phone and said, "Hey, Moon."

"Oh no, man," I said. "He can't do it again."

"Tell him I want to hear it again."

"Okay, but I'm pretty sure he's not going to be able to do it."

"Just tell him I want to hear it again," Elvis said. He knew George would do just about anything for him.

I called George again, and when he heard my voice he said, "No, man, I just can't do it again."

"George, I'm just telling you what the man said."

George played it again, and I can tell you he was taking a big chance with his job.

When we arrived at Graceland, all of our wives and girlfriends were there and, with the excitement of the homecoming, I forgot the song and my spirits began to lift. I went to find Elvis to see if he needed anything special before I called it a day.

As I went into the hall, I saw Elvis kneeling on the floor crying. I mean really sobbing. He was suffering as I had never before seen. One of the other guys was there with him, and alarmed, I said, "Elvis, what's the matter? What's the matter?" I was certain that he was sick or had been hurt.

He looked at me with tears streaming down his face and slowly choked out, "Marty, when I came in the door, I saw my mother."

"What do you mean, Elvis?" I asked.

"I saw her, man. She was standing there. I saw her."

His emotion and suffering got to me and I began to feel tears in my own eyes. I tried to comfort him. "Elvis, she's always here. As long as you are here, she will be here too."

Finally, he gained control of himself, got up, hugged me and went to his room.

We didn't see him for about a week. He stayed in his private quarters.

Chapter Eight

There Were Sad Times and Happy Times

The man and woman were old, black and very poor. The house, if you could call it a house, had two rooms separated by only a tattered curtain. It was a hovel in the poorest part of Memphis. I knew I was in the right place when I saw the old woman had no legs.

This story began one December afternoon at Graceland. It was Christmas time, but for the life of me I can't remember the year. Perhaps sixty-six or sixty-seven or even sixty-eight. Anyway, I was in the den, half-reading the local paper and half-watching television. Elvis was still upstairs in his room.

I read a short article, it was no more than eight or ten lines, about an old woman in North Memphis. That is the section where Humes High School is located and near the area where Elvis lived while he was growing up. The old woman, the article said, had been confined to a wheelchair all her life. She had no legs and her old chair had deteriorated simply from age. It couldn't be used anymore and she was unable to get around her home. The article was written by a charitable woman who knew of the old lady's situation and was trying to raise enough money to buy her a new wheelchair.

The story touched me and I tore the article out of the paper because I knew Elvis would want to see it.

Later, when we were sitting around talking, I remembered the story and said, "Elvis, let me show you something. Read this."

He read the article, looked at me and said, "Moon, take care of it for me. Get her a new chair."

I called the number which was in the article and said to the woman who answered the phone, "Are you still looking for a wheelchair for the crippled woman?"

"We're taking donations," she said, "and will very much appreciate anything you can do. It's a very pathetic case."

"How much do you have?" I asked.

"We've raised a little over eighty dollars but we still have a long way to go, even for a cheap chair."

"Well, I'll tell you what. I represent someone who would like to remain anonymous but he would like to buy the lady the chair."

She said, "Oh, you want to donate some money."

"No, we want to buy the chair for her. You take the money that has been donated and give it to her. We'll get the chair."

I think, at first, she thought I was a crank, but when I said, "Ma'am, if you give me the address of where the old lady lives we'll get her the chair," she seemed convinced.

"You are very kind," she said, "but I can pick up the chair and send you the bill, if you would like."

"No, ma'am. We'll pick up the chair and take it to the woman."

She asked several times if I was sure we would be able to do it, and I kept saying, "Yes ma'am, it's just somebody who wants to do this for the old lady."

"God will certainly bless you and your friend," she said, and she gave me the old woman's address.

I called a hospital supply company in Memphis and found a really nice electric, automatic chair. They said it was easy to use and the old woman wouldn't have to do very much to get around. I think it was the most expensive they had and they had only one left so I told them I would be right out to buy it. One of the other guys and I went out to the store and bought the chair, put it in the trunk of the car and went back to Graceland to see if Elvis wanted to see the chair before we delivered it to the old woman.

When we arrived at Graceland, Elvis and Priscilla were

dressed to go out. I said, "Hi, you want to see the chair before we take it?"

"I'm going with you," he answered, "Priscilla and I are both going."

Elvis, Priscilla and I got into his car and a couple of the guys followed in the second car. We usually used two cars for security, just in case something happened to the car Elvis was in.

We went to one of the poorest neighborhoods in Memphis. It was really bad. We couldn't understand how people were living like that and yet, most of us had begun our lives in little better surroundings.

I went to the door to be sure we were at the right place and an old man let me in. It was probably the poorest place I've ever seen. There were newspapers keeping the wind from coming in the windows and there was an old coal stove in the middle of the floor. Now this was in the city, not out in the country. It was a shack, not a house.

The old man didn't understand why I was there and I had to explain three or four times. I'm not too sure he understood even then, but I knew I was in the right house when I saw the old lady sitting on a wooden chair in the other room. I told the man I would be right back.

Outside, I told Elvis the old lady was in the house and the other guys assembled the chair. Elvis carried it into the house and Priscilla and I followed along with the others.

Tears came to all our eyes at the sight of these old people amidst such poverty. Elvis went to the woman and said, "Hello, I came to give you this chair as a gift for Christmas."

She didn't seem to understand why this white man had come to her house to give her a new wheelchair. She kept looking at it and at him as he showed her how it should be operated. Suddenly she seemed to realize it was really for her and she tried her best to get off the chair she was on and into the new one, but she was unable to do so. Elvis gently picked her up and placed her in the new chair.

The tears were flowing from her old eyes as she cried, "Praise God! God bless you! God bless you! God be praised! God bless you!"

She held Elvis and Priscilla and their tears mixed with hers. Priscilla was on one side and Elvis on the other, sharing with this old woman a moment of happy sadness. There was no member of the tough Memphis Mafia in the room that night who didn't succumb to the emotion. Each of us went over and put our arms around the old lady and clasped the old man's feeble hand. We loved the old couple, we loved Priscilla and we loved each other but most of all we loved Elvis and the sincerity with which he gave his true gift, himself.

Before leaving, Elvis turned to me and said, "Look at the way they're living."

The sight made each of us thankful for what we had. He then said, "Marty, give me some money."

I usually carried the cash and as I reached into my pocket, I asked, "How much, Elvis?"

"Give me a couple of hundred."

I gave him two one-hundred-dollar bills. He placed them in the old woman's hand and said, "Merry Christmas."

He kissed her, then turned and walked out.

The old people had never heard of Elvis Presley and if they are still alive I doubt that today they know him as anyone other than the man who gave them a better Christmas one year.

All of us were experiencing an emotional high after we left the old people. We were sad, in a way, but also happy and jubilant and Elvis was now in a gift-giving mood. We were driving back to the house when he turned to me and said, "Man, that's great. Now who is going to be next?"

He had bought gifts for just about everyone we knew that year. Because the Christmas list was always so long, Joe and I usually prepared it, with suggestions for a gift for each person on the list. Elvis would add, take away or change as he saw fit when the list was given to him. Sometimes he would go shopping with us but if he was busy he would ask us to buy the presents. He would, however, always select the gifts for his father, grandmother, Priscilla and for Lisa, after she was born.

Elvis continued, "I want to buy somebody a car, a new Cadillac. Who is deserving, Marty?"

"How about George?" I asked.

"Damn right, George Klein. Let's go!"

When we reached the Cadillac dealer, Elvis said, "Call

George and tell him to come down here but don't tell him why."

"Elvis," I said, "he's on the air. He can't just leave the station."

"Tell him I'm in trouble and need him right away. Get him down here, Moon."

Elvis often said I could find a way to do anything I wanted and I think he got a kick out of throwing difficult tasks to me to watch my reaction.

"Find a way to do it," he said again. "Get him down here. Call Gary Pepper too, and have his mother bring him down. I'm going to buy George the Cadillac then give George's Chevy to Gary and his mother. George's car isn't more than a year old and it's a lot better than their old car."

"I'll do my best," I said.

I called George at the station and asked him if he could meet Elvis at the Cadillac dealer, but he said, "Man, I'm on the air. I can't get off now. What's up?"

"All I know, George," I answered, "is that Elvis called me and said he's in bad trouble and for some reason he needs you."

"How can I get off the air, Marty? Does it have to be right now?"

"Yeah, now. Tell them you have an emergency. There must be someone who can take your place. Tell them you have a chance to cover an exclusive story about Elvis. Tell them anything, but get there. He said he needs you real bad."

I knew George cared enough about Elvis to come down but he also loved his job, and radio in general, and wouldn't do anything to jeopardize either.

He did find a way to get off and before long he drove into the dealer's parking lot, jumped from his car, ran over to where Elvis was standing and said in an excited voice, "What's wrong, man? What's wrong?"

"Come here, G.K.," Elvis said, "I've got a real problem." He led the way to a new Cadillac and stopped by the door.

"What is it, Elvis? What's wrong?" George asked again.

"I've got a real problem. I just bought this Cadillac and I don't know what to do with it. Here are the keys, you better take it. Merry Christmas!"

George nearly fell down. He looked at me and said, "Is he serious?"

"Yeah," I said. "It's your Christmas present."

All George could do was look at Elvis and me and say, "You guys are too much. I don't know what to say. It's beautiful!"

Elvis said, "Go back to work before you get fired, but before you go give me the keys to your car. I want to give it to Gary Pepper and his mother."

George was so happy he said, "Man, give it to anybody. I don't care what you do with it."

He threw me the keys to the Chevrolet, jumped in the Cadillac and sped out of the parking lot. From then on George traded the Cadillac every year for a new one, and as far as I know, he is still doing it.

Gary Pepper was the founder and president of the first Elvis Presley Fan Club. Gary, when Elvis first met him, was a teenager. He had cerebral palsy and was confined to a wheelchair but his mother drove him almost anywhere he wanted to go. He lived with his father and mother and had pictures of Elvis all over the house and copies of every record Elvis had ever made. He wrote to other Elvis fans and did everything he could to boost the popularity of his favorite personality.

Since they both lived in Memphis, Elvis got to know Gary rather well and often invited him to join us at the movies. He and his mother would come to the theater and join the group, or she would bring him to the roller rink when we were there. He never seemed to mind that he could do no more than just sit and watch. As a matter of fact, he always seemed happy and spent many hours talking with all of us, but especially Elvis.

His parents were not well off but they managed to take care of Gary until his father lost his job. When Elvis heard that Mr. Pepper needed work he hired him as a security guard at Graceland. This helped to keep the family going for several years until Mr. Pepper became ill and died shortly thereafter. Elvis, after the father's death, began to send money to Mrs. Pepper to help support Gary and continued until she, too, became ill and had to go into a hospital. Rather than have Gary try to manage on his own, Elvis hired a man to look after him and paid this man's salary as well as Gary's full support. Until Elvis' death, as far as I know, he continued to do this for Gary.

The year that Elvis gave George the Cadillac, Gary's parents were still alive. They had an old car until that night when they arrived at the Cadillac dealer's lot and Elvis gave them George's Chevrolet. It was a beautiful yellow convertible and less than one year old.

They were as happy as George and the old crippled lady, but Elvis was probably the happiest of all because that's the way he was.

There is another Christmas which I often think about. Elvis and Priscilla were divorced and he was seeing Linda. He had bought fur coats as Christmas gifts for all the guys' wives or girlfriends. We spent days selecting coats. They were all beautiful, mostly fur and leather and, of course, when the girls received them they went wild with joy.

One night before Christmas we were talking in the den when Elvis said, "Moon, I've got to find something special for Linda."

"Like what?" I asked.

"I don't know. Try to think of something really nice."

"How much do you want to spend?"

"I don't care."

"Why don't you give her ten one-thousand-dollar bills. That would certainly be different," I laughed.

"No, something really special," he said.

The next day I went downtown to pick up several of the fur coats we had selected earlier and I saw a beautiful, full-length, black mink and fox coat complete with a hood. It was like something a princess would wear, absolutely stunning. That, I thought, would be perfect for Linda. If Elvis liked the idea of giving Linda a fur coat, I knew he would want hers to be the most spectacular of all, and this coat was it.

I took it back to Graceland and Elvis thought it was perfect. Linda was ecstatic when she opened the gift, and the coat was beautiful on her.

The night before Christmas was the traditional time for all of us to gather by a big tree in the dining room. The floor would be covered with gifts for everyone, including Elvis.

Some years we would each give him a present but usually we chipped in and bought him one very nice gift. Finding the right gift usually fell to me or Joe.

One year, none of us could think of a thing to give Elvis. We talked about a dozen or so different ideas but none seemed right until one night when I was alone in the den watching television and doodling on a piece of paper. I started drawing a tree with Elvis' name on the trunk and each of the guys' names as branches. Now, I'm certainly not a great artist but this came out just right.

The next day I showed it to the guys and they liked the idea but none of us wanted to have it done as a painting. We wanted something special and decided to have it made into a gold medallion which Elvis could wear. This changed, however, when I was in a book and stationery store and saw a large, hand-bound, white Bible with gold-leaf trim; a beautiful book. I decided then that this would be the perfect gift. We would have the *Tree of Life* drawing inscribed in the front in gold.

All the guys agreed it was just what we wanted when I told them about the Bible and we decided to include as part of the drawing the words *And ye shall know the truth, and the truth shall set you free.* This was one of Elvis' favorite quotations. We had it inscribed in English, Latin and Hebrew to represent the religions of all the men who were his friends.

Just before Christmas, Larry Geller was cutting Elvis' hair in his dressing room. Of course, Larry, as part of the group, knew what we were doing when we all marched into the room and presented the Bible to Elvis. He liked it so much that from then on the Bible always went with him when he traveled and he showed it to damn near everyone he knew.

We gave him a gold medallion of the *Tree of Life*, with the same inscription, for his birthday two weeks later. He wore it constantly.

Chapter Nine

The Wedding of the Year

In early April of 1967, we were in Bel-Air and had just finished filming *Clambake*. Joe Esposito called from his home in Beverly Hills. When I answered the phone, Elvis was in the room just next to me.

Joe said, "Marty, now I don't want you to get mad, but Elvis asked me to find out if you would mind if I was best man with you at the wedding."

I was surprised, and said, "Well, Joe, why didn't he ask me? He's right next door."

"You know how Elvis is, Moon. He just asked me to ask you."

"No, I don't mind," I said. "As a matter of fact, Joe, if you want to do it, why don't you just be best man and I'll hang out."

"No way," he said, "Elvis wants you to be best man but he just asked if I would do it too. He wouldn't do it any other way."

"Okay, but I don't mind if you want to do it alone."

"No, damn it," Joe said with some anger. "He specifically wants both of us, not just me and not just you."

Joe and I then became dual best men for the coming wedding. It had been postponed once, but in April Colonel Parker held a meeting with Elvis, Joe and me. Plans were made for Joe to handle part of the arrangements and I was to take care of the rest.

We didn't, of course, want the reporters to get wind of the wedding but they somehow learned, even though they had no specific details. Colonel Parker arranged with Milton Prell, who had just bought the Aladdin Hotel in Las Vegas, for the wedding to be held there. To get the reporters off the track, Elvis, Priscilla, Joe, his wife Joanie and George Klein would fly to Palm Springs on the night of April 29th. The wedding was scheduled for May 1st. Mr. Presley and his wife, Dee, were going to take the train from Memphis and they were to get off the train in San Bernardino to avoid any reporters at the Los Angeles station. Jerry and Sandy Schilling and I picked them up by automobile and drove them to Palm Springs.

The rest of the guys sort of came in, one at a time, but by the time we were all at the house in Palm Springs the reporters were there by the dozens. When they saw all the people arriving they, of course, knew something was about to happen and that something was probably a wedding.

The reporters were trying to bribe the maids. One was offered five-hundred dollars just to tell what was going on but she didn't buy it. Everyone kept quiet. The house was surrounded by a special detail of Palm Springs police so the reporters were unable to get too close to the house. No one would talk with the reporters, we acted as though they really were not even there. We would get in the car and drive away without answering any questions or even looking at them and they would follow in their cars.

Once, Joe and I were going to a little store nearby to pick up some cigarettes and Rona Barrett, the Hollywood reporter, followed us in her car. When we saw her following, we decided to have a little fun. We drove all around just to see if she would stay with us. Sure enough she did, and when we tired of our game we went to the store near the house. Rona, too, went into the store so the game started again. She obviously did not know we recognized her and she stayed very close to us as we picked different items and then decided not to buy them.

I would say things like, "Boy, it's really great that it's finally going to happen."

Joe would answer, "Yeah, I wasn't sure it was ever going to come off."

Then I would say, "Yeah, after all this time we just might get that chick."

We stayed in the store a lot longer than necessary just stringing Rona along. Several years later she reminded me of that night.

Colonel Parker told all the reporters that there would be a news conference at one o'clock the next afternoon when they would answer all questions. He told them it would be held in the ballroom of the Aladdin Hotel in Las Vegas and if they wanted to know what was happening they should all be there. Most left Palm Springs to go and wait. Colonel Parker had made it sound as though nothing special was planned before then, whereas the wedding was scheduled for ten in the morning.

That night we rented a Lear Jet and Elvis, Priscilla, Joe, Joanie and George flew to Las Vegas as though they were just going for a good-time evening. We also chartered a DC-3, and at three in the morning I got everybody to the airport and we flew to Las Vegas. There we were met by a special bus and taken to the hotel where we went to our rooms by a rear entrance.

About four that morning, Elvis and Priscilla, escorted by Joe and a security man, were taken to the Las Vegas Courthouse where a license was issued. Except for the clerks, there were no other people, so no advance notice was leaked to the press.

When I was dressed in the morning, I went into Elvis' suite to see if I could help with anything. He was there with Harry Levitch, a Memphis jeweler from whom Elvis bought most of his jewelry. He had delivered the wedding ring to Las Vegas. Mr. Levitch had his jewelry cases with him and Elvis chose a set of cuff links and tie clasp for me, as a gift for being best man. Because of the ranch, they were in the shape of a bull's head with diamonds set as eyes. He also gave a set to Joe. They were handsome, expensive pieces of jewelry.

I had designed Elvis' tuxedo and one of the studio tailors had made it. The tailor kept the secret and did an exceptional job to make the tuxedo come out special. Elvis was, indeed, a stunning groom.

Everything necessary had now been done so I said to Joe, "Well, I better go tell the guys to get ready."

It was then that Joe informed me that none of the guys could be at the ceremony. I was upset because I knew how hurt the guys would be. After all the years we had been together, as a group, it seemed incredible that they were to be excluded. The reason given was that there wouldn't be enough room in the suite where the ceremony was to be held, but, as it turned out, there was plenty of room. I don't know who made that decision but I don't believe it was Elvis, he would not have done that. It was a bad decision.

All the guys took it very hard and thought, because I was a part of the wedding, that I had known about it all along and was even involved in the decision. This, of course, was not true. The first time I heard it was a few minutes before I had to tell them. They were upset and would hardly speak to me, and for a time after the wedding was over they still thought I had something to do with it.

For me, a bit of the gloss had been taken off the affair, but it was simply not possible to be anything but happy for the two lovely people who were about to join their lives as husband and wife. The marriage ceremony was performed by Judge David Zenoff who was a Justice of the Nevada Supreme Court. The ceremony was a simple affair, held in the private suite of Milton Prell. There were only a few guests present. George Klein, Billy and Jo Smith, Gee Gee and Patsy Gambill, Colonel and Mrs. Parker, Harry Levitch, Mr. and Mrs. Vernon Presley, Major and Mrs. Beaulieu and their son, Donny. In the wedding party were Joe and I as dual best men, Priscilla's sister Michelle as maid of honor and Joan Esposito as matron of honor.

The ceremony was simple but the news conference that followed was wild. The guests were escorted to the Aladdin Room where a wedding breakfast reception for a hundred people was about to take place.

Elvis, Priscilla, George Klein, Joe and I were led to a different room where there were reporters and television cameramen from all over the country. The press had not been at the ceremony nor were they to be allowed to join in the reception. This was the press conference which replaced the one o'clock meeting scheduled by the Colonel. Elvis and Priscilla sat at a big table at the front of the room, while the rest of us stood on the side. The reporters started firing questions at Elvis. "What made you finally get married?"

"Why did you give up bachelorhood?" "How long were you engaged?" Why this and how that. Elvis and Priscilla handled the questions nicely. Then the Colonel, in his way, let it be known that the session was over.

We left to join the others for the breakfast reception. Inside the Aladdin Room were representatives from RCA, Hill and Range Publishing Company, movie studios and other businesses whom the Colonel had invited. All the guys attended except two who stayed in their rooms. At the head table were Elvis, Priscilla, Vernon and Dee, Major and Mrs. Beaulieu, Joe and Joan Esposito, Colonel and Mrs. Parker, George Klein and me. To our surprise, the only celebrity invited was Red Foxx, and there he sat next to the Colonel at the head table.

The wedding cake was six-tiered, five feet high and decorated with pink and white roses. There were waiters everywhere serving champagne, but the breakfast was a buffet. It included roast suckling pig, ham and eggs, fried chicken, fresh poached candied salmon and clams and oysters. I don't know if anything special was ordered for Elvis but I do know there was little on the menu he cared for except the chicken and ham and eggs. However, he was so excited that I doubt he even noticed. The guests were seated at nine or ten round tables and a string trio played romantic ballads for the newlyweds, including *Love Me Tender*.

Later that afternoon Elvis and Priscilla flew back to Palm Springs for a short honeymoon in a house he had leased. The rest of us went back on the DC-3. We had to carry the remaining cake, flowers, liquor and other things which had not been used at the wedding back to Palm Springs with us. The tension in that plane was thick. None of the guys would talk to me and I had to carry all that stuff off the plane by myself and get it to the house. No one offered to help. As soon as we arrived at the house, most of the guys left for Los Angeles, they were mad as hell. I still didn't blame them. I soon left Palm Springs for Bel-Air with a couple of the guys who were at the ceremony. We were a house divided for only a short period of time. The problems created by the wedding were eventually resolved, forgotten or diminished.

After a few days in Palm Springs, Elvis and Priscilla returned to Memphis and hosted a huge party for their friends and employees at Graceland. The newlyweds cut a new wedding cake, and a large buffet was provided by a Memphis catering service. There was a huge crowd in Graceland that night and Elvis and Priscilla were radiant.

Gifts and cards poured into Graceland from Elvis' fans. Most of the fans were happy for them but some of the less gracious threatened to kill themselves or, at least, become nuns.

Elvis and Priscilla started talking about going to Europe for a longer honeymoon. They were encouraged a little by Joe, who always wanted to go back there and he and Joan were planning to go along. Well, the Colonel stepped in and said it would be a bad move as he had been telling the European promoters that Elvis' commitment in the United States gave him no time to perform overseas. If Elvis went there for pleasure it could not be kept secret and he would be hounded by promoters and fans to perform. So, Europe was out and the Bahamas was in. They went there for a few days but came right back. The place was beautiful but Elvis did not like it.

Shortly after the marriage, Elvis decided to purchase a house in Trousdale Estates. Before, he had always leased and even said he would never buy a house in California as he didn't plan to live there permanently since Memphis was his home. He and Priscilla lived there for a couple of years, with frequent trips to Graceland. He then purchased another house located on Monovale Drive in Holmby Hills and the cost was about $400,000. At the same time, he kept the Trousdale home. The Holmby Hills home was French Regency style with a huge pool, four large bedrooms and a beautiful living room with a breathtaking view of the city. There was also a gigantic den with pool table, soda fountain, indoor barbecue and a private 35 mm projection room. There was a loft above the den where Sonny and Judy West lived with their son. Priscilla invested a considerable amount of time and money to create a new country kitchen and to decorate and furnish the entire home.

During one of Elvis' extended visits to Graceland, he decided to take some of the wives along to Los Angeles to do our next picture, *Speedway*. Since he was married he thought we should all start doing things together as families. We left Memphis a week earlier than necessary as a side trip to the Grand Canyon was planned. The trip seemed longer than usual, even accounting for the extra week, because Elvis didn't drive as fast and we kept stopping to show the girls the sights that we had seen a hundred times before. Almost everybody enjoyed the trip except those of us whose wives weren't there. Because we had children in school, Billy's wife, Jo, and my wife, Patsy, decided to stay in Memphis. Even though they had never traveled cross-country by car, they didn't seem to be too disappointed.

Another so-called family outing was a trip to Hawaii by Elvis and Priscilla, Joe and Joan Esposito, Jerry and Sandy Schilling, and Lamar and Nora Fike. The rest of us stayed in Memphis. Instead of staying at a hotel, Elvis rented a beach house. Priscilla thought it was going to be just her and Elvis. I think she was a little unhappy.

As close as Elvis was to the group of guys, he was also close to most of his immediate relatives. All of his uncles worked for him at one time or another.

Uncle Tracy Smith had been ill most of his adult life and Elvis took care of him. Uncle Johnny Smith, who was one of the uncles that taught Elvis his first chords on the guitar, worked for Elvis until Johnny passed away. Billy's father, Travis Smith, was one of Elvis' favorites. He was an easy-going person, well-liked by everyone. Working as a security guard at Graceland, Travis was loved by the fans who visited. When he became very ill and could no longer work, Elvis kept him on the payroll until Travis died.

Patsy Presley Gambill was Elvis' favorite and closest female cousin. Her parents, Vester and Clettes Presley, are representative of both sides of the family. Vester is Vernon's brother and Clettes was Gladys Presley's sister. Vester worked as a security guard at Graceland and is still there. He is the other uncle who taught Elvis to play guitar.

Another cousin, Harold Lloyd, has been a security guard at Graceland for years and is another quiet, easy-going man. Many times Elvis would comment, "I'll always remember Harold, when I was a kid and didn't have anything he would always bring me candy."

Elvis' Aunt Nashville is married to Earl Pritchett who works at Graceland. Nash is an ordained minister and has a church in Mississippi. She, at times, discussed religion with Elvis.

One night in 1966, we were in the barn behind Graceland. Elvis was marking the names of the horses on the stalls when the phone rang. I answered and it was Elvis' Aunt Delta, Vernon's sister, wanting to speak to Elvis. While Elvis talked to her, tears started to come to his eyes. From what he was saying, I gathered that Delta's husband, Pat Biggs, had died while they were in Alabama and she was there in a motel by herself.

Elvis said, "Where are you exactly? Don't worry, I'll send someone down to get you." When he said that, I tapped him on the shoulder and gestured with my hands that I would go. He told Delta that Marty was coming and assured her again that she would be all right. He invited her to come to live at Graceland.

Pat Biggs, Aunt Delta's husband, had been another of Elvis' favorite relatives. Pat was well-known in Las Vegas and Biloxi as he and Delta often traveled there, but the thing which caused Elvis to most remember Pat was, as Elvis said, "Man, at Christmas-time when I was a kid I didn't get much, but here would come Pat and Aunt Delta with toys for me." After Elvis became successful, he helped buy a nightclub Pat had always wanted.

I took Richard Davis with me and flew to Alabama. Delta returned with us to Graceland where she still lives with her mother, Grandma Presley.

Exactly nine months after Elvis and Priscilla were married, Lisa Marie Presley was born. Jerry Schilling drove Elvis and Priscilla to the hospital where George Klein and I joined Elvis in the doctors' lounge. Many of Elvis' friends arrived to wait with him for the arrival of a son or daughter. Lamar Fike, Gee Gee and Patsy Gambill, Joe Esposito, Richard Davis, Vernon and Dee Presley were there to share the moment with Elvis.

George and I knew Elvis was nervous and we heard that the doctors didn't like so many of us being there, so we told Jerry that we were leaving and would return after the baby was born.

Later that afternoon we were told the baby had arrived and it was a healthy girl. We went to the hospital early that evening and Elvis had just left. There was no need for us to be concerned for the safety of the new baby or the mother as the hospital had arranged for the room across the hall from Priscilla's to be used for visitors and one of the guys stayed there as security. In addition, a hospital security guard sat outside Priscilla's room to keep away curious outsiders. During hospital visiting hours, two guards were usually necessary. After visiting a very happy Priscilla, we left for Graceland to congratulate the new father.

Initially, I think Elvis was hoping for a boy, but, as always happens, the realization of a daughter became the answer to his dreams. Elvis was beaming like a proud father, handing out cigars and feeling like, as he jokingly said, "A happy pappy."

Priscilla was in the hospital for four days and fans and newspaper reporters stayed nearby for the entire time. The little girl began to receive hundreds of presents from devoted Elvis fans who now loved his daughter as they loved him. Priscilla had been determined not to let the child become spoiled and even at that early age most of the gifts were given to less fortunate children and not saved for Lisa.

Chapter Ten

A Time for Change

Perhaps I should talk a little about the music industry in general and some of the practices and terminology within the industry before I get into the next story.

When we talk about a *number one* record we are referring to the rating of the record on the popularity charts which are compiled by the trade publications such as *Billboard, Cash Box, Record World* and the others which have come along since the time about which we are talking.

A *number one* record means that it is the most popular record in the United States at that time. There are also divisions within the industry such as Country Charts and Rhythm and Blues Charts, but the Pop Charts are the big ones, simply because they represent the greatest number of people. One record may sell a million copies and be only number four on the Pop Charts, or not even in the top ten, whereas another may sell only half-a-million copies and be number one on the Country Charts. The Pop Charts are the big ones.

A *million seller* is when a single record sells a million copies and earns a gold record. An album, on the other hand, is considered a *million seller* when it has reached a million dollars in sales, so there is a difference. An album earns a gold record with a million dollars in sales. Under the same system they can each earn a platinum record when the two-million mark is reached.

An Elvis Presley hit, to me, was when a record would

pass the million mark *and* be number one on the charts. This often happened in the early days and, as we'll see, began again after the movie period was over and Elvis got back to being seriously interested in recording good music.

A publisher, or a song writer if he does not have a publisher, issues what is known in the trade as a *mechanical license* to a recording company, to produce a song which they have written or for which they hold the publishing rights. The publisher earns two cents from each record that is sold. That's two cents from each side. This is divided between the publisher and the writer with one cent going to each for a given side or song.

Elvis had a special arrangement concerning these percentages. Because he was such a smash-hit in the early years, he was practically the only one who was sure to have million sellers. His people asked for, and got, twenty-five percent of the two cents which was the writer's and publisher's share. It was good business during the early years. A publisher knew he would sell records and Elvis' company made a lot of extra money, but as time went on it began to work against him.

When more and more good artists came on the scene, and began to reach the million mark with their records, many of us thought that fewer and fewer good songs were offered to Elvis. It was during this time that Sam Phillips, the gentleman who "discovered" Elvis, asked me, "Where in the world is Elvis getting those songs he's recording? He deserves better than that!"

Now, almost anyone would have been delighted to have Elvis record their song, but they just didn't want to give up a part of their earnings to have him do it if another performer could do anywhere near as well. The songs either were never offered to Elvis or someone in the Presley organization turned them down, without Elvis ever seeing them, when the publisher refused to relinquish the twenty-five percent.

In 1968, Elvis began to think about getting back on the right track as far as music was concerned. He cut *If I Can Dream, Guitar Man, Alabama Wild Man* and *Memories* during that period, and they were all good. He decided to do the NBC television special which so many people remember not only for his sensational performance but for the black leather suit he wore.

This was a totally different Elvis from what he had been in the past few years. He had returned to do what I call the real Elvis as opposed to the movie Elvis. He started to sing more and show more interest in the recording sessions. He wanted to get better music than what we all referred to as the movie songs for the past few years. There is a tremendous difference in songs. For example, almost everything he recorded in the fifties and early sixties were what I call Elvis Presley hits, they were *number one, gold records.* Between 1965 and 1969, when most of what he was recording was the movie songs, he had a number of *million sellers* or *gold records* but they were never *number one* on the charts. He needed good songs.

From the time I had left Elvis' payroll I had been very involved in the music business in Memphis. I worked with many of the people in the industry and had grown to respect their talents. They were tops in the nation as far as I was concerned.

Chips Moman, who owned American Recording Studios, had recorded over 125 chart records in five years with the same six-man rhythm section on all of them. I don't think there is another recording studio in the world with that kind of track record. They were cutting big name artists. Those guys in the rhythm section were really good.

I had become very close to Chips and knew he wanted to record Elvis but more important, I thought it would be good for Elvis, and I often mentioned it to him. Mostly, he would say, "Well, I'll think about it," or, "One of these days soon we'll try it."

We were at Graceland one evening in January 1969 and Elvis was talking with Felton Jarvis, his RCA producer, about an upcoming recording session in Nashville. For some reason I must have been shaking my head in a negative way because Elvis turned to me and said, "What's wrong with you?"

"Man," I said, "I just wish you would try recording in Memphis. I wish you would try Chips and American."

"Someday soon, maybe," Elvis replied.

About that time the maids told us dinner was ready. I had eaten before coming to Graceland, so I stayed in the den when the others went to the dining room. They were gone only a few minutes before Felton came back and said, "Elvis wants to record in Memphis."

"Are you serious?" I asked.

"It's true, he wants to talk to you about it."

I went into the dining room and said to Elvis, "Are you going to do it?"

"Yes," he said, "but you're going to have to make some fast arrangements. We have to start on Monday. Can you set it up in four days?"

"Damn right, man. This is fantastic."

"Okay," he said, "you and Felton work it out."

When I called Chips at home and asked if he could be ready, he didn't believe at first that I was serious. He knew I was aware of a scheduled recording session he had with another big artist. When I told him I was serious but we had to begin Monday, he said, "We're just going to have to switch some schedules around but, damn, we can do it. You know how much I want to record Elvis."

I called Felton to the phone and he and Chips worked out the financial arrangements. Elvis had an agreement with RCA which permitted him to record wherever he wanted, as long as he kept them informed, so all Felton had to do was call RCA about the change.

We went back to the dining room and talked until everyone had finished eating. I had something on my mind but I wanted to wait until after dinner just in case it provoked an argument. Elvis was unpredictable and there were times when he would become very upset over something that was said or done. I didn't want anything to spoil this new beginning, but I also felt it was necessary to talk with him about the type of songs he had been doing.

When we were all settled down I said, "Elvis, will you do me a really big favor?"

"What?"

"Man," I answered, "you have great musicians, those six guys are fabulous. You have two damn good producers in Chips and Felton. You have a really good studio. The sound in there is fantastic. We all know you can sing, so please, get some good songs!" I waited for the ceiling to fall but Elvis answered quietly, "I've got a few upstairs but I want all you guys to get me some more."

We went upstairs and began playing some of the demonstration records he had. These are records made by the songwriter, or publisher, which are then sent to the recording artists. Some of the records were good, especially those by Mac Davis who had written *Memories.* His new ones included *In The Ghetto* and *Don't Cry Daddy.* There was not, however, enough of what we would consider really good songs.

Lamar Fike, who was then representing Hill and Range Publishers in Nashville, came in with *Kentucky Rain,* which was a damn good song.

The musicians were great on Monday. All of them, Reggie Young, Gene Chrisman, Bobby Wood, Bobby Emmons, Tommy Cogbill and Mike Leech admired Elvis and were pleased to have the chance to work with him. We were on our way home after the first night of recording, it was 6 a.m. and the Memphis morning sun was coming up. Most of us in the car had a good feeling about what had gone down that night. We were all silent for awhile when Elvis said, "It felt good, man, those musicians are good. I really want this session to turn out. I just want to prove I can do it again, record some good hits, number one records."

I was overjoyed. What Elvis was really saying was that he again cared about recording. He was presenting himself with a challenge.

Fate, however, was to join the session and cause a delay. Elvis came down with a cold and had to stay home for several days. During his absence the rhythm section continued to work. They laid down some tracks, that is, they recorded some of the songs and Elvis listened to them at home.

At one point, in the beginning of the session, Elvis was concerned about recording *In The Ghetto.* He had never done what might be considered a message song and had often said he did not want to get into this type of music.

We discussed the matter quite thoroughly and I finally said to Elvis, "I really don't think it will hurt you. It's a good song."

Chips agreed and Elvis agreed, and *In The Ghetto* was recorded in the session.

Chips had a demo record which had been made of a new song by Mark James, *Suspicious Minds.* Elvis thought it was great, we all did. We began listening to the other demos to see if we could find some more that were good.

Several of the guys were in the suite with Elvis that night. Joe and I would play the demos and Elvis would say, "Yes," "No," or "Maybe," to signify what he wanted done with them. We didn't have to listen to the entire song, usually just a few lines were enough for us to know if the song was good.

When we finished the entire stack, there was just one record in the "Yes" stack. This did not, of course, include those songs previously discussed like *In The Ghetto* and *Suspicious Minds.*

Elvis said, "Man, I really want to cut some hit records but these songs are just not worth a good damn."

The time had come to continue my talk about good music, so I said, "Elvis, there's a reason you don't hear the good songs first anymore."

"Why?"

"Because they don't need you anymore. Now, before you get upset, let me explain what I'm saying. There was a time when you were the only sure thing for a million seller but there are a lot of artists now who are selling damn good. There are a lot of good songs which never get to you anymore because they don't need to pay you the twenty-five percent."

The room was absolutely silent and I thought Elvis was going to blow. He looked at each of us and said, "I want everybody in this room to hear what I'm going to say. From now on I want to hear every demo, every new song, and I'll be the one to decide if I want to record it. If we can get the damn percentage, fine, but if we can't get it and I still want to record the song, then I'll record it. I'll make the decision. I want you guys to let it be known that I'll listen to the demo and I'll personally make the decision about recording it."

That was a turning point. From then on he began again to do the good songs.

There is a footnote to this; we found Elvis meant business when he said he would make the decisions.

Chips was the publisher of *Suspicious Minds,* which, as I said, Elvis really liked. As a matter of fact, he had recorded it and was rehearsing something else when Freddie Bienstock and Tom Diskin, a couple of guys who worked for Elvis' publishing company, and the Colonel began talking with Chips about the percentage. It was their job, of course, to get as much as possible for Elvis, but Chips was a man who didn't ask for any extras and didn't give any. He just told these fellows that he didn't do business like that and he would not give up any of his or the writer's percentage of *Suspicious Minds* and that was final.

Well, the two guys kept after him until Chips finally told them they could take all the tapes and get the hell out if they wanted but he was not giving up a percentage.

Harry Jenkins, an executive from RCA, was at the session and he spoke up and said, "Gentlemen, the man is right. This is a good song. It will be a hit record and that's what we're here to cut."

Diskin was still not ready to give up and he went to Elvis and told him what had happened. I went along to be sure the story didn't become distorted. It would have been stupid to allow such a minor incident to ruin the sessions when Elvis was enjoying it so much and the results were so good. Elvis told Diskin, "I know you're just doing your job, but leave it to Chips and me. It's okay."

The Memphis session was the first time we used what we then called the new way of recording. This is the system where the rhythm section would lay down the rhythm track and Elvis would sing along with them, but that would not be the final vocal. Later, we would do what is called sweetening or over-dubbing of horns or strings or background voices. Then Elvis would come back and over-dub his voice. He would be the only one recording at the time. He liked the old way better with the whole thing being recorded at the same time but the new way allowed us to get a better balance on the records.

It was a super session. Elvis cut thirty-six sides in twelve days. They were released over a period of a year-and-a-half. Four were released as singles and all four were *number one, gold records*. The two albums which were part of this session were also *gold albums*.

A few weeks before Elvis began to record in Memphis, George Klein and I introduced Chips to Roy Hamilton. Roy was playing in a club in Memphis named T.J.'s. All of the guys, especially Elvis, really liked Roy. He was great, but he had never received the acclaim he deserved. He was famous but not nearly as much as he should have been. George and I went to T.J.'s one night to see Roy. George had been talking with Roy about recording at American under Chips' label because Roy didn't have a recording contract at the time.

As vice-president of the studio, I too was professionally interested in what Roy was doing as well as being personally concerned. We talked with Roy and he said he would like to start recording at American, so the next day we introduced him to Chips. They really liked each other and Roy signed with Chips. They scheduled their first recording session for the following week.

Because he had to be at the club in the evenings, Roy was recording in the daytime when Elvis began recording in the same studio at night. Elvis would come to the studio early just to listen to Roy, that's how much he liked him. They liked each other. It was great seeing them together, they had so much respect for each other's work.

Elvis said to me, "I sure would like to see Roy Hamilton get a hit." He seemed as concerned with Roy's recording sessions as he was with his own.

One night, when we were going over the demo records, we came onto a song called *Angelica*. It was a beautiful, big, dramatic song about a man who took his wife for granted. She died and he had never even told her he loved her. The song tells of his feelings. It's a beautiful song and was just perfect for Elvis or Roy, they both had big voices. When he heard it, Elvis said, "I want to give that song to Roy."

Rather than recording it himself, the next day Elvis went to Roy and said, "Here's a song I think will be great for you."

It was a touching moment. We all felt good about it and Roy really liked the song and appreciated Elvis having brought it to him. That was Roy's first single from the session and it was great.

About three months later Roy had a stroke. He stayed in a coma for weeks before he died. After his death, his manager in New Jersey called to ask if I would handle the press reports. During the conversation, he repeated a story told to him by Roy's wife.

She had been at the bedside before Roy died. He was in the coma but suddenly he sat up and said, "Angelica, Angelica." That's how much it was on his mind.

The recording became a hit!

Chapter Eleven

The Last And New First

In 1968, Colonel Parker announced that NBC television would produce an Elvis special which would be released during the Christmas holidays. Part of the package deal which the Colonel made with NBC was that they would also produce a motion picture which was to become known as *Elvis, That's The Way It Is.* The television special was to be the beginning of a new Elvis.

Colonel Parker was, of course, the moving force behind the special and he was fortunate enough to have some superior talent produce and direct the show and supervise the music. Steve Binder was selected to serve as producer and director. Steve had a list of successful productions behind him as did Bones Howe who would supervise the music. Both men were independent enough to accept those suggestions from Colonel Parker which were constructive and reject those which would have kept Elvis in the same old mold.

Bones had worked with Elvis some years before and the two were able to communicate with ease and feel comfortable together. Bob Finkel was the executive producer of the special but most of his time was spent meeting with the Colonel and convincing him that what was being done was best for Elvis as well as NBC.

Steve wanted to produce a modish show which would give Elvis the opportunity to rid himself once and for all of the movie image which had grown over the years. The

Colonel wanted a Christmas special which would essentially have been the same old Elvis singing a series of Como-type Christmas songs. It was an uphill battle for Steve who managed to gain an inch here and a step there by pleading, promising and conniving until he was able to produce the type of show he knew would be right for Elvis.

Bones and Steve wanted Elvis to be deeply involved in the production of the special. They had seen the electricity of the Elvis personality in the early days and they wanted to bring it back to the surface. To do this, they thought Elvis would have to become excited about the music and the whole atmosphere of the special. It would never work if he looked upon it as another of the same boring, movie-type productions.

It went back and forth, back and forth, with the two men spending hours meeting with Elvis and discussing what they wanted to do. They hired Billy Goldenberg as the show's musical director and, although at first he was less than excited about working with Elvis simply because he didn't think Elvis would be able to move into the world of modern rock music, he quickly changed his mind. Goldenberg changed his thinking about Elvis after he had an opportunity to sit and talk music with him. He was amazed to learn that Elvis didn't care anymore about the movie-type music he had been doing than Billy himself did. Elvis was every bit as much personally involved in modern music as Billy Goldenberg and as anxious to perform it as Billy was to write it. The two quickly came to respect each other's talent and began to work together as a unit.

Elvis tells a funny story about the time he and Joe Esposito were with Steve Binder discussing the special and the type of music which would be a part of it. Steve was really trying to make a point about how much music had changed and how quickly performers could come and go if they didn't keep up with the changes.

He kept talking about it and suddenly said to Elvis, "What would happen if we all walked out onto Sunset Strip? If we just went for a walk?"

He was a little afraid of the idea at first, but Elvis finally said to Steve, "Hell, let's try it and see."

In mid-afternoon they went out to the strip and walked up and down the busiest block without being recognized.

They even stood around in front of one of the night clubs and talked in very loud voices, but nobody paid the least attention to them. Steve had made his point even if it wasn't a valid test.

Confrontation after confrontation came with Colonel Parker, who would give just enough ground each time to keep the schedule going, and resist enough to keep Steve and Bones wondering if they would ever be able to complete the show. There were meetings after meetings after meetings. The least little change from pre-arranged plans would be enough to cause Colonel Parker to call everybody together for a discussion of the new idea. He was going to be damn sure nobody took advantage of Elvis for his own benefit.

The costume designer, Bill Belew, suggested that Elvis wear the now-famous black leather suit during part of the special and the idea was quickly approved. He also designed a gold lamé tuxedo but Elvis refused to wear it. It reminded him too much of the baggy gold suit the Colonel persuaded him to wear in the early years. He never forgot, and he never stopped hating it.

Steve Binder and Bones Howe brought Alan Fortas, Scotty Moore, D.J. Fontana and Lance LeGault to the rehearsals so Elvis would be surrounded by his old friends, and later decided to use these men in part of the live show. Steve and Bones thought Elvis would be more comfortable being in the company of men he knew and with whom he had been closely associated for so many years. They wanted Elvis to talk, to be involved, and the idea worked.

It was a return to the old days for Scotty. He, Elvis, and the rest of the group would rehearse for hours at a time. They would set up the instruments and, as Elvis said, ". . . bang around like back at Sun." They talked and played and talked and played until they were really at home with each other again.

The guys had a good time and Elvis performed like he did in the early days. He never just sat and sang a song, he moved around to get the feel of each number. The studio rhythm men, Hal Blaine, Don Randi, Tommy Tedesco, Larry Knectal and Mike Deasy worked with Elvis during the long sessions and did a superb job. It was one big happy group working together to achieve something beyond the ordinary, a very special, special.

Colonel Parker wanted Elvis to end the show with *Silent Night,* or one of the other traditional Christmas songs, but by then the flavor of the show had been set. After several meetings, it was decided that *If I Can Dream* would be the final song. It was written by Earl Brown, especially for the show as the closing number, and Elvis loved it. The song is a plea for peace and understanding among all men and after it was released it quickly climbed to the number twelve position in *Billboard,* the highest position an Elvis record had achieved in more than three years. The recording sessions were finished but the live show was still to be taped.

When the day arrived to begin videotaping before the studio audience, Elvis was nervous. He later told us about wondering what he would do if the audience laughed when he was trying to be serious or if they just wouldn't turn-on to him. He was dripping wet from nervous perspiration when the time arrived and he had to go out and prove he could still perform in front of an audience. Even though they were small in number, the unnerving part was that they were live people and it had been a number of years since he had performed for anything other than a camera.

The white stage, which was trimmed in red, was arranged in the NBC studio in such a way as to allow the audience to sit in seats around three sides of it. It was a good arrangement which allowed Elvis the security of not always having part of the audience behind him and still made it possible for him to become close to those who were fortunate enough to have acquired tickets. The entire audience was scheduled to be changed three times during the actual taping.

Colonel Parker arranged to seat some of the prettiest girls in the front rows and even had a few on the edge of the stage. Bones and Steve never ceased to be amazed by the genius of some of the ideas which the Colonel came up with on the spur of the moment, and, of course, the girls were delighted to be that close to Elvis.

When he came onto the stage anyone could tell he was nervous. His hand was actually shaking when he reached for the microphone, but the minute he began to sing, the fear disappeared. Elvis was in his element and he was terrific.

He sang many of his early hits, including *That's All Right, Mama, Lawdy Miss Claudy, Heartbreak Hotel, Blue Suede Shoes, Love Me* and *Are You Lonesome Tonight.*

Lance LeGault sat on the edge of the stage while Charlie Hodge, Scotty Moore, Alan Fortas and D.J. Fontana sat on the stage with Elvis. They talked between songs about the old days, fed Elvis lines and laughed at those he pulled naturally from his own memories. That part of the show was spontaneous with not the least hint of any rehearsing of spoken lines. It was a relaxed, informal group, which conveyed the impression of a group of good friends getting together for a jam session, with a few non-musician friends invited in to enjoy the music. Even though Elvis had long since lost his nervousness, his habit of always moving some part of his body was obvious. Between songs, while he was just sitting and talking, his left leg was never still.

They taped for several hours and Elvis was completely exhausted when the lights faded for the last time. He had put his heart and soul into this part of the special, and when it was aired, even though the *live* segment had been cut to less than half an hour, it was far and away the greatest part of an outstanding show. Elvis had demonstrated that he was even greater than ever and the critics reacted enthusiastically with words of warm praise.

Elvis was exhausted from the performance, but he was happy. He said that night that the Hollywood movie days were over, even though he was still under contract for two more. He would honor the contract but there would be no more beyond those two. Elvis seemed to realize what he had been missing during the years of phony movie making and he was going to stay on the new road, the road upon which he probably should have been for years past.

The evening of December 3, when the show was telecast, belonged to NBC. The other networks could have stayed off the air and few would have ever noticed. Those who missed the special learned what they had missed the following day when the New York *Times* heaped praise upon the "charismatic performance" of Elvis Presley. The king was on the path leading home again.

The night the special was telecast I was in Memphis and Elvis was in California. Because of the time difference, I saw the show two hours before he did. With my family, I watched the show and was extremely gratified to see him perform in his natural way again.

Seeing him joke and talk with Scotty, Alan and the

others got to me because he was letting the world see the real Elvis Presley, the person he was at home. This was not the motion picture Elvis.

When the show was over, I called him in California and he asked, "What did you think?"

I told him I was happy to see the natural Elvis come back at last and that he could be proud of the show, it was great. He said he would see me in a few weeks, he was coming home for Christmas.

The last two Hollywood-type movies, *The Trouble With Girls*, Metro-Goldwyn-Mayer, and *Change of Habit* for NBC-Universal were no better artistically than the first twenty-nine but, as usual, they made money for all concerned. I say Hollywood-type movies to distinguish these two films and the previous twenty-nine, from the two specials *Elvis, That's The Way It is* and *Elvis On Tour* which were also released as motion pictures but bore no resemblance to the others.

The last film, *Change of Habit*, co-starred Mary Tyler Moore, Jane Elliott and Barbara McNair who portrayed nuns who had changed their habit for street clothing to work in the ghetto. Elvis played the part of a doctor and the three actresses became nurses in what was an early-day free clinic. Of course, they didn't tell Elvis they were really nuns until after he had fallen in love with Mary Tyler Moore.

This dismal piece of Hollywood art offended Elvis and probably Mary, because she is a fine actress. Nevertheless, they worked their way through it and developed a lasting respect and fondness for each other. There was a fresh taste of the new entertainment in Elvis' mouth and he was anxious to finish with the old years and begin the new.

I've often been asked why Elvis continued to make the movies for so many years when they did little for his image and less for his personal fulfillment. I often asked Elvis the same question but never received what I consider a satisfactory answer. Speculation is the only thing I can offer as to the real truth because I'm not certain that Elvis himself knew.

For all his craziness and sometimes wild antics Elvis was basically a man of routine. Like so many people, he had a job and he was reluctant to leave it. All things are relative. We may think that he had enough money to quit making movies and do almost anything he desired, and there is little doubt that he did if we place my financial needs onto Elvis. But they are my financial needs and not Elvis'. He was accustomed to earning an astronomical income and spending most of it. His taxes alone were staggering, since he never tried to take advantage of many of the shelters which are available to those with high incomes and money to invest.

The motion picture industry has a charm of its own and even though most of the scripts Elvis had to work with were less than exciting that did not detract from the rest of the movie world. There was the glamour of being a big star in a universe of lesser stars where beauty is commonplace and usually available. And there was hope, there was always hope for a better script, and for that one bit of magic which would transform a financial success into an artistic success and win the acclaim of those critics whose opinions are respected. Hollywood is a city of hope which is as much a part of the greatest star as it is of the newest arrival.

Colonel Parker was happy with his role as manager of one of the world's most highly paid and famous stars, and he had a great influence on Elvis. Because he genuinely cared for Elvis, I have no doubt he would have changed his thinking and encouraged Elvis to change had Elvis ever voiced a real objection to the type of life he was leading, as far as his work was concerned. Elvis, however, was not a complainer. He seldom bared his soul to anyone and he never seemed to have the type of relationship with the Colonel which encouraged more than a business conversation. They were close in many ways, but their lifestyles were completely different and the generation gap was too great to permit any real communication.

Why, then, didn't Elvis change? Why didn't he set about to find a good script and, if necessary, to produce it himself? He was certainly capable of accomplishing any task he set for himself and intelligent enough to have formed his own production company, and financial backing, if needed, would have been available for the asking. Did he have the talent to be a good actor? Most of those in the industry who knew him felt that, with the proper guidance, he could have become a really fine actor.

If we find a reason for Elvis' staying on the job, does that same reason apply to the producers, directors, script writers, financiers and motion picture company presidents? Probably it does. Yet, it is no more expensive to produce a good movie with a meaning than to produce the banal trash which is pumped from the city of stars. It is, in fact, often less costly to produce an artistic film, but unfortunately, where the one requires only money the other requires performers whose talents have been cultivated, and material which utilizes those talents.

Do the *people* get what they want? Yes, I believe they do. Had the first Elvis movie been a financial failure there would have been few, if any, more. Isn't that also true of television? If we turned off our sets every time something offended our sensibilities wouldn't the quality of what comes into our homes quickly improve? But we don't turn them off, we sit and watch and go out and buy the products which are touted and the shows go on.

There is no simple answer. As always, a complex series of events, personality traits, and circumstances kept things the way they were for many years. Elvis was not an easy man to understand. His early life, and its insecurity, undoubtedly influenced his thinking and actions throughout his adult life. A boy who lived dirt poor for most of his early years would have to find it difficult to reject a million-dollar offer at any age. Mostly though, I think it was the *tendency of a body to stay in motion in a straight line unless disturbed by an external force,* the definition of the same inertia which afflicts most of us. Tomorrow will be different.

And then it was different. In 1969 the big decision was made to begin again to do live performances. At that time, the International Hotel in Las Vegas was preparing for its opening. It was billed as Las Vegas' largest hotel and the management wanted Elvis to be the first person to perform in the massive new showroom.

Elvis and the Colonel shrewdly declined the offer to be first. They wanted someone else to get the bugs out of the showroom, to get the flaws out of the sound system and to let the staff of the hotel become accustomed to the place. But most of all, they wanted to wait until the summer season when people usually go on vacations.

The Colonel left little to chance. He reasoned that people would come to Las Vegas for their vacation if they had an opportunity to see a live Elvis performance. It would be his first performance on stage in many years except for the television special. While the television special was a performance before a live audience, the audience was small in number, one hundred at most, and the audience was changed about every hour. Except for those relatively few people present the special was, of course, not live. Errors, mistakes and things which just did not sound right could be deleted and left on the cutting room floor before the telecast. A true live performance has to be right the first time, because that's the *only* time for that audience.

Elvis was excited about resuming the live performances and this time he thought Las Vegas would be good for him. By now he knew that performing before an audience was the most important thing in his life. It really turned him on, whereas the movies had been a bore and the recording sessions never had the thrill which comes with being before a large group of people.

Elvis began to get himself ready for the show. He became nervous but he was also enthusiastic and when he first told me about the plans, prior to their being made public, he was like a happy child with great expectations.

During the Memphis recording sessions in January of 1969, Elvis had talked of the possibilities of going back to Las Vegas to begin live performances and, at that time, he said he was thinking of asking Chips Moman and the American rhythm section to back him up on the stage. Chips, of course, would have been doing the sound engineering, but I didn't think it would be possible for him to close his studios for the necessary four or five weeks. When, however, I asked Chips if he would like to do it, he said yes. Unfortunately, no firm plans were made and when the time came, he was unable to leave Memphis due to bookings at his studio.

Elvis began to hold auditions in Los Angeles and Memphis for musicians and he finally chose James Burton for lead guitar. He and Burton assembled a great group including Ronnie Tutt on drums, Larry Mohouberac on piano, Jerry Sheff on bass and John Wilkinson on rhythm guitar. Both Tutt and Mohouberac were originally from Memphis so they had something in common with Elvis. Later, Glen D. Hardin replaced Larry Mohouberac on piano.

The return to live performances was a real challenge for

Elvis. He was a natural performer and a natural man of music who, when faced with a challenge in his profession, never failed to overcome it.

Every phase of the opening show was meticulously arranged and supervised by Elvis. Lists of songs were made and orchestra leader Joe Guercio, who worked for the International, was hired to lead the string and horn section. Bill Porter who had been the sound engineer on some of Elvis' early recording sessions was called back to perform the same task again, under the supervision of Felton Jarvis. The Sweet Inspirations were hired as the female background singers and the Imperials became the back-up male group.

Like all good rhythm sections, Elvis' used no charts or written arrangements. Everything was worked out during weeks of rehearsals in Los Angeles where Elvis set the pace and created the feel for each song. As time for the opening drew near the pace became more frantic but things were falling properly into place.

Two weeks before the show was scheduled to open the entire group moved into the International. There they rehearsed in the showroom, every afternoon, to get the feel of the huge room and set the sound system in the way that Elvis wanted it.

In the meantime, the Colonel continued to do his thing. The lobby and entrance way of the hotel were decorated with photographs of Elvis and other promotional material. Newspapers, billboards, radio and television carried promotion after promotion of the coming show. It was an Elvis summer festival for Las Vegas. The hotel had overflow reservations.

On the opening night of July 31, the showroom, which held twenty-two hundred people, was filled to capacity and it continued to be filled for two shows a night for the next thirty-two nights. There were no dark nights, Elvis performed seven nights a week with two shows every night.

Opening night was to be a special show with admittance by invitation only. Those in attendance included members of the press, celebrities and their families, and close friends with the hotel taking the majority of the twenty-two hundred seats for their best customers.

Colonel Parker scored another triumph when he decided not to use Elvis' last name on the marquee. Instead he simply used the name ELVIS. It was spelled out in letters so large, they dominated everything in sight. After all, the Colonel reasoned, there was only one Elvis.

Elvis was not a tuxedo-wearing man. He began a trend when he and Priscilla, who had a real flair for fashion, decided he should begin wearing karate-type outfits. He later turned to jewel-studded jumpsuits. They were custommade and cost over twenty-five hundred dollars each. As with most everything Elvis introduced, the jumpsuits were soon copied by other performers.

Charlie Hodge was assigned the task of being on stage with Elvis to supply him with water or Gatoraid, as he needed it and to sing harmony on some of the songs. Charlie would keep the list of songs Elvis wanted for each show and pass them to the musicians. He also replaced the scarves around Elvis' neck when he threw the one he was wearing into the audience.

Security was tight. Elvis and the guys used the service elevators to go from their rooms to the lower level where they would walk through the back halls to reach the dressing rooms. Elvis' dressing room was located one floor below the stage and consisted of a sitting room, a bedroom, a make-up room and two baths. The large sitting room contained a bar, color television, sofa and chairs, and a round table where meals could be served. All the rooms were quite comfortable and designed for relaxation before and between performances.

On the afternoon of July 31, Elvis got out of bed about five o'clock, ate a big breakfast, reviewed some notes he had made regarding the performance and then he and the guys went to the dressing room. There was about thirty minutes to kill before Elvis had to begin dressing for the performance. It was a nervous half hour for Elvis. His fingers drummed constantly on the table and his right foot, which rested on his left knee, moved constantly in the old Elvis fashion which we all knew so well.

Dressing, with the assistance of two of the guys, took about twenty minutes and when they were finished it was time to go to the stage. All the guys went upstairs and backstage with Elvis, to one side of the curtain, where they tried to keep his level of enthusiasm and excitement at a fever pitch until it was time for him to begin his performance.

Comedian Sammy Shore, who was later replaced by

Jackie Kahane, finished his act, the rhythm musicians began to play and then all of a sudden, Elvis was on stage. There was no introduction in Las Vegas, and none was necessary. If the audience didn't know who Elvis was, there was no reason for them to be there. They knew him, even though most had never seen his live performance. They gave him a fifteen-minute ovation.

While the audience was applauding, Red and two of the guys moved behind the stage to the opposite side. Sonny, who shared with Red the responsibilities of security, kept two of the guys with him at a position where they could remain unseen, but still have a good view of the audience. It was their job to keep the peace and politely escort back to their seats any overzealous fans who tried to get on the stage.

When the applause died, Elvis began a show which established once and for all that he was still the most exciting performer alive. The people who attended the show, including the critics, raved about his fabulous *comeback*. Credit, of course, must be given to all who worked to make the Las Vegas tour a success but it was Elvis who gave it the natural touch, his special feeling.

George Klein and I were in Memphis the night the Las Vegas show opened. We had planned to go, but Elvis asked us to skip the opening night and wait a few days until he was sure everything was right. He told me he was afraid he would be nervous and he didn't want us to see him until the show was perfect. George and I understood and respected his feelings.

We arrived in Las Vegas on the afternoon of the third day of Elvis' performances and called Joe Esposito from our rooms. Joe said that Elvis had told him he didn't want to see us before the show. Elvis wanted us to see his performance and then go backstage. Elvis respected George's opinion and mine, and I knew he didn't want our reactions to the show influenced by seeing him first.

Before the show began, Joe met us and escorted George and me to Elvis' booth, from which we would watch the performance. The excitement in the huge room was overwhelming. Even the balcony, which was the only one in a Las Vegas show hall, was filled to capacity. Twenty-two hundred people waited for the star to begin his performance, and in a flash there he was, Elvis.

As close as I had been to him for years, seeing him this time, listening to him and knowing that this was real and not a movie, I was spellbound. George and I began yelling and applauding like everyone else. The Elvis electricity was in the air, it couldn't be resisted even had we wanted to remain silent. Once, during the show when Elvis said something funny, he heard George's high-pitched laughter, looked in our direction, and said, "Cool it, G.K."

When the show was over we joined in the standing ovation and then went backstage and downstairs to the dressing room. Before we reached his door, Elvis walked out to greet us. We looked at each other and I could tell he was watching for a sign on our faces which would tell him what we felt about the show. What he saw, he liked, and we hugged each other and were so full of emotion we were all unable to speak. I felt like his biggest fan who was meeting him for the first time. We went into his dressing room where the first thing spoken was when I said, "M'boy, M'boy." It was an expression we all used, meaning, "It was something else, out of sight."

We sat and talked until thirty minutes before the second show when George and I went back to again become a part of the audience. With the exception of only a few shows, George and I always sat out front rather than staying backstage. We wanted to be where we could see the show, we just couldn't get enough. During the second week, our wives came to Las Vegas and we then sat out front with them.

Elvis cherished our opinion of his performances and was overjoyed with what he heard and saw. After the late show Elvis would change clothes and then greet the celebrities and guests who came backstage to see him. We would often stay in the dressing rooms for awhile and then the wives and girlfriends would go up to the suite through the lobby while Elvis and the guys went by the service elevators. This, too, was for security reasons. The guys and the women never went at the same time, or by the same route, just in case we had to escape from a rush of fans, or if some idiot tried something funny, we didn't want to be hindered from getting away from it.

We would sit in the suite and talk away the night, have something to eat and go to bed. It was like old times, but better.

Chapter Twelve

Honor and Heartbreak

For some years the Memphis Chapter of the Junior Chamber of Commerce had been trying to persuade Elvis to agree to be their candidate for one of the places in the *Ten Outstanding Young Men in America* awards. He was always flattered but declined the offer each time since he would be unable to attend the ceremonies if they were held at a time which could conflict with his tour schedule or in some city where it would be difficult to arrange security. Many awards had been presented to Elvis but he had never been to a ceremony to accept them. He felt the Jaycees award was too important to accept the nomination and then not attend the function.

January, 1971 was to be the first and last time he ever accepted an award in person.

Elvis and all of the guys were fairly close to the former sheriff of Shelby County, William N. Morris. Bill was a past president of the Jaycees and active in their work. He came to Elvis one day with news that the ceremonies for the *Ten Outstanding Young Men* of 1970 were to be held in Memphis. This was the first time in Jaycees history that Memphis had been selected as host city for the festivities. It would be a coup for the city and the Jaycees wanted to nominate Memphis' favorite son.

The age limit for the award is thirty-five and that year was the last time Elvis would be eligible. Bill Morris was a good salesman. He told Elvis about John F. Kennedy and Richard Nixon who had been past honorees and that there was a chance President Nixon would be able to personally present the awards. In addition, he told Elvis that the others who had been nominated for that year's awards included Presidential Press Secretary Ron Ziegler, scientists and doctors who were seeking cures for some of the world's most dreaded diseases and others who were working to help all mankind.

The setting was perfect and Bill was very persuasive and Elvis agreed to accept. The first small problem arose when we learned that the ceremonies were to take place at a time when Elvis would be in rehearsal for a Las Vegas engagement, but since they were scheduled to last for only two days Elvis agreed to be present for all of the final day. That made everyone happy but then a request was received from the Jaycees that he attend a dinner on the night before the awards. He simply could not get back to Memphis in time for that.

Elvis really wanted to do something special to honor the other candidates, but he did not want to be thrown among the thousands of Jaycees and their wives at a big public event which could cause problems for everyone. I suggested that rather than going to the Jaycees dinner, he should consider giving a cocktail party at Graceland and then a sit-down dinner either at Graceland or at one of Memphis' fine restaurants where there would be sufficient facilities for a large group. When I made the suggestion I didn't know what I was getting myself into. He turned to me and said, "Okay, Moon, it's all yours. I have to be in Vegas rehearsing and I can just about get back to Memphis in time for everything, and I'll have to leave again right after the awards. You're the best man for the job, you set everything up for me."

"Okay, Elvis," I said. "Any limit on the amount you want to spend?"

"None, just see that it's done right."

Bill Morris and I got together and made plans. He was going to take care of the security at the breakfast, the luncheon, the question and answer period in the afternoon, the cocktail party at Graceland, the dinner and finally the awards ceremony. With the exception of the cocktail party, dinner, and awards, everything was going to be held in the

Holiday Hall of Memphis' nicest and largest hotel, the Rivermont, on the bluffs of the Mississippi River.

Because the newspapers kept mentioning that Elvis would return to Memphis and personally accept the awards, we knew we would have a problem of getting to and from the hotel if Elvis stayed at Graceland. He decided to stay overnight at the Rivermont which made the life of the security men much easier. I reserved all the rooms on one side of the top floor of the hotel. Elvis had the biggest suite in the hotel. It was next to the service elevator so we could get in and out without being noticed. I then set about to complete the cocktail party and dinner arrangements.

I called upon my friend Harlon Fields, the owner of one of Memphis' finest restaurants, The Four Flames, and took him into my confidence about the plans. He was pleased to be able to help and to have the honor of arranging the cocktail party and dinner which would be for more than one hundred people. The florist was next on the list and the table pieces and decorations were chosen and ordered.

The night of Elvis' arrival from Las Vegas came and I went to the private airport to meet his chartered customized G-2 jet. We all got into limousines and had a motorcycle escort to the rear entrance of the hotel where Bill and I led Elvis, Priscilla and the guys up to their rooms. We went to Elvis' suite where we discussed what was going to happen. Bill worked out the security with Sonny and Red West and then went over the events of the next day. It was then that Elvis was told there might not be enough room for most of the guys at the breakfast and luncheon. Elvis told Bill that if the boys didn't go, he wasn't going. Room was made for everyone.

The breakfast went fine, as did the luncheon, and that afternoon there was a question and answer period for all of the nominees. One of the people present asked Elvis, "What kind of message do you hope to bring to the world?"

He answered, "I'm not here to bring anyone a message. I'm here to entertain people and make them happy. If that has any meaning then I'm accomplishing something of value."

After the question and answer session we changed to formal clothing and, along with our wives, then went to Graceland for the cocktail party. As each nominee and their guests arrived they were met at the front door and given a tour of the house. They were then taken to the huge trophy room where waiters from the Four Flames restaurant were serving their famed barbecued oysters, champagne and mixed drinks. After about an hour and a half we went with a motorcycle escort to the restaurant. There we were seated in a private room where we dined on Caesar's salad, chateaubriand, stuffed baked potatoes and cherries jubilee.

Elvis had an extra, extra well-done, cut-up filet mignon and a huge salad with Thousand Island dressing. That was what he wanted and I had it cooked especially for him. Everybody was happy and each man toasted the others. During the serving of dessert, which Elvis also had, he and Priscilla looked over at me and with his hand he gave me the *okay* sign for a job well done. After dinner we all got into the automobiles and followed the motorcycles to the downtown auditorium where the awards were presented. Elvis had, by this time, learned that President Nixon would be unable to attend the award ceremony. He was disappointed but still excited about the affair.

My job was over, the rest was up to Elvis. All the guys and the wives sat in the front rows which were reserved for the families of the nominees. Along with Priscilla, Vernon and Dee, we, too, were a part of Elvis' family.

During the awards ceremony Elvis literally glowed with the enthusiasm of a happy young man who has accomplished something great. I was thrilled to see him looking so good and acting so very much alive and interested in what was happening. It was a great day for all of us.

Elvis and Priscilla had worked together for many hours on his acceptance speech the day before the awards were presented and they were both justly proud of the results. He was introduced to the audience and presented the award which was placed around his neck. In accepting he began the speech, "I am very humbled by this award, not so much in receiving it but receiving it in the company of the other nine men honored here tonight."

The closing lines were, "I'd like to say: 'Without a song, a man ain't got a friend, without a song, the road would never end,' so, I'll just keep singing my song. Thank you." With that, the audience gave Elvis a standing ovation.

We all left and went to the hotel and when I went to his

suite he came over and hugged me and said, "Thanks for making this a memorable night."

Elvis did meet President Nixon sometime later, when the President issued him a Federal Narcotics Bureau badge. Elvis had always been crazy about law enforcement and he collected police badges like other people collect matchbooks. He was also a gun collector which went along with his ideas of what law enforcement was really like. I've often thought he could have been an intelligence agent and would have been happy in his work. That was the way his mind was. He went out of his way to make friends with police officials almost everywhere he traveled.

One of his favorite possessions, before he got the Federal Narcotics Bureau badge, was a police lieutenant's identification shield from the Los Angeles Police Department. It was the real thing. Elvis wasn't interested in an honorary shield, he wanted only the real thing. He was also a deputy sheriff in the Shelby County Sheriff's Department and a member of the Memphis Police Department, where he qualified on the pistol range just like any other officer. In fact, most of the guys were made special deputies because of the security nature of our work. We qualified on the firing range and were allowed to carry weapons. All of us learned respect for firearms, understood them and knew how dangerous they could be if mishandled.

Elvis helped a lot of police departments with their youth programs and became especially close to those in Denver, Philadelphia and Los Angeles. His greatest contributions, however, were in Memphis where for years he was intensely interested in the work the police and sheriff's departments were doing with young people.

The Federal Narcotics Bureau shield incident began when Elvis learned that a Hollywood celebrity was an undercover agent for the Federal Narcotics Bureau. He never talked about it but apparently he continued to think about how he, too, could become an agent for the Bureau.

When I went to Graceland one day to discuss Sonny's wedding, which was scheduled to take place in a few days and for which I was making final arrangements, I learned that Elvis had left the house without telling anyone where he was going. That was really unusual for Elvis and when we learned he was in Washington, D.C., we were astounded. He had made his own flight arrangements and had Jerry Schilling meet him there. Elvis was visiting the Deputy Narcotics Director, John Finlator.

Elvis offered his services to the Bureau in their anti-drug campaign and then asked for a Federal Narcotics Bureau badge. Deputy Director Finlator explained to Elvis that he would be glad to issue him an honorary shield, but it would be impossible to give him a real one. Of course, Elvis wasn't interested in the honorary status so he thanked the gentleman for his time and left the building.

From there he drove to the White House where he handed the guard at the gate a note addressed to President Nixon. He then went back to the hotel suite and Jerry called the White House to see if the note had been delivered. It seems the person to whom the guard had given the note had thought the whole thing was a prank, but after Jerry's call they checked and sometime later called back to let Elvis know when the President could see him.

In the meantime, Jerry had called us in Memphis and told Sonny that Elvis wanted him to come to Washington right away. My groom had been summoned by the very man who had asked me to make the wedding arrangements. Sonny caught the first flight to Washington and met Elvis and Jerry at the hotel, while I sat in Memphis worrying and wondering if Judy, the bride, would be the only person at the altar at the appointed time.

When they went to the White House, Elvis was dressed in a solid black outfit with a huge black cape. He carried a black walking stick and wore an enormous gold belt which had been given to him by the Hilton people for breaking so many attendance records with his performances. He was adorned with gold, that's about the only way his outfit could be described and he was wearing those big amber sunglasses. He was really done up!

Elvis, Sonny and Jerry were met by Egil Krogh who had an assistant take Sonny and Jerry into the Federal Building while he escorted Elvis to the President's office.

When he met President Nixon the President looked at Elvis' outfit and said, "Boy, you sure do dress kind of wild, don't you?"

Elvis said, "Mr. President, you've got your show to run and I've got mine."

From that moment, they hit it off, Elvis later told us.

He and President Nixon talked about law enforcement and Elvis told him of his interest in the Federal Narcotics Bureau and how he would like to help in the anti-drug campaign, if he could get an agent's badge. The President, Elvis told us, said he saw no reason why a man of his standing should not have one if he wanted to help. He assured Elvis he would get the badge and told him that the Bureau would be grateful for his assistance in trying to guide American youth away from the drug scene.

Elvis told President Nixon how much he appreciated his help, invited him for a visit to Graceland if he was ever in Memphis and asked if the two men with him could come in as they really wanted to meet the President. Jerry and Sonny were escorted into the President's office where they were given key rings and cufflinks with the presidential seal engraved on them. Both were grateful for the opportunity to meet the President and Elvis was ecstatic about the honor of being named a narcotics agent. Here these guys were, meeting the President and receiving gifts, while I was trying to complete the arrangements for the missing groom's imminent wedding. There were occasions when Elvis' timing presented monstrous problems.

His timing was always perfect, however, when it came to his profession. These were good years for Elvis. The tours were going great and Elvis enjoyed performing before live audiences again. His recording sessions were producing one hit after another and he was a happy husband and father.

I was, during this time, Chairman of the Board of Trustees of the Memphis Music Association and Chairman of the government-appointed Memphis and Shelby County Music Commission. One of the tasks I set about to accomplish was to have the city of Memphis erect a monument to Elvis, or at least name something after him in appreciation of what he had done for the city.

The city fathers had taken a survey and found that Elvis and the Mississippi River, in that order, were the two biggest tourist attractions the city had. Many of us felt that Elvis deserved some recognition by the city for which he had done so much and, of equal importance, we thought it would be good for the community. Elvis' fans were constantly trying to have things named after him and earlier there had been a big controversy about the Memphis Coliseum. His fans wanted the newly-constructed building named the Elvis Presley Coliseum but the city council refused and the whole mess embarrassed Elvis.

Elvis never asked for anything. He didn't do things for the city expecting anything in return, and when the newspapers began to print articles about the coliseum controversy he said to me, "I wish they would just forget all that, man. I don't care what they name the damn coliseum."

Later the city made a real blunder. Someone in authority decided later they should send Elvis a letter asking what he would like to have named after him. When the letter arrived Elvis showed it to me and we just couldn't believe what we were reading. Here was the city of Memphis asking one of its leading citizens what he wanted named after him. The whole thing really turned Elvis off. He said, "If they want to name something after me, of course, it would make me happy, but I'm sure as hell not going to tell them what to do or how to do it."

I went to see Lyman Aldrich, a friend who was active in local politics, and a close friend of the mayor, and told him that they had made a real mistake with the letter. I explained that Elvis just wasn't like that, it would be completely against his nature to suggest anything to them or try to tell them what to do.

Lyman said, "Well, we want to do something but we just don't know what to do. I guess it was a bad idea to ask Elvis."

"You bet it was," I said. "Why don't you just forget what happened in the past with the coliseum. There's been too much talk about that and I don't think Elvis would even accept the idea now."

"What can we do then?"

"The least the city could do would be to name the street where he lives after him," I answered. The idea came off the top of my head but as soon as I said it, it seemed like the right thing.

"My God," I continued, "it's not even named for anyone or anything now, it's just Highway 51. Think of all the people who come to the gate of his home and stand there just to get a glimpse of Elvis. It seems to me it would be good for all of us."

"That's not a bad idea," he said.

He went to the city council and introduced the idea at a meeting. In Memphis it takes three readings of a resolution such as this to pass. That's one reading a meeting for three consecutive meetings, allowing anyone who wished to object the opportunity to be heard.

The first two readings passed without any objections and when the third was scheduled I mustered together all the important people I could find and went to the meeting to speak in favor of the resolution. Objections, if there were to be any, would come at this time. The hall was full of bankers, people from the Chamber of Commerce and other important Memphis citizens who appreciated what Elvis had done for the city.

Sure enough, we had some opposition from an older group who would probably have complained regardless of what was on the agenda. Some of them were people with whom Elvis had done a lot of business, which somewhat annoyed me.

One man said he had a business on Highway 51 and he didn't want it to be located on Elvis Presley Boulevard. He didn't think it would be good for business.

Fortunately, one of the councilmen spoke up and said, "You know, I'm in business myself and if I wanted the location known, I sure would like to have it on Elvis Presley Boulevard. I can see my name and Elvis Presley's on the same billboard and people are going to know where to come. So I think your reasoning is a little unbelievable."

The resolution was unanimously passed and when I called Elvis, he was pleased to be honored in that way by Memphis, his hometown. The street was dedicated a few months later by Elvis' father, Vernon Presley, the mayor, Wyeth Chandler, and Sheriff Roy Nixon.

As time passed, more and more businesses which were located on Elvis Presley Boulevard advertised on radio and television. This caused Elvis to once remark, "It's kind of spooky to have the radio or television on and all of a sudden hear somebody saying your name, and then have it turn out to be an address."

Because it was such a time of warmth and pleasure for Elvis, I fondly remember the first time I met Priscilla. She had arrived at Graceland from Germany the previous day and when I went to the house Elvis met me outside and we began talking. He didn't mention her until I said I had to be leaving and when he heard that, he said, "Stick around a little, Marty. There's somebody here I want you to meet."

Whenever Elvis had something especially beautiful or unique, something of which he was very proud, he acted like a little kid. He wanted everyone to love it as much as he did. His eyes were laughing and he was bursting with excitement waiting to see my reaction to his surprise.

Priscilla came out of the house after a few minutes and she was everything Elvis had said. She was a charming young girl, very easy to talk with, self-assured and down to earth. She seemed far more mature than her sixteen years would account for, and she was breathtakingly beautiful. I sat there staring while we talked.

After a few minutes, Priscilla went back inside and Elvis looked at me, smiled and said, "Didn't I tell you?"

"Yeah man, she's lovely, a very nice person and really beautiful."

Elvis and Priscilla seemed to fall more in love each day and after the wedding and the birth of Lisa Marie, he was a very happy man. There is no question in my mind as to how much Elvis loved Priscilla and how much she loved him. They were right for each other and, had Elvis been in another business, I honestly believe theirs would have been a perfect marriage.

The success of the movies and then the tours demanded more and more of Elvis' time. Priscilla would sometimes travel with him but she didn't want to be a problem and he was really more comfortable being alone when on tour. Lisa, for all the enjoyment she brought, was born a short nine months after the marriage and neither Elvis nor Priscilla wanted their baby raised in a suitcase.

Even with all his modern music, Elvis was a very old-fashioned man and he wanted his wife and their child at home when he returned from work. Unfortunately, there were times when there would be six to eight weeks between the time he left for work and when he returned. The long periods of separation began to erode their marriage.

It just wasn't the life for a vibrant young woman like Priscilla. She wanted to see the world, be a part of it and make it a part of her.

Elvis was very possessive and protective when it came to any girl he cared about, and he was especially so with Priscilla. She wanted to be able to get out and do things but for awhile Elvis wouldn't let her, unless he or one of the guys were along.

Things gradually began to change. Priscilla started to take dancing lessons and became quite good at it. Because of her dancing talents and her agility, Elvis suggested that she begin taking karate lessons. She began the karate lessons and started going on shopping trips to New York and Dallas with one of the guys' wives. She was doing anything to break the monotony of being home alone while Elvis was away.

The trips became more frequent as did the karate sessions and we began to hear rumors that Priscilla was being seen a lot in the company of Mike Stone, her karate instructor. Elvis brushed off the rumors and didn't seem to think much about them until it became obvious that there was more involved than karate.

The marriage was falling apart without either of them knowing why and without either of them knowing what they would have to do to keep each other. Their love didn't seem to change, but they were unable to go on together.

One night when I was visiting Elvis at one of his California homes, we were standing outside talking. Elvis, almost a broken man, told me, "Moon, Priscilla is leaving me. I love her and she loves me but she says she isn't happy. She wants to leave and I don't know what to do. I don't want to lose her."

There were tears in his eyes, and in mine, when I said, "Elvis, are you going to change? Are you ready to stop traveling and spend more time with her?"

"No," he said. "Man, I just can't."

"You can't?"

"No, Moon, I can't. I just couldn't live without performing."

"Then you're going to have to accept it, Elvis. You're just going to have to accept it no matter how much it hurts."

I still can't figure it out and I don't believe anyone else can either, including Priscilla or Elvis, while he was alive. The only thing I know for sure is that they still loved each other when he died.

Chapter Thirteen

A Natural Resource

Elvis was a generous man. Those words don't even begin to express the overwhelming nature of his generosity. He gave and gave and never asked anything in return except to see or hear of the pleasure on the faces of those to whom he gave. There were special gifts to relatives, friends and often even to strangers, and there were regular gifts to charities both national and local.

Every year at Christmas time, Elvis would donate at least $100,000 to organized charities. Checks were usually delivered to one of the Memphis newspapers which had established itself, over the years, as a distribution point for funds being donated to charities by local people.

Some of Elvis' gifts became public knowledge but most were known only to the recipient and a few of us who were intimately involved in his life. I've discussed some of the gifts on other pages of this book because they seemed to fit best where I've placed them, or they were related to events being discussed. To comprehend the immensity of the amount involved they should be considered together.

The annual gifts to organized charity of more than $100,000 would amount to at least two million dollars during the period of Elvis' life when he was able to distribute that amount. Some were small, relatively speaking, such as the gift of the wheelchair to the crippled lady, but they were nevertheless important. Others, like the yacht *Potomac* and the Arizona Memorial, amounted to large sums of money.

The motorcycles, the Cadillac to me and then to each of the guys, the Cadillac for George, the help for the English girls, the $12,500 contribution to the Jewish Community Center, the help he gave his relatives and friends by putting them on the payroll or with outright cash gifts, the horses and trucks and TCB and TLC necklaces, and identification bracelets and Christmas gifts and bonuses were only a small part of his generosity.

Elvis built a beautiful new home for his father after Vernon and Dee were married. He helped buy the land on which my home in Memphis was built and he bought Joe Esposito a house in California. That happened one day when Elvis was out driving in Beverly Hills. There was a "For Sale" sign on a house he liked so he stopped the car, went to the house, knocked on the door and talked to the people who were inside. In a short time he was on the phone calling Joe to tell him he had bought a house for him. Just like that. Elvis bought Joe a house, because he knew Joe wanted one. $30,000 was given to Jerry Schilling to help him buy a house in California.

While filming a picture, whose title escapes me at the moment, I was told to make out a check for $50,000 to the Motion Picture Relief Fund Home and Hospital. This is a facility that is open to any actor belonging to the Screen Actors' Guild. The contribution from Elvis was one of the largest ever given and was accepted on behalf of the hospital by Frank Sinatra.

Before writing the check, I asked Elvis if there was enough money in his checking account to cover so large an amount. He laughed, and assured me that there was always a sufficient amount to cover a million-dollar check. Another of his idiosyncrasies. Imagine a checking account, drawing no interest, of one million dollars, always on hand, just in case he wanted to use it.

When it came to weddings, Elvis was the champion wedding giver. Over the years he paid for the weddings of Joe Esposito and Jerry Schilling and in 1970, he picked up the bills for three more. First was Dick Grob. Elvis paid for the wedding and then, as a wedding present, gave Dick and Marilyn a new automobile.

Then came George Klein. George asked Elvis to be his best man. He accepted, and told George he would like to pay for his wedding and reception in Las Vegas. Joe was asked to make the arrangements. The Rabbi and minister were contacted and Elvis' big suite on the top floor of the Hilton was decorated for the wedding and the food ordered for the reception. The task of transporting everyone to Las Vegas from Memphis was given to me. Reservations were made for everyone to go on the same flight, about fifteen couples, all first class.

We arrived in Las Vegas with just enough time to dress for the wedding. It was a beautiful wedding, and, for a little extra excitement, we were treated to some of Elvis' crazy antics. As is the custom in a Jewish wedding, the bride and groom stood under a canopy while the Rabbi performed the ceremony. As the Rabbi was talking, Elvis began repeating everything the Rabbi was saying. A couple of times, he even got ahead of the Rabbi, and then, he started talking to the Rabbi. This was not, at all, a part of the ceremony. Everyone was biting their tongues to keep from laughing and luckily, the Rabbi finished before Elvis took over. If it had been possible, I really believe Elvis would have officiated.

Later that year, on December 21st, Sonny, Elvis and I were sitting in the dining room talking when Sonny said, "E, do you mind if I get Moon to set up all the arrangements for my wedding?"

Elvis said, "No, I don't mind."

Well, that took me by surprise as Sonny had not asked or mentioned wedding arrangements prior to that moment. He saw the surprised look on my face and started laughing.

After meeting with Sonny and Judy to discuss what they wanted, I started the wheels in motion. Speed was necessary as they were planning to be married on the 28th of December.

The next day, Elvis called Sonny to meet him in Washington, D.C. and there I was trying to make the arrangements for Sonny's wedding to be held in a few days. Fortunately, they returned on the 24th and I was able to bring all the loose pieces together for the coming events. The day of the wedding, we went to the church for rehearsal and everything seemed to work out quite well. That evening, we met Elvis at the back of the church and, so he wouldn't be seen, went to the minister's office until time for the ceremony to begin.

As was his habit, Elvis was carrying a big police flashlight. When he started to leave the office to go to the altar, in his capacity as best man, he was still carrying it. I had to persuade him to let me hold it as he was determined to take the flashlight with him.

I later learned that Judy had fearfully anticipated that Elvis might start talking to the preacher as he had done with the Rabbi at George's wedding. She had asked Sonny to talk to Elvis before the ceremony and, except for the flashlight, Elvis behaved himself. However, he did do something typical. The reception was held at the church and, after an hour, Elvis came to me and said, "Let's move the reception to Graceland where I'll be more comfortable."

"Elvis, Judy and Sonny probably want to stay here with their families," I answered.

"Well, tell them to invite a few of them up to the house and meet us there."

So, that's what happened. The food, drinks, and some guests were moved to Graceland. Around midnight, Elvis decided he wanted to go to the movies. As we were all leaving in our cars, Elvis said to Sonny and Judy, "See you at the theater."

Judy laughed and Sonny said, "Okay, boss, we'll meet you over there."

Judy thought Elvis was kidding and she must have thought Sonny was kidding also. After all, this was their wedding night. However, neither was kidding but somehow Judy's good sense prevailed and they didn't show up at the theater that night.

The next day, the 29th, Sonny received a call at the motel where he and Judy were staying. "Elvis wants you to go back to Washington this afternoon."

Sonny and Judy went to Graceland and, as Sonny was kissing Judy goodbye, Elvis came down the stairs and said, "Let's go, I thought that stuff stopped after you got married." Everybody laughed and Elvis, Jerry and the husband of less than one day went to Washington. It was business as usual.

I guess Elvis felt that since he helped with the marriages, he was in some way responsible for the children. He paid the hospital bills for the births of many of the guys' offspring.

Elvis recycled things. Often when he gave someone a new car he would take their old car and give it to someone else, as he did with George Klein and Gary Pepper. Once, he gave a new Pontiac to Pat Parry, the Beverly Hills hair stylist, and then asked her what she wanted to do with the car he had replaced. She told him she would like to give it to her brother, who needed an automobile.

Elvis said, "Okay, now you see how it works. You got a new car and now your brother is getting a car, so two people are happy."

That happened to me and my wife in 1973. One afternoon. I brought my children, Sheri, Angie, and Marc, to Graceland to use the pool. My wife was entertaining one of her friends at home so she was not with us.

Elvis and Linda were sunbathing and Sonny was in the pool. Elvis started talking about his cousin who came to see him only when he wanted something. He said, "That sonofabitch came up here last night and said he wanted a new car and a motorcycle. Man, he doesn't ever come here just because he wants to see me, only because he wants something."

Knowing that Elvis was more hurt than angry, I changed the subject and tried to joke him out of his mood. A few minutes later I jumped in the pool. Elvis went back to sunbathing and talking with Linda.

Sonny and I were in the pool and our conversation turned to car trouble. There was a mechanical problem with my wife's car and I was asking Sonny's advice. Suddenly I heard Elvis ask, "What car, what's wrong with it?"

Sonny and I were a good distance from Elvis and we were talking low, but old "super ears," as we sometimes called him, had heard us. It was always disconcerting as we never grew accustomed to his ability to be speaking to someone else, but be able to hear what others were saying across the room.

He again asked, "What are you talking about?"

Sonny answered, "Oh, nothing. We were just talking about fixing cars."

Elvis said, "Moon, what were you saying?"

Trying to be funny, I said, "I was saying that I want a car and a motorcycle." We all started laughing and then he said, "Do you really want a car and a motorcycle? I'll buy them for you."

"Hell no," I answered, "I'm just joking around because of what you told me about your cousin."

"No, you've given me a good idea and I want to get them for you."

We went back and forth on this for about ten minutes when I said, "Look, if you want to do that, buy the car for my wife and give Sonny a motorcycle. I already have a good car and Sonny would like to have the chopper his brother brought over the other night for you to see."

Elvis said, "Okay, what kind of car does Patsy like?"

"Well, she has a Grand Prix now and likes it."

"Call the dealer and get her a new Grand Prix with everything on it and tell them I want it here in an hour. Then call Patsy and tell her to be here in thirty minutes."

I called the dealer and then called my wife. She said it would be awhile before she could come because of her company. Of course, Elvis wanted her there immediately and took the phone from me. Patsy knew Elvis didn't like strangers at Graceland, so she told him she would be there as soon as her friend left. He countered, "Bring her with you, fool."

About fifteen minutes later, Patsy arrived without any knowledge of what was going on. The new Grand Prix was just coming in the driveway as we were walking out the front door to meet her. Elvis waited until it got to the top of the hill and then said, "Patsy, that's yours."

At first, she was so shocked she couldn't speak, and then she began crying. Elvis was laughing and, after awhile, everybody calmed down and went inside to talk. During the conversation, Elvis said he had given the car to my wife because he had never really given her or Jo Smith much of anything, compared to what he had given to some of the other wives. Patsy said, "Jo really needs something like this, she doesn't have a car and she's always wanted a Grand Prix."

Elvis said, "Then we'll buy Jo one tomorrow, what's her favorite color?"

Patsy answered, "Green."

The next day, Jo Smith got exactly that.

The story doesn't end here. That night, George and Barbara Klein were having dinner at Graceland and Barbara was telling me that her car was about to fall apart. Elvis came in just a few seconds later and, taking him aside, I mentioned Barbara's ailing car. He told me to give Barbara my wife's one-year-old Grand Prix. Patsy had a new car and Barbara had a fairly new one and again, two people had been made happy through his recycling process.

Later, Elvis handed my wife a check for $2,000 and said, "Here Patsy, I want you to go out and buy a new wardrobe to match your car, you can't go around driving it in jeans all the time." The man was amazing.

The car giving continued when Elvis started buying Mercedes for some of the guys. He bought one for Dave Hebler, Charlie Hodge, Sonny West and a couple of the other guys while he was in California. He, himself, had a beautiful light blue Mercedes 600 sedan. It was worth over $20,000 and he gave that one to Lamar Fike. Upon his return to Memphis, he bought a Mercedes for Dr. Nick and another for Bill Morris. Unfortunately, the second was quite widely discussed in the Memphis newspapers as Bill was running for mayor of Memphis at the time and his opponent created a big sensation because he had accepted a gift of such value. Bill was a good friend to Elvis and the car was given to him because of the friendship. The newspapers were unfair to insinuate otherwise.

I came to Graceland one night in 1974, and noticed two beautiful Mark IV automobiles parked in front. I'd never seen the cars before so I assumed someone was visiting or Elvis had bought two new cars. I went upstairs and Elvis, Linda, Billy and Jo Smith were there. Elvis had just finished breakfast and looked as though he was preparing to leave.

He asked, "Did you see Linda's new Mark IV outside? It's the one that is two-tone blue, and I bought Billy and Jo the maroon one last night."

"Sure did," I answered, and felt happy for them as I offered my congratulations.

"Glad you got here, Moon," Elvis said. "You need to go with us."

"Why, where are you going?"

"We picked out one for you last night and it's down there waiting."

I thought he was either kidding or, because I was there,

had decided he felt like buying another car. I smiled and said, "Yeah, uh huh."

"I'm not putting you on, Moon, let's go. When you see it you'll know, it's your favorite color. They just held it until today to get it ready and serviced."

When we arrived at the new car service department, there was a gleaming, dark blue Lincoln Mark IV. The salesman gave the keys to Elvis and he handed them to me, saying, "Now, am I kidding?" I couldn't believe what was happening, he really had bought it for me the night before.

An unusual incident occurred in 1975 when Elvis went to the car dealer with whom he had been doing business for years and bought Mark IV automobiles for some of the guys. Six were purchased and he gave them to Lamar, Dave, Red and a few of the others.

The next evening, Vernon came to Elvis with the bill and showed him that the salesman, with whom Elvis had also done business for years, had not given the customary discount on the cars. No fleet rate, no cut at all. Elvis usually never concerned himself with prices, but this time he was really angry that the salesman and dealer were so unappreciative of past business. He thoroughly resented being taken advantage of and said, "Call the sonofabitch and tell him to open the showroom. We're bringing his damned cars back right now. If he doesn't want to open tonight we'll leave the damned things in front of the place. Then call the Cadillac dealer and tell him I'll meet him at his place in an hour. I'll buy you guys Cadillacs instead of the Lincolns."

The Mark IV salesman, and then his sales manager, came running out to Graceland. Elvis refused to talk to the salesman but did speak with the sales manager for about ten minutes. He would not change his mind. We formed a caravan of six Mark IV Lincolns, with Elvis, Billy and I leading in another car. The guys took the Lincolns back, while we went to the Cadillac dealer where Elvis bought Sevilles and then to another dealer where he bought two Mark IV Lincolns.

Later he bought various cars for others. A Grand Prix for his cousin Patsy Gambill, a Porsche for Al Strada, a car for Dean Nichopoulas. A Corvette for Lamar and he gave cars to the maids, to girls he dated, to certain doctors and to a few

Denver policemen he befriended. He also gave cars to Pat West, Judy West and a girl Joe Esposito was dating while they were vacationing in Vail, Colorado. He gave so many to so many people, it is impossible to remember them all.

The thousands of Christmas cards, birthday cards, and flowers which arrived at Graceland, were also recycled. They would be taken to the local hospitals where the patients, especially the children, would make things from them or simply keep them intact as souvenirs from Elvis Presley.

Elvis liked to wear jewelry and enjoyed giving it to his friends. Once, I think it was in 1974, George Klein was at Graceland and Elvis decided he was going to give him a ring as a present. This was a spur of the moment thought. He called the jeweler and had him bring an assortment of rings to the house. A beautiful, square emerald and diamond ring was selected by Elvis and given to George. There was no special occasion involved or anything. He simply decided to buy G. K. a gift, and that was that.

During the same year we were all at the movies one night and I was sitting directly behind Elvis. He turned around and said, "Let me see your hand."

"What?" I said.

"Let me see your hand!"

I thought he was goofing around so I held out both hands and said, "Which one do you want to see?"

He grabbed my right hand, on which I was wearing a ring given to me by my parents twenty years before. Elvis said, "Take off that ring."

"I can't take it off, Elvis. That's been on there since I was thirteen. My parents gave it to me. Here, use this hand." I put my other hand up to him.

He slipped a ring on my finger. It was an eighteen karat gold ring mounted with the largest black star sapphire I had ever seen. Elvis had worn it before and I always thought it was a beautiful ring, but never realized how beautiful until I saw it on my own finger.

I said, "Hey, man, what are you doing?"

"Just shut up and keep still," Elvis said. "Now, let's watch the movie."

"Wait a minute. Did you want to see how this looks?" I held up my hand for him to see, and then started to remove the ring to return it to him.

"Keep it on that finger," he said.

"Come on, man, here, take it back before something happens to it."

"Damn it, I said keep the ring." He turned around to watch the movie and my wife and I looked at each other in total disbelief.

Another time, Elvis decided to give jewelry to everyone. The big airplane had been purchased and he called his jeweler with an invitation to join us for an airplane ride. Elvis also asked that he bring his sample case full of jewelry.

The pilot took us for a short ride from Memphis to Nashville. There was a large group of friends on the plane and, one by one, or one couple at a time, the friends were asked to go to the rear compartment where Elvis was waiting. As soon as they entered, Elvis, sitting with the jeweler, would pick something from the cases of jewelry and present it to the friends. Now, these were not trinkets, they were expensive pieces of jewelry. He chose each piece himself and it was something special for each person. Something he felt matched their personalities. I have no idea of the dollar amount he gave away that night, but it was a bundle.

I was on the airplane one night with Dave Hebler, Elvis and a girl he was dating at the time. We had earlier flown in the small jet to Texas as Elvis wanted to see the progress of the refurbishing of his larger jet. We were on our return trip to Memphis when Dave noticed a new ring Elvis was wearing. It was a large ruby surrounded with diamonds, worth about $25,000. Dave said something about it being beautiful and Elvis took it off and handed it to him. Dave, of course, thought Elvis was giving it to him to see, so he looked at it, then passed it over to me. I was sitting between him and Elvis. I looked at it and also commented about how nice it was and then gave it back to Dave. He slipped it on his finger for a minute, then gave it back to me to hand to Elvis. When I held it out to Elvis, he didn't take it. He looked at Dave and said, "You want it?"

Dave just laughed because he thought Elvis was joking.

Elvis said, "It's yours."

"Oh no, man," Dave said, "I can't take that. I just wanted to get a look at it, up close."

I had, when Elvis said, "It's yours," begun to give it back to Dave, and when Dave said no, I held it out to Elvis. It was like a tennis match with me being the mover of the ball because they kept saying yes and no. Finally I said, "Okay, you guys make up your damn minds and let me know who gets it."

We all started to laugh and Elvis said, "Well, I'm not taking it back so you might as well put it on your finger, Dave."

That was the end of the subject as far as Elvis was concerned so Dave had a beautiful ring.

We were in Texas again to see Elvis' big jet and T. G. Shepherd, a country singer, and his wife, whom Elvis had known for awhile, went along. They were talking about music and Elvis asked how his career was progressing. Everything was fine, he told Elvis, except for the difficulty in getting from one gig to another and added that he planned to solve that by buying a bus when he had the money.

As we left the small jet, Elvis hung back as though he wanted to say something to me. "Moon, get on the phone, call J. D. in Nashville and tell him I want a bus at Graceland tomorrow."

He was referring to his friend, J. D. Sumner the gospel singer, who was quite knowledgeable on the subject of customized buses.

I wasn't quite certain what Elvis meant, so I asked, "What kind of bus?"

"I'm going to buy them a customized bus," motioning toward the singer and his wife. "J. D. will know what I want."

I called J. D. in Nashville and said, "J. D., we're down here in Texas, and Elvis wants you to do something for him."

"What's he want?" I caught the little laugh, we were all accustomed to Elvis and the crazy things he requested.

"He wants you to get a customized bus for him and have it at Graceland tomorrow afternoon. He's going to give it to some people."

"Well, damn. I know of a good one, but it's in North Carolina."

"I'm just telling you what he said."

"Okay son," J. D. answered. "It's going to be a night of hard driving but tell him it will be there."

When I rejoined the group, I gave Elvis the okay sign and he smiled his approval. Elvis couldn't keep a secret, so when we were all on the airplane heading back to Memphis he said to the singer, "Well, T. G., I think I've got your transportation problem licked."

"What do you mean?"

"I don't think you'll have too much trouble going back and forth to your gigs anymore because I'm buying you a bus, a customized bus."

Of course, Shepherd was ecstatic. The next day he came to Graceland about two in the afternoon and the bus was there waiting. J. D. had picked it up in North Carolina and driven it to Memphis. All of us piled into the bus for a ride through Memphis and Elvis was just as happy as the singer who received the gift.

When Elvis gave a gift, he didn't want continuous gushing. As far as he was concerned, a simple "Thank you," was sufficient. That was the end of it. No further thanks were expected and he disliked reading about his gift-giving in the newspapers. He gave gifts because he wanted people to be happy and his enjoyment came from seeing them that way.

Alan Fortas' father became very ill and, in fact, was not expected to live. Elvis saw the effect on Alan and called me to say he wanted to visit Mr. Fortas in the hospital. He didn't want a large group to accompany him, so he and I, with only two other guys, went to the Baptist Hospital.

Alan was outside his father's room when we arrived, and was really grateful to see Elvis. He told Alan he wanted to say hello to his father and asked if it was all right for him to have visitors. Alan went into the room with us and Mr. Fortas was pleased that Elvis had come. They talked for a few minutes and Elvis tried to encourage Mr. Fortas, telling him everything would be fine and that he would soon be able to go home.

When he felt he had been there as long as he should stay, Elvis reached in his pocket and brought out a beautiful, gold, pocket watch. He had received it as a Christmas gift and it was engraved with his name. He handed it to Mr. Fortas and said, "Here, I really would like for you to have this."

Everybody in the room became a little emotional. We knew the watch was a very expensive, imported gift which Elvis liked, but we also knew that it did not mean nearly as much to him as the smile of happiness on Mr. Fortas' face.

Since 1971, I had been in business for myself, working in marketing and promotion for the record and publishing industry. My company was doing well until the economic slump which affected the entire country. We were hit pretty hard and in late 1973, started sinking badly. I became depressed and constantly worried about the welfare of my family.

I was in bed with a bad case of flu when the phone rang one night. Billy Smith was on the line. "What are you doing?"

"I'm lying here in bed with the damn flu!"

"Wait a minute," Billy said.

A familiar voice asked, "Moon, what the hell have you been doing? Billy tells me you're in bad shape." It was Elvis.

"Yeah, I've got the rotten flu bug."

"I can hear that, but that's not what I'm talking about. He told me you're having a rough time financially."

"Well, the economy is beginning to get me, but I'll be all right."

Elvis snarled, "Don't give me that bullshit. I know you're hurtin' for money and you're worried about your business."

"I'll be all right, don't worry about it, I just need to get over the flu."

"Yeah, yeah, I know," he answered. "Look, I don't want to see you in this position. I'm your friend and I want to help."

"Look, friend, I appreciate it but you don't have to."

"I know I don't have to, but I already have. Charlie should be at your door about now."

"Charlie? What for?"

"Just hang up and answer the door when he knocks," and with that he was gone.

Charlie arrived and handed me a check without saying a word. I looked at the check and my eyes popped out. It was for $10,000. I immediately called Elvis and said, "Thank you, you're unbelievable, but I can't let you give me this much money."

"You're welcome, but I don't want to hear anymore about it, I know what I'm doing. Use it wisely and I'll see you when you're over the flu," and he was gone again.

Another special memory of his generosity to me, is a time in 1975, when my financial situation had worsened and money problems, as they so often do, were taking their toll on my marriage as well as my mental health. Elvis sensed that something was wrong and talked with some of the others about me. They told him my wife and children had gone to Ohio that day to visit her brother and that I was extremely depressed.

I went to Graceland that evening and was in the den talking to Richard Davis, who was also having some real problems. Lamar Fike walked in and, when he saw us, went upstairs to Elvis' suite and told him I was in the house. Billy was with Elvis at the time and called to me to come upstairs to see Elvis.

I went to the suite and we talked a little about different things. Then Elvis said, "What's the matter, Moon?"

Had I been thinking clearly, I would have held back, but it was a relief to share my burdens. They came tumbling out as I explained how things were going and what was bothering me.

He asked, "Why did Patsy leave?"

"It's just for a little while, Elvis. We thought it would help clear the air of some of the tension, while I'm trying to get things straight. We just want to see where we're at."

"Man, we can't have that. I want you to call Patsy and tell her to bring the kids and get herself back here. I'm going to give you some money, I'm going to buy you a new car and I'm going to send you and your family to Hawaii for a vacation."

He knew how much I liked Hawaii and, while he was talking, he pulled a page from a desk calendar and began to write. When he finished telling me what he was going to do, and before I could answer, he handed me the calendar page. On it he had written: *Pay bills. Think positively. All expense paid vacation in Hawaii. New Car.* I folded the scrap of paper and placed it in my wallet, where it remains to this day.

While I was trying to choke back tears and mumble some words of gratitude Elvis wrote a check for $10,000 and handed it to me. He then had me dial Patsy at her brother's home and impatiently told her to get on the next plane home. I interrupted their conversation long enough to tell him to let her stay a few more days, get some rest and visit with her brother.

Words could not express how much I appreciated his help, but I tried. Then I remembered Richard and his problems and mentioned to Elvis that Richard was downstairs and also in rather bad shape. He asked me about Richard's trouble and when I had finished relating as much as I knew, he said to have Richard come up to the suite.

When Richard came in, we talked for awhile and then Elvis asked, "What's the matter with you, Richard?"

The problems were repeated again, and when he had finished, Elvis looked at him and said, "Well, Richard, there's nothing I can do," he hesitated for a long pause and then added, "except to send you to Hawaii if you would like to go."

Richard almost fell over when Elvis said that, because he, too, loved Hawaii. But Elvis had not finished. He added, "I'm going to give you some money and buy you a new car, and if you want to take somebody to Hawaii with you, you can. Marty will make all the arrangements. Now you guys wait about thirty minutes until I get dressed and we'll all go down to the Cadillac dealer and buy you each a new car."

Almost simultaneously, Richard and I said, "Man, you've done enough. You don't have to buy a new car."

"I told you I want to, and I'm going to, now shut up!" Elvis' tone was harsh, but his eyes were laughing and we knew him well enough not to waste time arguing.

We waited until Elvis was dressed and, after calling the Cadillac dealer to open his showroom, drove down to buy new Cadillacs in the middle of the night.

We were walking around the back of the lot, looking at

the different cars which the dealer had in stock when Elvis stopped before one and said, "Marty, that's for you. That looks just like you."

I could barely tell the color because it was so dark where we were, but he was a good judge of beauty and when we moved it into the light I saw I owned a Cadillac in a striking burnt-orange color.

A white Cadillac Eldorado was chosen for Richard and, believe me, we were two happy guys that night. But Elvis wasn't finished buying cars. As we were walking back to the showroom he saw a handsome, young couple looking at one of the Cadillacs. Elvis walked over to them, introduced himself and began to talk. They were, of course, pleased to meet Elvis and told him they enjoyed his music and appreciated his taking the time to say hello.

Elvis said, "You like that car?"

"Sure, it's beautiful," the man answered.

"Well, why don't you get one?"

"Man, I sure would if I could, but we're just looking now."

"Go ahead and get you one," Elvis insisted.

"We just can't, Mr. Presley."

"Yes, you can. I'm going to buy it for you."

They thought he was kidding and the man said, "Aw come on, now."

"I'm serious. I want you to pick out the one you want and I'm going to buy it for you. Come to the office after you've decided which one you want and the man there will take care of the paper work."

The woman almost fainted and the man was just about speechless, but before the night was over they owned a new Cadillac. That one made all the newspapers and television news reports, probably because the couple was so grateful they told everyone they knew.

I came home one night and my wife wasn't in the house. Patsy was almost always at home when I came from work so I asked my daughter, "Where's your mother?"

She said, "Elvis called and asked her to come up to Graceland."

That was extremely unusual and I was afraid something had happened which had caused him to need us there. I quickly drove to Graceland and met some of the guys when I entered the house. I asked if Patsy was there and was told she was with Elvis.

When I went into his suite, they were talking and I said, "What's going on? Is something wrong?"

Elvis said, "Sit down. I want to talk to you."

"Why? What's up?"

Elvis said, "Man, I'm worried about you and Patsy. I've just had a feeling you were having it rough and I thought I might be able to help."

"No, everything is all right," I said.

"I think there's something wrong. Now what is it?"

"No," I said. "Everything's cool. There's no problem. Things are not the way I would like them to be, but there's no big problem. We're making it."

"Well, that's not enough. How much money do you have in the bank?"

"I've some money in the bank, Elvis. Everything's cool."

"I want to know how much you've got."

"About two hundred and fifty dollars."

"Is that all?"

"Yeah, but everything's all right." I had thought things were improving and was proud that I had managed to have a savings account at all but, of course, to Elvis it was peanuts.

"No, everything's not all right. I'm going to give you some money."

"Now listen, Elvis, I don't want you to give me anything. You've already done too much and I don't know when I'll ever be able to repay you. We're okay. There's nothing to worry about, man."

"I said I'm giving you some money."

"I'm not going to take your money, Elvis. I don't need it."

He looked at Patsy and said, "Will you take it?"

"No," she answered. "Not if Marty doesn't want me to."

"Look," Elvis said, "I'm not going to argue with either one of you." He called one of the guys and told him to bring the checkbook upstairs. Elvis wrote out a check for $10,000, handed it to me and said, "Damn it, don't argue with me now. I want you to have this."

There was no point in trying to argue with Elvis when he had decided to give you something. That's the kind of person he was.

On the way home that night, my wife and I were talking about Elvis' concern for our welfare when she said, "Guess what I have?" She reached in her purse and showed me another check for $2,000. He had given it to her before I arrived.

I asked, "What is this for?"

"Well, he called and asked me to come to Graceland because he was worried about us. When I got there, he said he knew we were having a rough time and he thought I should leave you because we're not happy together. He said he knew I could make it on my own.

"So help me, Marty, he said, 'Leave the miserable sonofabitch, nobody will blame you and I'll help you in any way I can. If you want to open a business for yourself, I'll back you, anything you want to do.' "

Patsy told me that all she could do was look at Elvis in astonishment. She didn't understand how, if he cared about me as much as he said, he could suggest such a thing. I smiled as she told me this and thought to myself, "That crazy bastard."

She told Elvis she couldn't leave me because we loved each other. He then handed her the check for $2,000 and told her to spend it on herself and the kids, not me. A few minutes later I had walked in and he changed the subject.

I thought about the strange conversation and then dismissed it realizing that one of the reasons we called him "Crazy" was the unusual things he said and did when least expected. Looking back, I now know there were other reasons, about which we'll talk later, and I'm no longer sure there wasn't at least some sense in what he had said to Patsy, considering the condition I was in at the time.

These were some of the instances when Elvis helped me and my family and he did the same for most of the other guys in the group. There were also bonuses after each tour, and numerous gifts from time to time.

Throughout the years, Elvis often said that what the group gave to him was more important to him than money. Our love, our friendship and our loyalty were worth more to him than all the gifts he gave to us.

When he gave George Klein his Cadillac and George thanked him, Elvis said, "What good is all my fortune and fame if I can't share it with my friends?"

When he bought a Cadillac for Sonny, Sonny remarked, "I can't take this, E, you're always giving us things and we can't give you anything in return."

Elvis answered, "You're giving when you don't know you're giving."

He gave us his friendship, and at the same time wanted to make some of our dreams come true. He cared that much for us. The things written about Elvis buying friends and the guys being opportunists, hangers-on and blood suckers are pure nonsense, written by people who knew little of the relationship between us and, even if they had known, would probably have been unable to comprehend anything so unique.

Most important though, these writers didn't know Elvis and weren't aware of his ability to judge people. It is impossible to buy friendship, love and loyalty and Elvis was able to recognize those who feigned these feelings simply as a means of ingratiating themselves. Fortunately, there were only a few of this caliber.

All of the examples of generosity related in this chapter are only those of which I have personal knowledge. Since I was not with Elvis at all times, since he did not like publicity regarding his generosity and since I was not aware of all his gifts to the guys in the group, a complete rundown is not possible. I have read many accounts of this facet of Elvis' personality and, even though most of what has been written about him is not true, I cannot doubt the accuracy of the reports regarding his generosity. This is the way he was.

Chapter Fourteen

Elvis by Satellite

After the success of the first Las Vegas appearance, Elvis was really enthused and happy about doing live performances. It was set for him to return to Vegas the following year, but that was not enough. He and the Colonel began talking about going on tour with the show. They put their thinking into action after Elvis played the big annual Houston Livestock show and broke all records. A tour was planned for late 1970.

Elvis again performed in Las Vegas in August, and everyone was still in top shape, so no rehearsal was necessary for the tour which began in September.

Elvis was ready to take his show to the people, many of whom had heard him sing only on records or seen him in the movies. The first concerts were sold out before Elvis left Graceland, and that was to remain true of every tour he went on until the day he died.

Two big airplanes were chartered, one jet was for Elvis and the guys and the other for the musicians and the rest of the show. The Colonel made the arrangements in each city and would arrive a day ahead of Elvis. Sonny traveled with Colonel Parker because he had to be at the new location early to check security in the hotel and concert hall.

In 1971, Elvis asked George Klein and me to go on tour with him. I owned my own marketing and promotions company then and I was free to go. George was program director of the number one radio station in Memphis and he, too, would be able to take some time off. Coincidentally, we were both going to a radio and record convention in New Orleans on the twelfth of November and the tour would arrive in Houston just in time for us to make the short hop to New Orleans. The tour began in Minneapolis on the fifth and George and I flew to Cleveland on the night of the sixth and joined Elvis and the guys at the hotel. It was a big, old hotel as were most of the tour hotels. It seems the Colonel liked old hotels, Elvis didn't.

It was snowing the next afternoon when we boarded a bus for the airport and then flew to Louisville. We were going there to do a show in Louisville's Freedom Hall and from there we would fly to Philadelphia.

We landed in Louisville and went to a hotel to rest and to allow Elvis to change into his jumpsuit. We then went to Freedom Hall and arrived during the show's intermission. The music began and Elvis was on stage. I thought Las Vegas was exciting but being there on the side of the stage and seeing 19,000 people stand up and applaud was overpowering. The show was filled with the same intensity and excitement as those in Las Vegas and looking into the dark and seeing thousands of flashbulbs exploding with light was a new experience.

After the show we returned to the hotel, packed and then headed for the plane and Philadelphia. The airplane we used on this tour was a beautifully customized F-28 jet. It was decorated in beige and rust colors, a flying living room with couches, tables, game tables and comfortable reading chairs. There was a private room, complete with a shower, in the rear for Elvis. We later learned this was the same plane used by President Nixon during his campaign. We were met at the airport by some fine Philadelphia policemen who were assigned to us as a security force for the entire time. They were led by Inspector Mike Mangione who was a dynamite guy.

We went from the airport to the Bellevue-Stratford Hotel, one of Philadelphia's oldest. It's now closed, but before closing it became famous as the home of the Legionnaire's Disease. Within a period of three days we were to do shows in Philadelphia, Baltimore and Boston. The plan was to stay in Philadelphia all three days.

The first night we played at the Philadelphia Spectrum. The crowd was unbelievable, there were almost 20,000 people in the audience. When I think about it, I am still amazed at the crowds of people who were always drawn to Elvis. Even while it was happening, it was hard to believe. Interestingly enough, I think Elvis was also astounded by his immense impact. It never failed to thrill me that millions of people loved Elvis just as much as he loved them.

The routine in all the cities was that the Sweet Inspirations would perform first, then Jackie Kahane and then a twenty minute intermission. It was timed so Elvis arrived at the concert hall during intermission. This was done to avoid huge crowds at the stage entrance when we arrived. Elvis would do the show, then when he began singing, *Can't Help Falling In Love,* which was his final song, we would all head for the cars to get ready to leave. Joe, Sonny and Red would stay at the stage and when Elvis was finished, all four would run to the limousine and we'd speed away to the hotel. This was all done while the audience was still applauding. There was never an encore, we never gave the crowd a chance to block the stage entrance.

After we left, someone would announce to the audience that Elvis had left the building. When we returned to the hotel, Elvis changed clothes after showering and we all gathered in his suite. It would take hours for him to unwind and since we slept most of the day, we were far from tired. Sometimes girls were invited to the suite as he wasn't traveling with a girlfriend on that tour.

George and I had arranged for Jay Cook, a close friend of ours, to come by and spend some time with us. Jay is program director of WFIL radio, Philadelphia's number one station. Jay is from Memphis and a good friend so Elvis was always pleased to have him for a visit.

The day after the Philadelphia show, we had a little trouble getting out of the hotel because of the crowd but managed to get to the airplane for the flight to Baltimore. Elvis changed into his jumpsuit on the plane and when we arrived at the Baltimore airport we went by limousine to the auditorium, arrived there at intermission, did the show, went back to the plane and flew to Philadelphia spending the night there again.

Elvis was a little crazy on stage in Baltimore. But then,

antics were a part of his behavior, and I believe a portion of his effect on an audience was this mischievous part of his personality. Except when singing a serious song, and sometimes even then, he always appeared to be on the verge of laughter, with sparkling eyes shifting around the audience as though looking for someone with whom to share a very funny secret.

In this instance, the very funny secret was aimed at Red and me. He was drinking water between songs, when he looked toward the side of the stage where Red and I were standing. He walked a little closer to us and, while talking to the audience, turned and threw the water at us, turned back to the crowd and, without missing a beat, began singing.

An unusual incident happened in Baltimore which almost ruined our precision timing for leaving the auditorium. Elvis finished his last song, we ran to the backstage doors, and they were all locked. One of the auditorium guards had forgotten to unlock them and we managed to get out only moments before a human barricade of fans blocked the stage entrance driveway.

The next day we flew to Boston where the people were hanging off the balconies in the Boston Garden for the show. Again, we boarded the plane, then flew back to Philadelphia for the night. Our last night there was spent having a big going away party. The next day we flew to Cincinnati for another performance. From Cincinnati we flew, the next day, to Houston where George and I left for New Orleans in time for our convention. As hectic as it had been, I hated to leave the tour. I went on several after that and enjoyed the last as thoroughly as the first.

Shortly after the New Year, in 1973, Joe, Elvis and I were sitting in the den at Graceland when Colonel Parker called. Elvis talked to him for a few minutes and then came back with a smile on his face and said, "Moon, the final arrangements have been made to do a television special in Hawaii. It will be beamed all over the world by satellite. The Colonel has outdone himself."

I took it in stride until Elvis said, "The Colonel estimates that over half a billion people will see it at one time."

I was astounded. Elvis said to Joe, "Everything is set, we leave next week."

He got up and went into the next room. I looked at Joe and said, "Do you think there's room for one more?"

"I don't know," Joe answered. "Let me see what happens."

Elvis knew I loved Hawaii as much as he did and I think he gave Joe and me a little time to talk. When he walked back into the room he had a sly smile on his face. He sat down and said in a very serious tone, "Joe, I want this show to be great, no slip-ups, I went everybody on their toes. We need an extra guy or two with us."

He said all this without looking at me and Joe answered, "Look, Marty volunteered to help out."

Elvis looked at me for a few seconds and didn't say anything, then he started smiling and just nodded his head yes. He was making me sweat but from the moment he first mentioned the show, he knew I would want to go and he wanted me to be a part of it.

I was overjoyed when I learned that all the wives would be joining us in Hawaii, three days after we reached the island. I made arrangements for Patsy, and all the guys paid for their wives' airfare. We planned to make it a fun time, with the wives joining in, but at the same time we knew that the most important thing was the show.

When the departure date arrived, we flew from Memphis to Los Angeles where we spent the night at Elvis' Holmby Hills house, and left the next night for Hawaii. It was my first ride on a 747 and Elvis knew it. Joe and I sat in front of Elvis and Linda and when it was time to take off, Elvis began telling me about the computers on the plane and how they helped with the takeoff, flying and landing. He explained everything about the plane to me and when we were in the air he insisted on giving me a guided tour of the 747. Elvis didn't want me to miss a thing.

When we landed in Hawaii we went to the Hilton Hawaiian Village hotel where the Colonel and Sonny were waiting for us. They had arrived earlier, as usual, to check the accommodations and security. We had one entire floor to ourselves.

In the daytime, we were free to do as we pleased. Elvis slept most of the day, but the rest of us were up early in the mornings and together on the beach. For the first time in years all the husbands and wives were together having a good time away from home. We played volleyball, rode the outrigger canoes, went to dinner together and visited Pearl Harbor to show the wives the *Arizona* memorial. It was a truly wonderful vacation for all of us with the only disappointment being that Elvis was unable to join in. It was impossible for him to go on the hotel beach without being mobbed by a crowd and, of course, he needed more sleep than the rest of us. He was the one who had to go on stage and perform, and he was doing his best to make sure he was ready for it. Elvis had been watching his weight for weeks and he looked sensational.

Marty Passetta, a very talented man, was chosen to direct the show. He and Elvis hit it off great from the start, and that was essential for Elvis and the show. Rehearsals were held every night at the Honolulu International Center auditorium. Elvis was in rare form and the set was fantastic. The wives went to the rehearsals with us and Elvis used them as an audience to play to during his performance. RCA and NBC executives were all over the place. This was a first in the history of television, a one-man performance to be beamed all over the world via satellite. The RCA and NBC executives were anxious to see that nothing went wrong, but their dealings were with the Colonel. The show itself was left to Elvis. He wanted it to be great, and knowing that was enough for the Colonel.

The night before the show, a dress rehearsal was held and everything came off right. A spectacular white jumpsuit with an American eagle on back had been designed for the satellite show.

Elvis was keyed up. We were all excited and tense, and after the dress rehearsal we went back to the hotel and talked away the hours. The show was to take place the next night at midnight Hawaiian time so it could be shown at prime time in each of the foreign countries.

Even though it was a television show, the audience was charged admission because Elvis and the Colonel had arranged for every penny of the proceeds to go to the Kui Lee cancer fund. Kui Lee was a talented Hawaiian songwriter who had died from cancer at an early age. He had written one of Elvis' favorite songs, *I'll Remember You.* Elvis and the

Colonel each paid $100 for their own tickets. The fund's goal was to raise $25,000 for the show, but in the middle of the show Elvis announced that they had raised $75,000.

Over 5,000 people, which is an overflow crowd for the Honolulu International Center, packed the place. A special row was roped off for Linda, the wives and Pat Parry, who was there as a guest of Elvis. The guys were stationed on each side of the stage to keep an eye on the audience.

The strains of *Also sprach Zarathustra* began, a powerful piece which only increased the tension of the audience; in seconds Elvis would be on stage and they knew it. After all the waiting, these final moments were the most difficult to bear. The orchestra and vocalists built to a crescendo and the suspense was intolerable, then the drum began rhythmically beating out a compelling series of rolls and Elvis flashed on stage like a champion coming out of his corner.

The audience was up in unison, creating so much noise we wondered if the microphones were transmitting a roar to the rest of the world rather than the sound of Elvis. He smiled, began to laugh, the left leg trembled and his voice was like a knife cutting through the applause. Our spines tingled and the girls went wild.

A thunderous applause after *C. C. Rider* was acknowledged by Elvis with a softly spoken, "Thank you very much," and the music picked up the rocking beat of *Burning Love* and everyone's temperature rose as Elvis sang the words.

At the conclusion, in response to the applause, Elvis said, "Thank you very much. Thank you. Thank you, ladies and gentlemen. Good evening, and, I hope you enjoy our show tonight. We're gonna try to do all the songs you want to hear." The audience was as quiet as possible, trying to hear what he was saying, but one girl sitting quite close was unable to restrain a half-sob, half-shriek which set off a few others and Elvis smiled at her and said, "Thank you, dear."

Then he went into the beautiful words of *Something* and every female in the audience, regardless of age, knew he was singing about her. That was his appeal, his ability to make every girl and woman feel that he loved her, if only he could just someday meet and be close to her. The incredible part is that it was true, he did love them all and he was able to communicate this message in such a personal way that it made no difference that the girl in the next seat was screaming, Elvis was singing only to the girl who was seeing him with her own eyes.

The oldest, the youngest, the prettiest and the homeliest were lost in the Elvis magic and did, in fact, become more beautiful because of him. Elvis had seen the true woman within each of them and their own estimation of their worth had been confirmed. They would remember his caressing words, *something in the way she moves*, and would walk with just a little more grace and awareness than before.

They were his. The audience belonged to him and he knew it. His every move, every sound, every musical note was calculated to keep the electricity flowing. He was a master performer who used his body to support his voice, to accentuate the sharpness and mellow the sweetness. Elvis was in complete control.

The musicians backed him perfectly, they were a single, finely-tuned instrument assembled for the sole purpose of being a part of the star, and the star was shining in all his glory.

Something was followed by one of Elvis' all-time favorites, *You Gave Me a Mountain*, and the audience suffered all the trials and tribulations with him. *Steamroller Blues* was next. Red and I had brought this song to Elvis from Chips. The original recording was great but, for some reason, we never thought it worked right for Elvis. *My Way* was given the full treatment and Elvis used the immense volume of his voice for a dramatic conclusion which brought down the house. When completed, he said, "Thank you. Whew! Thank you very much. I'd like to do a medley of some of my records for you, ladies and gentlemen."

A girl yelled something we were unable to hear but "super-ears" answered, "We'll get it later, kid, just hang on."

Then he started to sing, *Treat me . . .*, stopped and said, "What?"

Again, he heard what we could not and answered, "Okay, I'll do it, all four hundred and twenty nine of them," no doubt in response to a request that he sing every one of his songs.

Again, he started to sing the song *Love Me* and the years melted away and we were all back in the fifties because his voice was the same and therefore we had to be the same. This was followed by *Johnny B. Goode,* another solid Elvis song. *It's Over* had a special meaning to him and this came across in the tender feeling Elvis gave to the words.

Blue Suede Shoes, an Elvis oldie, was followed by *I'm So Lonesome I Could Cry* and *I Can't Stop Loving You. Hound Dog* always put Elvis and the audience in a light-hearted mood which quickly changed with the powerful *What Now My Love.*

Fever really turned the women on. For Elvis it was a very visual song which always wrenched forth every body movement he knew. Strangely, he didn't like doing it, even though he liked the song. I believe this was because he wanted the people to like his voice, rather than the body movements over which he had little control, particularly when the drums punctuated every line as in *Fever.* He was unable to keep still and his natural rhythm took over.

Welcome to My World and *Suspicious Minds,* another visual song, led to the Kui Lee song, *I'll Remember You.* From there Elvis went into a medley of *Long Tall Sally* and *Whole Lot-ta Shakin' Goin' On* and, believe me, there was.

American Trilogy, which he first did in Las Vegas, was another very moving song. On the stage it is very impressive and should be seen as well as heard. It is a very sensitive medley of *Dixie, Battle Hymn of the Republic* and *All My Trials.* While the audience was trying to recover from the immensity of feeling Elvis had conveyed, he broke into *A Big Hunk O' Love,* another fun song for Elvis and the audience. His closing number, *Can't Help Falling In Love,* brought the usual wild response.

Even after all the rehearsals, we were as mesmerized as the rest of the audience. Almost at the end of the show, Elvis did something completely unexpected, a spur-of-the-moment finale so typically Elvis that we should not have been surprised, but instead left us breathless. In one spontaneous movement, Elvis removed the cape from his shoulders and tossed it far into the audience. It had been a fantastic crowd and they had done their share to make it a memorable night. In return, he had given them his heart and soul and there was nothing left for him to give, other than his clothing.

The cape, which had cost thousands of dollars, was caught by one man who, God only knows how, was able to fend off other fans and keep it intact.

The show was over and we were emotionally exhausted as we walked toward Elvis' dressing room. He met us with enthusiasm, hugging each and every one, and once again took us back to the heights of his joy.

The next afternoon the Colonel came to Elvis' suite where we were all talking. He had the newspapers with him and it was then we learned that over one billion people had viewed the show. The largest single audience in the history of television, and it has never been surpassed.

That evening some of us were in Elvis' suite and he and Joe were talking in the bedroom when I heard a yell, "Moon, come on in here."

It was Elvis. I went in and closed the door as he asked. Then he said, "I want to buy each of the wives a gift, they really provided me with inspiration during the rehearsals and the show, and they've kept the atmosphere great."

Here he had approved the wives coming to Hawaii with us, they were having a vacation but he felt they did him a favor and now he wanted to show his appreciation. He then said something crazy, "I want to buy them each a fur coat."

Joe and I started to laugh and I said, "Elvis, this is Hawaii, it's hot here all year, they probably don't stock fur coats."

He said, "Call some department stores and see."

I called and sure enough, they thought I was crazy, no fur coats. Then he said, "Joe, call downstairs to one of the jewelry shops and tell them we're on our way down."

The Hawaiian Village is not an inexpensive place and the jewelry shop was no exception. Elvis, Joe and I sneaked out the bedroom door of the suite and out the service entrance of the hotel. Even the people in the suite didn't know we were gone. We walked about half a block to the jewelry shop. It was after hours so there was no one inside except the owner. Elvis picked out beautiful emerald and diamond rings for each of the wives. We sneaked back upstairs and into the bedroom, then the three of us walked into the living room. By that time all the guys and their wives were gathered there. Elvis started to hand out the rings and the wives were overcome with emotion.

There they were in Hawaii, we had all, earlier in the day, agreed that this was the nicest time we had ever had together,

ELVIS, PRISCILLA AND "THE GUYS"

Colonel Tom Parker, the world's greatest promotor, with (left to right) Elvis, Joe Esposito, Marty Lacker and Colonel Parker. The Colonel gave Marty this picture several years ago.

The set of Kid Galahad, Idlewild, California, 1961 (left to right) Lamar Fike, Ray "Chief" Sitton, Elvis, Marty, Alan Fortas and Joe Esposito.

Elvis with children from the Maori tribe of New Zealand at the Polynesian Cultural Center during filming of Paradise Hawaiian Style.

On the set of one of Elvis' movies (left to right) Jerry Schilling, Marty, Larry Jost, Elvis, Los Angeles Dodger pitcher Don Sutton and Richard Davis (front row) George Klein and Joe Esposito.

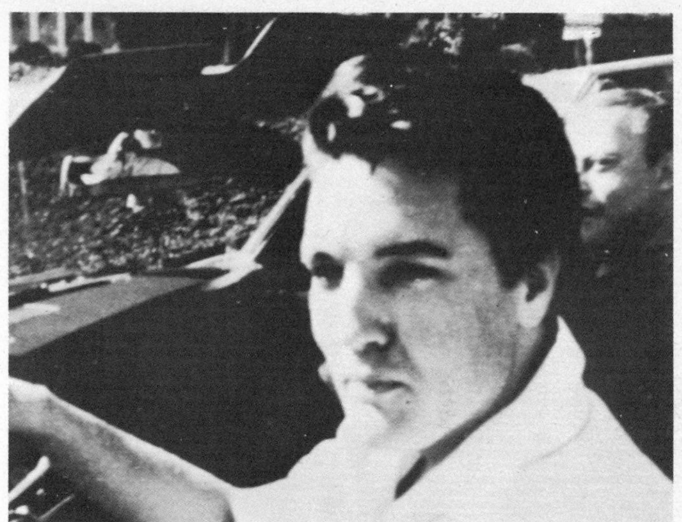

Elvis and Marty at Rocca Place in Bel-Air on a Sunday afternoon drive.

The set of Roustabout, 1964 (left to right) Billy Smith, Alan Fortas, Richard Davis, Jim Brown, Elvis, Joe Esposito, Marty and Jimmy Kingsley.

Elvis and Jackie Wilson in Los Angeles, 1967.

Elvis donating President Roosevelt's yacht Potomoc to Danny Thomas for St. Jude Children's Research Hospital, Long Beach, California (left to right) Joe Esposito, Billy Smith, Alan Fortas, Marty, Jimmy Kingsley, Richard Davis and unidentified sailor.

From the inside looking out—Graceland gates, 1969.

Elvis and Priscilla in front of the Graceland Nativity scene Christmas, 1965. This is the only Christmas card picture Elvis ever personally sent and they went to about twenty friends.

May 1, 1967, Elvis and Priscilla at their wedding. Elvis' brocade tuxedo was designed by Marty.

Priscilla, Marty and Joe during the ceremony.

The Aladdin Hotel in Las Vegas where Elvis and Priscilla's wedding reception was held (left to right) Richard Davis, Jerry Schilling, George Klein, Joe Esposito, Priscilla, Elvis, Charlie Hodge and Marty.

The wedding party, May 1, 1967 (left to right) Marty, Judge David Zenoff, Joe Esposito, Elvis, Priscilla, Michelle Beaulieu and Joanie Esposito.

Elvis with the American Recording Studio group band.

American Recording Studio, Memphis, Tennessee (left to right) George Klein, Elvis, Roy Hamilton and Chips Moman. During this time, Elvis was recording at American at night and Roy Hamilton was recording there during the day.

Elvis accepting his award from the Jaycees, January, 1971.

Award breakfast for the Jaycee's "Ten Outstanding Young Men in America" in January, 1971 at the Holiday Inn Rivermont in Memphis (left to right) Priscilla, Elvis and William N. "Bill" Morris.

Displaying Shelby County, Tennessee Deputy badges at Graceland, 1970 (back row, left to right) Billy Smith, Bill Morris, Lamar Fike, Jerry Schilling, Roy Nixon, Vernon Presley, Charlie Hodge, Sonny West, George Klein and Marty (front row, left to right) Dr. George Nichopoulos, Elvis and Red West.

Priscilla and Jo Smith with their 60's bouffant hairdos,
Summer, 1964.

Elvis was Best Man and Priscilla, Matron of Honor at Sonny and Judy West's 1970 wedding. The wedding party (left to right) Charlie Hodge, Jerry Schilling, Red West, Priscilla. Judy, Sonny, Elvis, Richard Davis and Marty.

and then to top it all off here was Elvis giving them emeralds and diamonds. There were a lot of happy tears, and a lot of hugging and kissing, but that wasn't the end of it. All of a sudden Elvis started handing each of the guys an envelope and said, "Thanks for helping make this special time a great time for me."

I opened the envelope and inside there was a check for $1,000. That's what he and Joe were up to before he called me into the bedroom. I was overwhelmed, he never quit. We all said our thanks and then he said, "I'm still tired, I'm going to bed."

He left the room.

We were all still unglued from his gifts, and decided to go downstairs and have a drink, even though some of us didn't drink. It was such a happy time we didn't want to waste any of it sleeping.

The next night some of us had to return to Memphis but it was hard to leave. Elvis and some of the guys stayed a few extra days and Elvis was able to renew his acquaintance with Jack Lord and his wife, Marie. We all look back at that trip to Hawaii as one of the best times we ever had together.

Our lifestyle was, to say the least, unusual. During the movie years we spent most of our time in California which caused a lot of problems for the guys who were married and had wives and children in Memphis. Elvis had a *no wives* policy when we were traveling during most of our years of association, and even if he had not objected to the presence of the wives it would have been difficult for those with children. For the most part, then, our wives stayed home while we were on the road.

During one year I was away from my family for eight months. To say the prolonged separations put a strain on the marriages would be an understatement. Most of them ended in divorce.

Some of the wives became very good friends. My wife and Billy Smith's wife, Jo, became close and did a lot to keep each other going through some of the more trying times. They had a lot in common, children, love of home life, and a desire to see their husbands give up what they were doing and begin to lead a normal life.

Resentment built in the minds of some of the wives

toward Elvis because they felt he was responsible for the husbands being away so much. Of course, our being away from home was not Elvis' fault. We worked for him and all we had to do was quit if we didn't like the job.

But we did like it.

There were times when we wanted to stay at home and had to leave. There were times when we wanted our wives with us and couldn't have them. There were times when we were ready to quit, but mostly we became accustomed to our way of living and we continued to do it regardless of the price we were paying with shattered marriages.

When we were not making movies we spent most of our time in Memphis, but we slept all day and spent our nights with Elvis. Again, that was our job. When he needed us we were expected to be available, but the result was that we saw very little of our families.

There were exceptions to the *no wives* rule, of course. The satellite show was one, and right after Elvis and Priscilla were married he honestly made an effort to do things which included all the families and there were many happy days spent together. Unfortunately, the theme of togetherness did not last very long.

Special occasions and holidays brought us together. Christmas was a very special time. We all enjoyed being together and exchanging gifts. New Year's Eve was another time when we would all try to get together. During the sixties Elvis would rent a nightclub for a New Year's party and, in addition to all the guys and their wives, we would invite a small group of friends and even a few fans were allowed in. But often the parties would turn sour, as did the one in 1967.

That year, we arranged for Isaac Hayes, Willie Mitchell and David Porter to entertain and Elvis had even persuaded Grandma Presley to go with us. We drove from Graceland to the nightclub where we were met by a crowd of fans who had learned of the party. They were so anxious to see Elvis that they kept us from going inside.

We actually could not get out of the cars the crowd was so large. We even drove away and returned later to see if they had dispersed, but they were still there. Elvis became annoyed and we all went back to Graceland.

As soon as we reached Graceland, Elvis and Priscilla

went upstairs after saying they would be right back down. They did not return and the rest of us sat there waiting until midnight when he called down on the intercom and wished us all a "Happy New Year."

I went to the club, paid the entertainers and help, and gave everyone Elvis' greetings and went home. That just about ended the New Year's parties at nightclubs. In 1969 we did try again, and even though we were able to get inside, it wasn't much of a party. Elvis stayed about forty-five minutes.

We had a party at Graceland to welcome 1973, but that one was not much either. Elvis, whose idea it had been to have the party, came downstairs about ten-thirty, greeted everyone and was back in his suite by ten-forty-five. The guys started a poker game and played most of the night while the wives sat around and talked.

1974 was different. We were determined to have a good time that New Year's Eve. Elvis wanted a rerun of the previous year but we decided we would have a party at my house. Everyone chipped in for drinks and the wives each made a special food dish. Elvis said he was staying home.

We were having a grand time, just being together, when about 11:45 the doorbell rang and in came Elvis. He stayed until midnight but we couldn't get him to stay any longer. It seemed that more and more he was enjoying himself less and less, on what were once happy occasions.

When Priscilla was a part of Elvis' life he seemed much more content than he did after their separation. Our lifestyle was the basic problem with Elvis' marriage, as it was with the marriages of many of the guys. We probably forgave ourselves our own situations because we were taking orders, whereas Elvis was giving them. We could not have changed without leaving our jobs but Elvis could have had Priscilla with him every day had he wanted it that way.

Eleven months after their separation, Elvis filed for a California divorce from Priscilla. She had been a part of his life since his army days in Germany and they had been married for over five years. Lisa was to live with her mother.

On October 11, 1973, the divorce became final. Priscilla had not contested it and the two kissed outside the courthouse before going their separate ways.

There was, fortunately, no bitterness and they seemed to

continue to care, and even love each other. Their daughter was an important part of both their lives and their concern for her was great. Elvis and Priscilla both wanted Lisa to have as normal a life as possible. They had always wanted to protect her from the emotional damage which could come so easily to the daughter of a famous entertainer, and now they wanted to protect her from the hurt of being a child of separated parents.

Elvis continued to send gifts to Priscilla and she did the same to him, but they were to have another day in court before things were finally settled. A California law firm filed a petition in Los Angeles on behalf of Priscilla in which she claimed Elvis had failed to make full disclosure of his assets during their settlement negotiations.

Priscilla's attorneys said the $100,000 settlement did not represent anywhere near her share of the community property and the $1,500 per month for her and Lisa would not support them. A new settlement was worked out with the attorneys and Priscilla received about two million dollars.

Even after the new court action and settlement, Elvis and Priscilla remained on good terms and Lisa spent a lot of her time at Graceland. Priscilla opened a fashionable, and expensive, boutique in Beverly Hills which she operated for some years before selling her interest so she could concentrate her talents in other areas.

One night in July, 1972, we went to one of our all night movie sessions in Memphis. Elvis and I were sitting in front of everyone else and just before the show started George Klein came over and said, "Hey, Elvis, I just came from Friday's nightclub and saw a girl I know. I invited her to come to the movies. I think you'll dig her. Her name's Linda Thompson."

"Okay," Elvis said, "let me know when she gets here."

About fifteen minutes later George came back to our seats and said, "Elvis, she's here. You want me to get her to come down and sit with you?"

"No, I'll meet her in a minute."

A little later Elvis got up to go to the men's room and on the way he saw Linda sitting next to George. Evidently, he liked what he saw because he asked George to move over and he sat with Linda for the rest of the show. From the theater they went back to Graceland.

A few weeks later Elvis asked Linda to join him in Las Vegas where he was about to begin a series of performances. She accepted and then returned to live at Graceland with him after the Las Vegas tour was finished.

Linda was good for Elvis during a very bad period of his life. He was terribly depressed after his separation and needed someone to boost his morale. Linda was the one who was able to do it. She is a beautiful, outgoing woman who, in 1972, earned the title of Miss Tennessee.

Linda seemed to love the excitement which went with being close to Elvis. She was very different from Priscilla in appearance and personality, which was probably also good for Elvis at the time. He needed to forget the hurt of the separation and divorce.

Elvis showered gifts on Linda as he did with his previous girlfriends and would do with those who came in the future. Elvis gave Linda her own credit cards and personal bank account into which he would deposit money. She loved new clothes and often went on shopping sprees, much to Vernon's annoyance when he received the bills. Some of the guys even began to talk about her spending without realizing that it was Elvis who told her to do it. He bought Linda a beautiful new house a few blocks from Graceland and provided two more houses, which remained in his name, for her brother and her parents.

Linda was a very special girlfriend who seemed to love Elvis as he seemed to love her. They had a lot of fun together and became constant subjects of news reports and marriage speculation stories.

Whether or not Elvis and Linda ever planned marriage is unknown to me and Linda is probably the only one today who really knows. Those of us who were close to Elvis would have welcomed a marriage if it would have brought a new happiness into his life. But Elvis probably wasn't ready. In fact, he may never have been ready for the commitment of marriage which was, perhaps, the real reason for the failure of his marriage to Priscilla.

There are many stories concerning Elvis and Linda, some may be true, but most probably are not, and none warrant being told or re-told here. It is enough to say that they had a few years of happiness together and when the time came to part they did so with a grace which was a credit to both.

I honestly believe that if Linda had been with Elvis on August 16, 1977, he might not have died. At least, she would have discovered him much sooner and called for assistance to try to save his life.

Linda was probably the last girl about whom Elvis was, in any way, serious. There were many others who were with him a day or a week or even a month or more and to whom he gave expensive gifts of rings or other jewelry. Some today talk of their "true love" and how they planned to marry, and flash their diamonds as living proof for an anxious press, but those of us who knew him only laugh. We've seen too many girls and too many rings over the years of association to be very impressed.

Lisa Marie became, if possible, an even more important part of Elvis' life after his separation from Priscilla. He was a truly proud father who wanted his beautiful daughter near him as often as possible. When Elvis was in California she lived at his home as much as she was with her mother. Except for the times when a visit may have interfered with school, Priscilla permitted Elvis to take Lisa to Graceland whenever he asked. She was often there to brighten Elvis' life and bring joy to the rest of us who also love her.

Elvis protected Lisa, perhaps he overly protected her, but the fear of kidnapping was always present and because of that he tried to keep her from becoming a public image. There were times when he would take her places, but mostly he would bring entertainment to her.

Elvis was quick to tell us about every new thing Lisa said or did when we were not around. He could talk about her for hours at a time. He loved her and she loved him. They were a beautiful pair.

Chapter Fifteen

The World of Music

From Tupelo gospel to Las Vegas rock, Elvis Presley traveled the music road to success, fame and riches. There were roadblocks such as the *Grand Ole Opry* and Arthur Godfrey's *Talent Scouts,* and even Las Vegas at first, but he overcame and changed these rather than letting them change him. There were detours which led through Hollywood where, in passing, he became a motion picture star, but he found his way back to the path of pure music and became even greater the second time around.

Music affected Elvis and he affected music, and the music industry.

A rebellion began in America in the fifties and spread through most of the world within the next few years. It was a youthful rebellion against the mores of sexual repression which somehow became attached to, and a part of, the music of the times. It was not a new rebellion, each generation has undergone some form of the same thing, but this time it was a little more dramatic, a little more open and a little more positive. The young people knew what they wanted. They wanted Elvis, and they wanted for themselves the freedom of expression which was his.

Pop music, prior to the arrival of Elvis and rock 'n' roll, was pure presbyterian in thought and substance. There was an almost total ban on sexual thoughts even through innuendo by radio stations and recording companies, more because of the inquisitorial temper of the times than any desire to keep the youngsters chaste.

The exciting music of the twenties skipped the depression of the thirties, and the music of the forties was about to skip the fifties. The teenage war babies had little in common with Bing Crosby, Perry Como or Rosemary Clooney, they needed their own idol and that idol became Elvis Presley.

One of the first, and perhaps one of the most important, achievements of Elvis' career was the awareness which he brought to the white race of the music of the black. The black sound, or race music as it was then called, was the soul of modern music, but it was mostly ignored by all whites prior to the meteoric rise of the young man with the long hair.

Things began to change. Elvis dug the black sound. He respected it and he respected black musicians. He never covered a black hit for gain as other white artists had done before him. In other words, he did not take the cream of the black hits and record them for a white market and thereby divert recognition and money from a black singer. When he recorded the music it was always long after the song had ceased to be a hit and often it was never a hit until he recorded it.

Conversely, black musicians began to gain more respect for their white counterparts as the market for black music expanded. Rhythm and blues charts suddenly included more and more white musicians, as the pop charts included more blacks. The once rigid line of musical segregation began to disintegrate and all music and all mankind was better for it.

Country music was also changing. The *Grand Ole Opry* has rejected Elvis, and the country music purist hated him and the popularity he was bringing to what had been an elite pickin' fraternity. Those who saw the new light were quick to change to the rockabilly sound and style, but the regulars resist even unto today. The split between the two groups created havoc in Nashville where the pure country clique became more deeply involved in their music, and the splinter group moved in the new direction. Talent, as usual, rose to the top. Johnny Cash, Marty Robbins and Jerry Lee Lewis were only three of a large group of gifted country singers who began to appear regularly on the charts with the new sound.

Radio stations changed, too. More than one hundred changed their program formats from country music to rock 'n' roll. They, like the record companies, discovered the rising tide and economic strength of the teenage market. Dollars and cents made sense to those who saw the increase in advertising and record sales. Even Ed Sullivan changed.

Elvis was changing the industry at the same time he was changing the music it produces. Before Elvis began recording for RCA, almost every singer, regardless of stature, was only a cog in the great record-making machine. There were well-planned, lengthy rehearsals prior to cutting a record and the recording artist was usually only one of the decision makers. Often his thoughts were the least considered by those who had the final word.

Elvis changed all that. He had his own way of making records and his associates quickly found him in control of the recording sessions. There was usually little, if any, rehearsing. Elvis selected the songs to be recorded and he decided if there were to be any changes in the musical arrangements. If a change was to be made, he made it. His decisions were spontaneous, but they were usually correct. Elvis was the recording artist, and the producer. This was an unheard of arrangement when he began. It's common practice today.

Memphis, Tennessee grew with modern music until it became one of the largest and most successful recording centers in the world. In 1969, I assumed the vice-presidency of American Recording Studios and quickly became very involved in promoting the Memphis music industry. With several others, who were also a part of the trade, I helped form Memphis Music, Inc. This was a non-profit organization dedicated to the promotion of the music industry in Memphis.

Memphis has a deep musical heritage and its musicians have always been known as innovators. W. C. Handy, the father of the blues, wrote *Saint Louis Blues* and *Memphis Blues* in Pee Wee's saloon on Beale Street. From the great blues and jazz musicians, who were in abundance on Beale Street, came one of America's true art forms, race music or rhythm and blues or soul music, three different names for the same thing.

By 1970, many record companies and recording artists from all parts of the world were coming to Memphis to cut their discs. The sound was special and it was what they wanted. I was, at the time, chairman of the board of trustees of Memphis Music, Inc. (MMI). We decided to honor those who had helped throughout the years to make Memphis a music center of the world, and at the same time, of course, we wanted to turn a spotlight on the city and bring even more of the music industry to Memphis.

The board of trustees selected me to write, produce and direct what was to be our first annual Memphis Music Awards show. The entire membership of MMI, which totaled over five hundred, would submit nominations for the *Best Record of the Year* and then select the winner, by ballot, from among those which had been nominated. The qualification for being nominated for the award was that an artist had to work, live or record in Memphis.

In addition to the award for best record of the year, the board of trustees of MMI presented *Founders Awards* to the six known people who were most responsible for the creation of the Memphis sound.

The recipients of these six awards were W. C. Handy, Sam Phillips, Chips Moman, Jim Stewart, who was the founder of Stax Records, Joe Coughi, founder of Hi Records, and Elvis Presley. I had the honor of presenting the *Founders Award* to Elvis who, unfortunately, was not able to attend the ceremony because he was on tour, but Vernon accepted for him. When presenting the award, I talked about how proud Elvis was of Memphis and the role he played in Memphis music.

A funny thing occurred about three weeks after the awards show. Elvis was back from tour and Patsy and I went to Graceland. Elvis, Priscilla and some of the guys were in the trophy room when we arrived and, when he saw me, a big smile came on his face and he said, "I want to thank you for all the nice things Daddy told me you said when you presented the *Founders Award*. I was surprised at what you said."

"Surprised?" I questioned. "Why were you surprised? What do you think I'd say about you?"

He just smiled at me but I knew he was serious about what he had said. Elvis really puzzled all of us sometimes.

He was happy about receiving the *Founders Award* and for years kept it in his bedroom rather than in the trophy room with all the others. But the *Founders Award* wasn't the only honor Elvis received at the first annual Memphis Music Awards show.

The roster of nominated artists with hit records was staggering. Neil Diamond, Dusty Springfield, Wilson Pickett, Joe Tex, Petula Clark, Isaac Hayes, Al Green, The Staple Singers, Dionne Warwick, The Box Tops, and Booker T and the M.G.s are only a few of those who had recorded their hits at various Memphis studios. Most had been nominated for the top award and were in attendance along with many of the nation's leading music executives, industry people and civic personalities.

The entertainment was excellent. Our thirty-five piece orchestra was comprised of the famed Memphis musicians and Dionne Warwick, B.J. Thomas, Isaac Hayes, Willie Mitchell, Al Green, and the Gentrys all performed.

That night, even though it was up against records like Neil Diamond's *Sweet Caroline,* Elvis' *Suspicious Minds* was voted record of the year. It was a happy night for all of us who loved Elvis.

Elvis was influenced by various singers and by different types of music. During his early years in Mississippi and in Memphis he heard country music, gospel and the music of the black people. These three forms of music merged to become the Elvis Presley style and they remained his personal choice of music forms throughout his life.

When Elvis became a big star he opened the door to success for many singers and for types of music which had not been previously accepted by the majority of people. He was, of course, a pioneer of rock 'n' roll and I think it's safe to say that many of the now famous rock singers would have had a much more difficult time had Elvis not set the pace for the new music.

What Elvis did for country music and race music was as significant socially as it was musically. Country music was popular within a small segment of the United States, but when Elvis began singing country, he exposed it to much of the world simply because his fans were buying every record he made.

The impact on race music was so significant that it amazes me so few people have ever recognized it. Race music, the music of the black race, was thought to be worthy of being performed only by black people, and many white parents did not want their children exposed to it. The kids, however, loved it and spent many hours listening to the radio stations which played this segregated sound. Elvis smashed through the music color barrier and was followed by most of the world.

Elvis would never say publicly which singers he liked best or which were the most influential on his style. During his early years he listened to most of the blues singers including Arthur Cradup, Big Mama Ella Mae Thornton, John Lee Hooker, and Jimmy Reed. Hank Williams and a few other country singers also influenced him.

One night at Graceland he opened up to George and me. We were in the dining room and had just finished dinner. Elvis was talking about music and musicians, when he said, "Those who I've always liked and who I try to combine with my own style are Brook Benton, Roy Hamilton, Jake Hess, Arthur Prysock and Billy Eckstine, but I don't want anybody to know I said that."

He didn't want to make a public statement on the subject. As a matter of fact, that was the only time I ever heard him make that type of statement. There were times, of course, when he would say he liked a certain singer but he would never say who influenced him.

One instance comes to mind regarding Elvis' unwillingness to publicly talk in terms of favorites. It happened in 1965, while we were filming *Paradise Hawaiian Style*. Elvis agreed to meet a singing group, Herman and the Hermits, from England who were doing a concert in Hawaii at the time. They visited us one day at the Polynesian Cultural Center where we were shooting the film. The group had made a few hits and Herman, the leader, seemed to have let success go to his head. Throughout the visit, he wisecracked and talked about how much they were doing, to the point where no one else could say a word.

All of the rest of us, including his group, were becoming somewhat bored with his monologue when he said to Elvis, "Who is your favorite group?"

We all knew that he naturally expected Elvis to say that their group was his favorite, but instead Elvis said, without hesitation, "The L.A. police force."

We all cracked-up laughing, including the English group but Herman shortly decided they had to leave.

Something which has bothered those of us who were close to Elvis is the failure of the music industry to pay proper tribute to him since his death. A few artists on some of the television specials have acknowledged his contributions to the world of music and spoken of how he influenced their lives, but the shows have failed to reflect what he accomplished.

Dan Forte of *Guitar Player* magazine interviewed some of the musicians who have worked with Elvis and their thoughts reflect the respect and admiration which many of today's top musicians felt for him. Don Menn, editor of *Guitar Player,* and Dan Forte have been kind enough to permit me to use parts of the interviews.

Chet Atkins said, "Elvis played pretty good guitar but he didn't utilize it all that much. Of course, he didn't need it, and on stage he used the guitar more or less as a prop. But he played pretty good guitar, and he played piano. He played an old Gibson guitar, I forget the model number now but it was the jumbo that Ray Whitley designed.

"The first time I ever met Elvis, he came up to me and said, 'Hi, I'm Elvis Presley and my guitar player wants to meet you.'

"He was talking about Scotty Moore. That was when Elvis worked the *Grand Ole Opry.* A few months later, of course, RCA bought his contract and I was on his first few recording sessions. I don't remember if he played guitar on those sessions more than just holding it and maybe strumming a chord now and then.

"Those were the first hits like, *Heartbreak Hotel* and *I Want You, I Need You, I Love You.* I played rhythm and Scotty Moore played lead guitar and later Hank Garland played lead. Elvis played rhythm sometimes and accompanied his singing.

"I think he could have been a good guitarist and piano player if he had worked at it.

"Elvis was a shy sort of person, and I am too, so we

never talked very much. We worked in the studio together but never had any real conversations to speak of. I always liked Elvis and admired him very much."

James Burton said, "Elvis loved guitar, he didn't play a lot but he liked to fool around on guitar. He loved guitar in general and as a part of his business, but as far as playing was concerned he mostly just fooled around for his own enjoyment. But guitar playing was a big part of his life and career.

"There were times when we sat and played together. He liked the bass string runs, the type of thing he did on *That's All Right Mama.*

"It's a shame that so many people who wanted to see him never had the chance. I've had people call me since his death and talk about how they had planned to see him at a coming tour and say, 'It's such a loss in our lives. We'll never see him.'

"I was with him since 1969, when I put the group together for him and out of all those years, I never missed a show with him. I remember the day we first met. It was just like we had known each other all our lives.

"It was a terrible shock to the world of music to lose such a great man. He was loved by everyone. I've worked with a lot of people and, I'll have to say, he was the king."

John Wilkinson said, "James Burton suggested me to Elvis in 1969 because I'm a rhythm guitarist. I play a little lead but rhythm is really my thing. I went to a rehearsal in Hollywood where I first met Elvis. It worked out real well right from the start.

"It was a thrill for me. I was a fan, an honest to goodness fan. I started playing guitar when I was seven years old and I was a Kingston Trio fan until Elvis came on the scene. I saw him on television and I remember thinking, 'Gee, if he can play, then so can I.' I didn't realize then that he didn't play that much. He knew A, E and that other chord, but he could play some pretty good blues, rhythm and the gospel things he was into.

"If it wasn't for Elvis Presley there's a lot of entertainers today who wouldn't be where they are. Some of them admit it and some don't, but they should. A lot of the big names are quick to say that they were very much influenced by Elvis. Everybody grew up with him. Look at what he spanned, almost thirty years, three generations. There are kids ten years old today that are going by the basics of that old sound, that old rock 'n' roll sound that Elvis evolved into or built for for us.

"Everybody benefited from Elvis Presley. There are classical guitarists who will tell you the very same thing. Even if they were not influenced by him at least they appreciated what he did for other guitarists. Some very strange things happened musically when Elvis came around.

"There are two instances which stick in my mind particularly, in regard to just fooling around. One was very close to the time when I first began to work for Elvis. We were on a break during a rehearsal for the Las Vegas show in 1969. I never could play *It's Now Or Never* correctly, I never could get it, although it's relatively simple, but I couldn't get it the way he wanted it. I was in a corner going through it and trying to get it the way James had shown me, trying to get it down that way instead of the way I was doing it. Elvis came over and I was singing the thing softly and trying to do it, and all of a sudden he's singing with me in harmony. When we got to the end I said, 'Is that the way you want it?'

"He said, 'That couldn't be better.'

"I remember another time at his house when we were listening to gospel records and then started playing and singing until five in the morning. He sang some old, old songs that I just never knew even existed.

"There were rehearsals when he would pick up the guitar and, as he was singing, he would beat on the top of the guitar and his rhythm was just perfect, you couldn't beat it, it was incredible. He knew what he wanted to hear, he never missed a thing, he could hear on stage something fierce. He'd know if something was wrong and he'd stop and say, 'That's wrong.'

"There was so much happening on stage that it was amazing, all the lights and the noise but if something was wrong he'd hear it.

"He never told us what to do. He would suggest what he would like to hear, he never told us anything, he suggested. On new songs we heard recordings by new people and the whole band would listen together and work things out. We were so tuned to what Elvis liked, what made him comfortable that it was easy. Basically, everything he wanted was simple because all he ever worked with in the early days was a rhythm section.

"As far as rhythm patterns were concerned, we always had a chance to listen to what we were going to play first on a demo record, and then we'd work it out with Elvis. He'd sing it the way he felt it and we would work around him.

"There were major changes in some songs. *Kentucky Rain,* for example, is a hard tune to play. I remember when we first tried to get it ready for the stage. Elvis thought some changes should be made but what he was feeling inside we couldn't quite get, until he beat the rhythm out himself. But it was a difficult number for the stage and he never did include it in a show.

"We had no problems, we were all so accustomed to Elvis and he was so easy to work with, that learning a new song was just a matter of listening, feeling it, hearing it and finding a key he liked.

"Just to meet the guy, I never thought that would ever happen. I just idolized him and I'm not ashamed to say so, and then to get to meet him, much less work with him for all those years. I guess we all got pretty close to him, as close as anyone could I suppose, and then to have him die, it just shattered me. But at least I realized a boyhood dream and I got to know a man who influenced my life, I guess everybody's life. What a beautiful cat he was."

Chapter Sixteen

Airplanes and Death Threats

After years of not liking to fly, Elvis grew to love airplanes and began, in 1975, to assemble a small fleet of his own. He bought a twin-engine Jet Commander, which he later sold to singer Wayne Newton for a little more than a quarter-million dollars. He bought a Jetstar and then leased it to one of the smaller airlines. He bought a Falcon DH-125 and a Gulfstream jet, which was later sold for almost three-quarters of a million dollars.

The pride of the fleet was the Lisa Marie, a Convair 880 which Elvis bought for about one million dollars and then spent an additional three-quarters of a million to have renovated. The Lisa Marie has a private bedroom with a queen-size bed; a sitting room; a dining room which will accommodate eight people; a galley with a stove and refrigerator; a lounge and conference room; two bathrooms, one with a shower; lounge seats for over twenty-five passengers; four television sets and seven telephones.

The pilot earned over forty thousand dollars a year and the co-pilot and flight engineer each earned just slightly less than that amount. Elvis had a stewardess on the Lisa Marie who was also well-paid.

Before he began to buy airplanes, Elvis would charter them for use when he was on tour. There was an assortment of different aircraft leased during that period, including Frank Sinatra's jet.

When he decided to buy a large airplane for himself, Elvis looked for a long time before deciding on the Convair. One airplane which he wanted belonged to Robert Vesco, the financier who went into self-imposed exile in Costa Rica. There were all sorts of legal problems surrounding the Vesco airplane and Elvis' lawyers decided he should not try to buy it.

After Elvis located the Convair and purchased it, Joe began to work with a company in Texas where it would be renovated. They were going to gut the airplane and completely rebuild the inside, but, of course, the project was going to take some time to complete. Elvis bought a smaller airplane to use to fly to Texas to follow the progress of reconstruction on the Convair.

To keep track of the work, and because he was so excited about it, he would fly to Texas once or twice a week to see the Convair. Everytime someone would come by the house who had not seen the plane, nothing could stop Elvis from taking them to Texas to view his new *Air Force One,* as he liked to call it.

When the Convair was ready, Elvis was like a child with a new toy. There were times, when he was on tour, when he slept on the airplane rather than go to a hotel. It was probably more comfortable than most hotels anyway, but his main reason for staying on the plane was that he really loved it.

As the years went by the Las Vegas shows became more routine. J. D. Sumner and the Stamps Quartet replaced the Imperials, as the background group. The shows weren't changed that much. One or two new songs were added for each engagement but songwise, there were no major changes.

As a gimmick, Elvis started to throw stuffed hound dogs into the audience but that got a little hectic. So he decided to start giving out the scarves he wore to the women in the audience. He knew how to get a crowd worked up, especially the women. Sometimes he teased them so much they would attempt to jump on the stage. The guys hated to see him do that because they would have to come out from the side of the stage to stop the fans. Naturally, when he went to the edge of the stage the women were screaming for him or for a scarf or a souvenir, but mostly for a kiss. He often obliged them with a kiss, especially the attractive ones. All of this was part of his natural talent. He knew what he was doing but it wasn't rehearsed.

Sometimes his crazy humor would take over. He could be singing or saying something and, at the same time, in his mind he would be substituting different words. Words that were crazy and offbeat. Sometimes he'd get mental pictures of the funny thing he was thinking about and he'd break out laughing. A few times he'd actually say or sing what he was thinking out loud, like when he would sing *Suspicious Minds,* he did this karate exercise where he would crouch on stage with one leg straight out to the side, and sing, "I hope this suit don't tear up, baby."

It usually got to the audience, especially the women who really wanted to see the inseam of his pants split. He definitely knew what he was doing!

Most of all, he was really enjoying himself. Elvis never did anything to get himself up before going on stage, he just heard the music, walked out and it was magic. In later years, he would combat the famous dry *Vegas throat* by inhaling a salt solution that was prescribed for him by a Las Vegas doctor. When Elvis came offstage he would be sweating profusely, he lost an average of six or seven pounds a day. He normally sweated a lot anyway, but with all that movement under the lights and wearing those jumpsuits it was very hot.

As the years went by, Elvis didn't stay in the dressing rooms after each show, he went upstairs to the suite. Between shows he'd rest and after the late show we'd sit up and talk or watch television. He never really critiqued his shows unless something out of the ordinary happened.

Throughout the years, especially from 1969, when Elvis began performing in front of an audience again, death threats became more and more numerous. There were bomb scares in the concert halls when he performed and at the hotels where he stayed. Fortunately nothing happened and most were not taken seriously.

In 1971, a threat became very serious. Elvis had just begun an engagement at the Hilton in Las Vegas and everything was going fine until one day when Joe Esposito received a phone call from his wife, Joan, who was in Los Angeles. She nervously told Joe she had received a telephone call from an unidentified man who told her to call Joe and tell him what he was going to tell her.

The man said he knew the identity of another man who was driving to Las Vegas at the time with the intention of shooting Elvis during a weekend performance. The man on the phone told Joan he would give her the name of the man, the type of car he was driving, and the license plate number. The price for this information was $50,000. He told Joan to call Joe and have him get the cash for her and then to wait for another telephone call.

After receiving Joan's call Joe immediaetly called the FBI. They installed a listening device on Joan's telephone but she did not get another call from the man.

Nothing was said to Elvis and the rest of us assumed it was another hoax, but as a precautionary measure the FBI checked out the hotel and remained nearby. One of the things they felt was out of the ordinary was the fact that the guy contacted Joan rather than trying to reach Elvis, and they were puzzled about how he had managed to get Joe's unlisted telephone number.

All of us were beginning to relax until someone brought the mail up from the front desk. While looking through it, one of the guys found a hotel menu with a picture of Elvis on the front. Someone had scratched out the face and sketched a gun near the heart. The words, "Guess who, and where?" were written on the menu.

Everyone began to take the threat seriously again. The menu had not been mailed but placed in Elvis' special mailbox behind the desk. The person who did it was obviously in the hotel and able to get behind the desk without being questioned.

Elvis was told and he became upset, then angry. Discussions were held, more FBI agents were called in and then the Secret Service appeared on the scene. Elvis absolutely refused to cancel the show even though everyone said they would advise his doing so. He said, "Look, these people paid good money to see me perform and I'm not going to disappoint them. They've probably been saving their money to come out here. Most of all, I'm not going to let some sick sonofabitch scare me off the stage. If I did that everytime some idiot threatens me, I'd never be able to perform again."

The president of the hotel came to him before the show and told him not to go on, but Elvis said he was doing the show and that was that.

Elaborate precautions were taken. A full-scale emergency medical squad, complete with Elvis' type blood and two doctors were stationed backstage. They were to immediately get him to the hospital, if something happened, in one of the two ambulances that waited outside the hotel's stagedoor.

Secret Service men, FBI agents and the guys were strategically placed throughout the showroom during the shows and each could be recognized by the others by some special item they wore.

A code word, *floor,* would be yelled by any of the guys or agents who spotted anyone making an unusual move towards Elvis. If Elvis heard the word he was to immediately fall flat on the stage and thereby give a gunman a smaller target. Agents were stationed at the entrance to the showroom to carefully scrutinize those who entered.

Before going on stage, Elvis called Priscilla and Lisa in Los Angeles. He didn't tell them what was going on but just that he was thinking of them and wanted them to know he loved them. He spent some time alone with his father and then went on stage, not knowing how he would come off.

None of the people in the band or vocal groups were told what was happening. Elvis didn't want to scare them and he may have thought some wouldn't do the show if they knew of the danger. Once he was on stage he was on his own and all of us marveled at how he managed to do the show.

Elvis told me that while he was standing on the stage singing, all the time he was thinking to himself, "Is that sonofabitch really out there?"

During the show, when he began singing *You've Lost That Lovin' Feeling,* his back was turned to the audience and the room was dark except for a small spotlight on his back.

Elvis shared with me later the thoughts that were running through his mind. He said, "I thought, this is it. I'm a perfect target like this. Then I looked at Ronnie Tutt who was sitting at the drums right in front of me and I thought, 'You poor bastard, if he misses me he's going to hit you.' "

Elvis Presley's mind and strength were amazing. I know

most of us would never have gone on that stage. Thank God nothing happened. It was either a hoax or the man was scared off. It was the one time things got too scary to ignore.

After the Las Vegas assassination threat, Elvis was really happy to be alive and unharmed. He told all of us how he realized the value of love and friendship and to show his feelings he had a Beverly Hills jeweler create gold bracelets for each of the guys. They're beautiful pieces of jewelry with our names engraved on the front and our nicknames on the back. We treasure them as a token of a bad time which, perhaps, brought us even closer together because it turned out to be less serious than it could have been.

Many strange things have happened with fans but their actions always stemmed from love and over-exuberance. There were others, however, who for one reason or another, either didn't like or resented Elvis.

When the decision was made to return to live performances we all knew the risk of something ugly happening would be great. For the most part the incidents that happened were minor. Sometimes fans became over-enthused or someone in a crowd would mouth off but there wasn't anything physical. The major exception occurred in 1973 and again, it was at the Hilton in Las Vegas during one of Elvis' performances.

I was in Memphis when this happened but Elvis told me about it a few weeks later. As customary, the tables next to the stage were arranged lengthwise, each seating about fifteen to twenty couples.

On this particular night there were a bunch of unusual-looking men, and a few women, seated at one of the tables near the stage. Just before Elvis went on, the supposed leader of the group arrived. He was dressed in a white cape, white hat, white suit and white shoes. He was carrying a long walking stick that Elvis swore had a dagger or sword hidden in it.

As this man approached the table, his group and the women rose and began applauding as if they were paying homage to their leader.

Elvis came on and began to sing. One of the men jumped up from the table and onto the stage and started toward Elvis. Red came from behind the curtain, grabbed the man in a headlock and walked him backstage where he threw him to a hotel security guard.

Another man from the group jumped on the stage. J. D. told him to get off and when he didn't leave, Sonny knocked him off the stage onto a table where another security guard grabbed him. A third man from the group jumped on the stage and Jerry picked him up and threw him into the arms of a waiting hotel security guard.

While all this was happening Elvis said he was keeping himself ready in a karate stance. He had his eyes on the leader. Elvis was raging mad and Vernon had to come on the stage to calm him down.

When Vernon was talking with Elvis another one of the men jumped on the stage and started toward them. Elvis said he karate-kicked that guy across the stage to a hotel security guard. To the audience, he cursed the troublemakers and then finished the show. It didn't end there though.

As in most cases when he was really enraged, Elvis worked himself into a bad state of mind. He found out the name of the girl who was with the group's leader and where she was. He called her and she told him she was afraid for her life if she told him anything. She said the guy and his gang were dangerous people who were mixed-up in drugs and pornography.

Elvis then called down to the hotel security office where some of the men were still being held. Elvis told the security men to give them a message for him. The message was that if they didn't leave town that night they wouldn't leave alive.

The group supposedly asked the hotel security men to escort them to the airport because they were afraid they wouldn't make it without protection.

A few days later Elvis obtained pictures of each of the men and copies of their police records and later showed them to me.

Elvis had some strange thoughts about death, his own death and the death of others whom he admired. An unnecessary and violent death could put him in a terrible mood. It wasn't just a matter of being depressed, he would rage against the perpetrator of a crime of violence.

I remember one morning in November, 1963. We had been up all night, as usual, and when we finally decided to go to bed, I turned on the television set in my room. I was going to watch it while I undressed and got ready to go to sleep but I didn't make it to bed for a long time.

A bulletin on the television announced that President Kennedy had been shot. I couldn't believe my ears. I went to Elvis' room and knocked on the door. He was not yet asleep so I told him what happened. We told the other guys and within minutes we were all watching the television set in the den.

President Kennedy was a favorite of ours. We greatly admired his spirit and what we thought he was trying to do for the country. Elvis began to change from being overcome with sadness to being angry. When they began to show pictures of Lee Harvey Oswald, Elvis started banging his fist on the marble coffee table and screaming at the picture on the television. "You dirty rotten bastard," he yelled. "You sick sonofabitch."

He looked at us and said, "That will never happen to me. No sonofabitch is going to be arrested or sit in a court room and tell the world how he killed Elvis Presley. If anybody ever shoots me I want him dead before he even sees a policeman."

He was really vehement about it. As the days passed he said the same thing many times and when Senator Kennedy was killed he repeated the same words to us.

The same intense feeling came out when Doctor King was killed and Governor Wallace was shot. Elvis never made us promise, but we all knew what he expected of us if some bastard tried to make a name for himself by killing Elvis Presley.

Chapter Seventeen

Downhill Racing

By 1974, Elvis had again begun to look upon recording as a drag. RCA had a backlog of Elvis' records which had not been released, but the time came when the supply began to run low and he was told he had to go into the studio again. For many reasons, he hated the thought of doing another session.

Elvis loved to sing and there was a time when he enjoyed recording, but the petty problems and bickering among those who were around him began to make the sessions more and more tedious. He worked well with the musicians and production people, but some of his business associates put a sour taste in many of our mouths.

During the fifties and early sixties, the results of the sessions were the gauge of how much Elvis enjoyed doing them. He produced one hit after another and, as far as I can remember, there was only one really unpleasant incident associated with recording.

This happened while Elvis was making movies and we were living on Perugia Way in Beverly Hills. On the weekends, Elvis would allow some of the girls, who were always hanging around the gate, into the house. Occasionally, men he trusted and considered friends would also be invited. One such man was a young singer whom Elvis had befriended. He spent many nights at the house talking about music and records with Elvis.

Before coming to Los Angeles to begin the film, upon

which he was working, Elvis had completed a successful recording session and one record held great promise. We all felt it would be a hit when it was released by RCA. We brought the dubs with us to the Perugia Way house because we all liked the song and it was not going to be released for several months. Elvis was proud of the record and would often play the dub copy of it.

One night, the singer was at the house and he and Elvis were talking about recording when Elvis said, "Man, I want you to hear the dub of a new record I made. We all think it's going to be a hit."

Elvis played the record and when it was finished, the guy asked to hear it again, and at the request of the young singer he played it a third, a fourth and I don't know how many more times. It's not unusual for a musician to repeatedly listen to a piece of music which he likes, so none of us thought anything about it and we, in fact, had an enjoyable evening.

That was the last time we saw or heard of the guy until one day when we were driving to the motion picture studio. As usual, we were listening to the radio. A disc jockey announced, "Here's a brand new record that sounds like it's going to be a hit."

It was a recording by the young singer doing the song Elvis had played for him, even the arrangement was exactly the same. We couldn't believe our ears. Here was a man whom we had all trusted, a man Elvis had welcomed into his home and he had taken the song and the arrangement. Elvis was angry, as were the rest of us, but he handled it better than we did.

This happened during the time in Elvis' career when every record he made was a hit and a big seller. If another artist had a record and Elvis recorded and released the same song, the other artist didn't stand a chance of getting any airplay by the disc jockeys, and thereby the promotion needed for sales. Elvis would get it all. We begged Elvis to release his record immediately and not let this man get away with what he had done.

Elvis was hurt and angry, but he said, "No, let the little bastard have his hit, he has to live with himself. I hope he has all the success in the world, but I don't want to see the sonofabitch again!"

A few years later, the closing line was written on this when the guy came to the house one day. I happened to be outside when he rode in on his motorcycle and I told him to get the hell off the property, none of us wanted to ever see him again.

As a part of the whole picture, the above incident may have been small but it had a bad effect on Elvis and his recording sessions. The movie songs which he began to record added to his discontentment.

The 1969 Memphis recording session put a new spark in Elvis' life, but when it and a few more recording dates he did in Los Angeles were finished, the sessions began to bore him again. For one thing, he was into the live performances, which was really his thing. He liked to be on a stage in front of an audience. It was a challenge for him, and he enjoyed it.

During 1974, Elvis tried to make the recording sessions as pleasant as possible but the continuing hassle over new songs plagued him. He tried to eliminate the inconvenience of going out of town to record. He wanted to do the sessions with the least amount of effort and get through them as quickly as possible. One day he said to me, "Moon, I want to record in Memphis again. Get me a good studio."

American Studios, where he had recorded in 1969, had moved out of the state so I suggested he use Stax where a lot of hits had been recorded. When he agreed, I made the nccessary arrangements with Jim Stewart and Al Bell, who were the owners of the company. Because of the part of Memphis where the studio was located, they had their own security guards and procedures so Elvis had the maximum amount of privacy. He was treated well at the studio but it was not a good session in terms of songs or desire.

Through the years, Elvis' source of new songs was his own publishing company. Anyone who tried to get a new song to Elvis, without going through his publishing company people, would run into a series of petty hassles. If a new song was presented to the publishing company, it would often never reach Elvis unless the writer made unreasonable concessions to the company. Even though Elvis had said, during the 1969 recording session, that he wanted to hear every song which was offered to the company, it never worked out that way. It was just not possible for him to know everything that went on or to be constantly available to listen to new music. He had to trust the people who worked for him.

Because I was in the music industry, Elvis depended on me to find good, new songs for him and asked me to bring them directly to him. I had many contacts with successful writers and music publishers. Some were clients of mine and from those I received a royalty, or commission, whenever I placed a song. I explained this fact to him and told him I would try to find him the best, but if they came from a client of mine, I would be making money when he recorded the song. He said, "Hell, I don't care. If they're good. I hope you do make something on them."

That was in line with what he had said to George Klein some years earlier. He had told George, "G. K., I don't mind any of you guys making money off of anything I do, as long as it doesn't hurt me."

Lamar and Red also brought songs to him without going through the publishing company, and even though I never heard him say it to them, I assume he told them to do so in the same way he told me. The resentment from his publishing company came to a head during the Stax session.

On the first night of the session, Elvis came to me and said, "I know you have some songs for me but let me hear this other stuff first and then I'll get to yours."

"Cool with me, Elvis," I said, "I've got plenty of time."

Red, Lamar and I waited until the publishing company songs were finished and then Elvis asked, "Does anyone else have any songs?"

I said, "Yeah, I have some, Elvis."

Red also had some and Elvis said, "Okay, I'll hear them as soon as I get back." He left the room.

Freddie Bienstock of Elvis' publishing company, who I feel had resented us for years, looked at me as soon as Elvis was out of the room and said, "How come you always have songs by that publishing company? Are you making money off what Elvis does?"

There were a lot of people in the room at the time, including one of Colonel Parker's assistants, and they all looked at me. The question may have seemed harmless to someone from the outside but, feeling as I did about this man, I thought it was malicious and was said in an effort to intimidate me. He thought I wouldn't want Elvis to discover that I was making money from the songs.

I said, "I sure do make money on some of the songs I bring Elvis, but I bring him a lot more from companies from which I receive nothing. If a song is good I try to get it for him, regardless of where it comes from. By the way, Elvis knows all about my business and what I get for placing a song, so I wouldn't worry about it if I were you."

I'm not trying to say it was that hassle, about which Elvis later heard, which caused him to lose interest in recording, but it and others like it were contributing factors. The fun had gone from the recording sessions.

After that, things went steadily downhill. In 1976, Elvis decided he would record a scheduled session only if he could do it at Graceland. It was an absurdity, but he insisted and RCA sent a remote truck, complete with the latest equipment. All the furniture was removed from the den and spaces marked for the musicians and backup singers. There was no possible way to get the proper isolation for each instrument, but Felton and the engineers did the best they could.

To add to the problems, Elvis stayed upstairs for hours beyond the scheduled starting time so everyone would be upset by the time he came to the den. Each night he was in a different mood, all bad, which, along with the poor recording facilities of the house, reflected in the finished records. One night he became angry because one of the playback speakers was making a strange noise, so he pulled out a gun and acted like he was going to shoot out the speaker. The recording session was a disaster.

He finally consented to do a recording session in Nashville but when he arrived there he had an argument with the girl he was dating and refused to leave the hotel. Elvis stayed in the hotel for three days and never recorded.

Elvis' health, as well as the recording sessions, was disintegrating. He was always prone to catching colds or other respiratory infections. His tonsils were often inflamed and should have been removed but, since no doctor would guarantee his voice would be the same after an operation, Elvis refused to have it done. He often had problems breathing. One night, many years ago, he awoke and was almost unable to breathe. We had oxygen rushed to Graceland where it was administered to him, and from that night on, a fresh supply was always kept at hand. There were blood pressure and weight problems in addition to the throat troubles. His health was a major concern for many of us.

One day in 1973, I was driving to an appointment in the northern part of Memphis when a bulletin came on the radio. The announcer said Elvis had just been rushed to Baptist Hospital for emergency medical treatment. I turned my car around and drove to the hospital. On arrival, I learned he was in a suite on the eighteenth floor. The hospital security guards had a list of people who could be allowed in the area and since my name was on it, I had no trouble getting to his rooms.

The private suite consisted of two rooms with a foyer separating them. Some of the guys were in one room and they told me Elvis had been unable to breathe when he was rushed to the hospital. The official announcement stated that he was suffering from hypertension and headache. I learned he had been at the hospital for several hours before I happened to hear it on the radio and was upset that none of the guys had called to let me know. That, however, was often the way things went. If someone wasn't on hand when something happened, he was likely never to learn about it. No one ever seemed to think about the feelings of the rest of the group.

Elvis was in good spirits when I went in to see him and I sensed that he needed a rest more than anything else. He seemed comfortable in the hospital and remained there for about two weeks. I visited him every day and we would sit and talk for hours or share the roast beef and mashed potatoes which were sent from Graceland for his dinner.

Elvis had a second hospital bed moved into his room and Linda stayed with him every night. Several of the guys always stayed in the second room at night and it was a regular meeting place during the day. During this stay in the hospital, as well as those of subsequent years, Elvis distributed the many flowers he received among the patients of the hospital. There were always thousands of flowers and he felt they could brighten the day for some of the patients who, perhaps, were not as fortunate as he.

Security, as usual, was tight. When it was necessary for Elvis to go to a different part of the hospital for tests we always used the service elevators. Elvis, more as a joke than anything else, began to wear sunglasses when he was being wheeled from one place to another. Often, as we would go through the halls, the patients would be standing by their doors so they could see him. He wisecracked with everyone. Once, when he had on the sunglasses, we passed an elderly lady who said, "Hi, Elvis, how you feeling?"

He touched his sunglasses and said, "Now, you know you can't recognize me." They both laughed.

During 1975, he was in the hospital three times. Once was for an eye problem, which was rather serious. Elvis told me that it was so bad the doctor, who came to the hotel where Elvis was staying, had to immediately insert a needle into his eye or he would have lost his sight. It was apparently a very painful procedure which Elvis said was done with no anesthetic. He said it hurt so much that he grabbed a metal tray and crushed it with his hand while the doctor was working. After the emergency treatment, he went to Mid-South Hospital for several days of extensive eye examinations. He was told he would have to begin to wear glasses, so Elvis had sunglasses made with the proper prescription.

The hospital reports for the other two visits, each of which were for about two weeks, stated he was being treated for hypertension and an impacted colon. Elvis didn't like to discuss his illnesses or treatment so I never questioned the reports. There was a time, however, when I went to the hospital on the day he was admitted and tubes were coming from every possible place in his body. Needless to say, I was frightened by what I saw.

Elvis was back in the hospital in April of 1977, for, the hospital said, gastroenteritis and anemia. Over the years, there were frequent visits to doctors when we were on the road. Sometimes the doctors would come to him but on other occasions he would go to their offices. He always saw them alone so I have no firsthand information regarding the visits.

By the end of 1975, Elvis had begun to retreat more and more into himself. Christmas was the same as usual but, for the first time, he decided to work on New Year's Eve. A special show was booked at the new Silverdome Stadium in Pontiac, Michigan and his magic continued to work. At midnight, 80,000 people were on their feet ushering in 1976 by singing *Auld Lang Syne* along with him.

Elvis began doing tours of ten to fourteen days in length, and stopped playing Las Vegas. He would average about one tour each month and spend the rest of his time at Graceland. There was an occasional trip to Palm Springs or Los Angeles, but for the most part he remained at home when he was not on tour. He began to draw Billy and Jo Smith nearer and nearer to him, almost to the point where he didn't want or need anyone else. Billy had quit working for the railroad and was again working for Elvis and living at Graceland. Billy did not travel on tour with Elvis, as he wanted to remain in Memphis with his family. During these times, Billy would work with Vernon, but when Elvis was at Graceland all of Billy's time was devoted to him.

Things soon reached the point where Elvis came out of his suite only when he had to go to work. About the only people, other than Billy and Jo, who saw Elvis were Joe Esposito, who spent most of this time on the West Coast, Charlie Hodge, Dr. Nick and sometimes one of the other guys.

On July 5, 1976, Elvis finished a tour with a show in Memphis. This show was to become something of a turning point in his relationship with me, as well as others with whom he was very close.

He arrived in town the night before the Memphis show and went straight to bed. It had been arranged for most of the guys, their wives and children to meet at Graceland and be taken to the show in a chartered bus. I went to Graceland a little early because I wanted to visit my mother, who was ill, before going to the show. I also wanted to pick up some backstage passes for my children. Joe gave me the passes and said that Elvis did not want to see anyone before the show. My wife and I decided to drive to the Coliseum with our children, rather than go on the bus.

Backstage, we joined those who had come by bus and Elvis arrived about thirty minutes later. Joe, Red, Sonny and Dick Grob were with him and he was already dressed for the show. He went to his dressing room for a few minutes, then came out and walked right past us, without so much as a nod, and went on stage.

Elvis put on a good show for the hometown folks and when the performance was finished he ran to the car and went back to Graceland. The bus followed, but my wife and I decided to go home. I had a strange feeling about the way he acted toward all of us that night, and I later learned that as soon as he reached Graceland he went to his suite without seeing anyone.

About a week later, I received a phone call from Red who told me he had just been fired. I couldn't believe it, and asked him why. He said he had a call from Vernon who told him they had to cut down on expenses and were letting some of the people go. Vernon had also fired Sonny and Dave. Elvis was in Las Vegas.

A few days after the firings, Elvis returned to Memphis and stayed in his suite. He didn't want to see anyone except Billy and Dr. Nick. I called Billy one day to see what was happening and he said, "I'm glad you called. I was going to call you and George to let you know that, for now, Elvis doesn't want anyone up at Graceland. I didn't want you guys to come to the gate and not be let in. I knew you would be hurt."

After the next tour, I talked with Billy again and mentioned coming by Graceland, but he said Elvis didn't want anyone there.

Billy began to go on tour with Elvis. Joe Esposito would fly to Memphis a few days before each tour, go with Elvis and then fly back to his home in Los Angeles. There was really no reason for him to hang around Graceland as Elvis continued to seclude himself in his suite.

The only time anyone saw Elvis was during the tours and very little was seen of him even then. Elvis appeared at the Las Vegas Hilton at the end of 1976 for ten days. It was a disappointing ten days for many of the people who had paid twenty-nine dollars for a ticket to see Elvis perform. There were nights when he seemed unable to remember the words for the songs and simply stood there while the backup groups did most of the singing. There were other nights when he went on stage and talked more than he sang. It disturbed me greatly.

Christmas was different that year. We didn't go to Graceland for the customary Christmas Eve gathering. Elvis didn't want anyone there other than a few family members and Lisa. He settled into the life of seclusion, except for a few visits to the movies and an occasional motorcycle ride with Billy and Jo in the early morning hours.

In March of 1977, Elvis made a brief trip to Hawaii, taking his new girlfriend, Ginger Alden, most of her family,

Billy, Jo and some of the guys and their wives. When they returned he resumed the tours and, in June of 1977, taped a CBS television special, but his strange attitude had not changed. He refused to see the designer of the wardrobe for the television special when she flew to Memphis. He kept her waiting for four days, while she tried to see him for fitting. He simply would not see her.

Elvis was having real problems with his weight. Keeping it down had always been a life-long chore. He had a natural tendency toward obesity, as many of us do. During the movie years, Elvis fought the weight problem with a combination of appetite depressants and long hours of work. At that time, he was constantly reminded that just a few extra pounds would be magnified by the camera and the results on the screen would be devastating.

He would gain weight very quickly and then go on a severe diet to rid himself of the extra pounds before a scheduled performance. Some of the diets were very hard on him. There were times when he simply ate nothing and there were times when he tried everything new, about which he had heard, that was supposed to cause weight reduction. There was one gimmick diet after another but all had one thing in common, appetite depressant pills.

Chapter Eighteen

An Era Ends

On August 16, 1977, I was driving on Interstate Five near Newport Beach, California where my family and I had moved to a new home and new life some months before. My wife had not been well and I was going home early in the afternoon. It was not a typically-beautiful California day. The sky was black and raindrops, the size of marbles, were pounding on the automobile. I reached over and turned on the radio and heard the announcer say, "... ley is dead, more details as we get them."

He began to play one of Elvis' records. My stomach turned over. Had he said Presley is dead? Elvis Presley is dead? It was a long time before the record ended. I'm not sure I wanted it to end because I was afraid of what I would hear. And then I heard it, "We have lost a good friend, Elvis Presley is dead, more details as we get them."

I almost ran into a light post as I started speeding home, telling myself it was just another one of those damn rumors. When I reached the house, my wife and daughter came running out to me in hysterics. They were crying and asking me if it was true and asking at the same time if I was all right.

My insides were churning when I called Graceland to find out if it was true. Larry Geller answered, and as soon as I said, "This is Marty . . ."

He said, "He's gone, Marty. He's gone."

I didn't think my heart was going to stand it. We were both silent for a moment, then I began to cry. Between the tears, I listened as he told me what had happened. Elvis and Ginger had gone to his suite about six-thirty that morning after playing racquetball for a few hours with Billy and Jo.

Elvis was apparently feeling good and not very tired, so he took a book he was reading and went into the bathroom. According to interviews she has given, Ginger went to sleep.

She says she awoke once and Elvis was still not in bed, but instead of checking on him she went back to sleep. She awoke a few hours later and since he was still not in bed, she went to the bathroom door and knocked. There was no answer so she opened the bathroom door and found him lying on the floor.

She immediately yelled for help and Joe Esposito and Al Strada ran upstairs to see what was wrong. While someone called an ambulance, Joe tried to find a heartbeat or pulse, but could not. Vernon arrived a few minutes later and then Dr. Nick and some of the guys arrived as the ambulance came up the driveway to the house. Dr. Nick and Joe rode in the back of the ambulance with Elvis' body to the hospital while some of the guys followed in a car. Dr. Nick tried to restore Elvis' breathing but it was too late. Elvis was dead when they found him on the bathroom floor.

I was so emotional, I couldn't listen anymore. My wife was hysterical and I tried to comfort her but wasn't much help. We kept watching television and listening to the radio to try to get some further news. Perhaps we expected someone to say it was all a dream.

A few hours later, I called Graceland again and when George Klein answered and I spoke to him, we both broke down. George said everyone was sitting around in total disbelief. When I told him I would be there the next day, he said Joe or Billy would arrange air transportation for me, but the next day I had to call back and tell them I could not leave my wife, she was just too upset.

The arrangements for the funeral were, I believe, the way Elvis would have wanted them. Sixteen long white limousines followed the huge white hearse. That was his style, and I'm glad Joe arranged it that way. Fans were allowed to file by the open casket and then a small, private ceremony was held.

Ann-Margret was there to say goodby to someone for whom she cared, as were James Brown and George Hamilton. Caroline Kennedy was admitted through the gate because of her father but it was not known at the time that she was there as a reporter. I've read reports that said John Wayne and Burt Reynolds were there, but they were not. Priscilla and Lisa stood alongside Vernon during the service, and she and Vernon were the last to say goodbye to Elvis before the casket was closed.

There were tens of thousands of people lined up along both sides of the highway between the gates of Graceland and the gates of the cemetery which, I'm sure, would also have pleased Elvis.

Some months after the funeral, Elvis' body and his mother's were moved from the cemetery to Graceland. They now rest in the meditation garden my brother-in-law built at Graceland, the peaceful, serene and beautiful garden Elvis loved so much. In 1966, as a Christmas gift for Elvis, we had a sculptor in Memphis create a huge statue of Jesus. We had it placed in the garden and he was overjoyed with the gift. The statue of Jesus, with outstretched hands, serves as a footstone and looks over Gladys and Elvis Presley.

In the past, Elvis and Vernon had often joked about Vernon's misspelling of Elvis' middle name when he was born. On the birth certificate it read Aron, instead of Aaron, as it is in the Bible. The name had been changed legally and on Elvis' grave it reads Aaron.

The autopsy of Elvis Presley required almost two months. It contains the reports of laboratory specialists and pathologists from California and several other places, as well as from those in Memphis. It is probably as complete as any autopsy has ever been. There are conflicting opinions concerning the results.

Dr. Jerry T. Francisco, Shelby County Medical Examiner, announced that Elvis had died of cardiac arrhythmia due to unknown causes. He also said there was no evidence of drug abuse. Dr. Francisco is reported to have said his diagnosis is often used by medical examiners who arrive at their findings through inference; that is, by interpreting what is found during an autopsy when no specific cause of death is apparent.

Dr. Eric Muirhead, Chief of Pathology at Baptist Hospital, and an internationally recognized authority on hypertension, has said that he does not consider heart disease as a possible cause of death.

The autopsy report of Baptist Hospital lists Elvis' death as a drug-related death known commonly as polypharmacy. This has to do with the action of more than one drug where the combined effect is greater than if each were used alone. Some of the laboratories, used by the various authorities, reported finding ten different drugs while others found eight, and Dr. Francisco has said only four were significant and these were not present in sufficient levels to cause death.

All of the authorities had access to the same reports. The kindest thing to say is that someone is mistaken.

I am not a medical doctor nor was I at Graceland when Elvis died, or present at the autopsy. I do not know the cause of Elvis Presley's death, but I do know that Elvis had a drug problem! That's a direct and honest statement by someone who was as close to him for over twenty years as any human being in this world. More important, it is a statement by someone who shared the same drug problem with him.

There are those who have blown the drug use out of all proportion, and there are those who would prefer that it not be mentioned. Both are wrong. The truth is no less the truth because it goes unspoken, as the truth ceases to be the truth when it becomes distorted.

Elvis contributed much to the world, as much, I believe, as almost any man who has ever lived. He has now the opportunity to make one final contribution to the millions of fans to whom he brought so much joy. He can share the results of drug abuse.

Elvis had a drug problem. I had a drug problem. Let me define the words *drug problem,* before any of his critics begin to say, "I told you so."

Aspirin is a drug and if someone takes too many, he then has a *drug problem.* This is true of alcohol, tranquilizers, diet pills and the host of other things which the American people administer to themselves everyday with, and without, the blessings of the medical profession. The more commonly accepted definition of the words *drug problem* is someone using marijuana, LSD, heroin, or something of that nature.

I can categorically state that Elvis *did not* have a drug

problem if we use the second definition. He did not use what are known as hard drugs. He did, however, have a drug problem and it began with the diet pills.

The diet pills, which were prescribed, allowed him to stay up and work for long hours. These pills have the side-effect of being stimulants, they make those who take them feel good. They turn people on to the excitement of the world around them, sometimes real, but more often not. They're easy to get, easy to take and, unfortunately, easy to continue taking.

Most of us began taking the pills because we kept the same hours as Elvis and some of us also had weight problems. We used the pills throughout the movie years. The diet pills can make the user feel great one minute and depressed and miserable the next. There were times when we would go two or three days without sleeping and be irritable as hell.

One type of pill leads to another.

To counteract the diet pills we began taking sleeping pills, tranquilizers or sedatives in order to sleep. All the pills were easy to obtain. They came in every color, shape, size and variety. They made us feel good during the day, they made us feel rested when we were tired, they gave us courage to do what we were afraid to do, and they made us sleep when we went to bed.

They caused me to lie in bed and wonder why the television set was turned on its side, but they kept me from thinking it was my head, and they made me not care enough to worry about it very long. Where two first did the job, four soon became necessary and before long, it took eight to bring back that old feeling. The pills led us to believe they were doing us no harm, and we felt so good we knew we could quit when, if ever, it became necessary.

Fortunately, for some of us, it became necessary and we were able to quit. Unfortunately, none of us were strong enough to help Elvis. Perhaps he simply didn't have a reason to quit, or perhaps he was going to, or perhaps he never really cared. He was a strange and unusual man of strong feelings and strong desires, and that very strength may have kept him from doing other than he did. I don't know.

Drugs take you nowhere and leave you there.

But there was a lot more to the forty-two years, seven months and eight days of the life of Elvis Presley than the abuse of prescription drugs. There were years of understanding, generosity and friendship. There was a legend left for millions of fans who loved and respected him, and if any one of them can accept this moment of failure in a lifetime of success, and understand what can come from the abuse of any drug, then perhaps even that was of some value.

There has been so much said and written over the years about Elvis, his habits, his family, and his friends that it must be difficult for anyone to separate the wheat from the chaff. It was reported that Elvis and his mother were both forty-two years old when they died and because Elvis had always openly praised his mother, something mysterious was made from the age. The fact is Elvis' mother was forty-six years old when she died.

One noted columnist wrote that Elvis had said he would never live as long as his mother had. In all the years I knew Elvis I never heard him say anything even remotely similar to that. It has been written that Elvis had a death wish, but in fact he often told us about how he wanted to live forever. He would say we were all going to live to be old and gray. What he did have was an immense thirst for a knowledge of life, the meaning of it, and how it began.

He constantly read about religions and the supernatural. Elvis was curious about reincarnation and life after death. He had a great faith in God upon which he built his life, but he was in no hurry to find out what death was like.

I have read about how cruel Elvis was to the people around him. I've read about how he took pleasure from inflicting physical pain upon those who worked for him, but I remember a time when Elvis and I were horsing around, as we often did, and a ring he was wearing scratched my face enough for a little blood to appear. Elvis saw it, jumped back and said, in an almost frantic voice, "That's not me, man. I'm not like that, I didn't mean that."

I started to laugh, but thought to myself, "You damn fool, who do you think you're talking to? I know what you're like."

Was this the man who supposedly enjoyed hurting people?

Elvis was truly a remarkable and special human being. I am convinced that he was put on this earth for a special purpose, but he was just as much a human being as any of us.

He suffered from human faults and frailties. He had the material things about which people dream, but often they were not enough to make him happy.

As considerate and understanding as he was most of the time, so was he inconsiderate and not understanding. The charisma and magnetism for which he was known was real. He had a smile that could turn the whole world on, and he had a strong hold over those who were associated with him.

It was hard to say no to Elvis, and there was no way I could tell him a lie. All he had to do was look at me and he would know immediately if I was trying to make him believe something that wasn't completely true. His eyes were probably the most expressive part of him. They told us when he was happy, mischievous or angry. Sometimes I thought he tried to change their expressions to hide his true thoughts, but he was never able to quite do it.

This world is a better place for Elvis Presley's having been here, and I know that as long as there is one of us alive, whose life he touched, he will still be alive, but I miss him. I miss the years of kindness and the years of love, and Elvis had a lot of love for all of us. I remember, God how I remember, the happy days of companionship, the days when we felt so very close to each other.

Ain't it funny how time slips away?

PART TWO

Wife Was a Four-Letter Word

Patsy Lacker

Chapter One

A Wealthy Commune

When I was a teenager in Knoxville, I was an Elvis fan, as were most of the other girls I knew. Elvis was a beautiful, virile, young man with a subtly-suggestive voice, something we had never before heard, and body movements which we had never before seen. He awakened emotions in many girls which they had kept hidden, even from themselves. Nice girls did not feel such things, only boys were allowed to possess sexual desires.

Instead of putting girls down for responding, Elvis actually encouraged wild abandon, and seemed to love them all the more for it. He was genuine and honest in his appreciation of girls; there were no games, just an open, sincere, sexual attraction between one boy and millions of girls. The entire world was appalled at his behavior and shocked at the hysteria he created. Even those of us who did not participate in the screaming and crying were secretly pleased that worn-out taboos and repressions were finally crumbling.

I remember a cool Sunday night in September of 1956, when my friend Carolyn and I slipped out of church early to watch Elvis' first performance on *The Ed Sullivan Show*. The church was across the street from my grandmother's house where I was living at the time, and since Carolyn's grandfather was pastor we had to be especially careful. We sat in the back of the church so there would be less chance of being seen when it was time to sneak out.

My black suede penny loafers, white bobby sox, white turtleneck sweater and black wool skirt, together with my blonde ponytail hair style, probably made me look exactly like a million other teenage girls throughout America who were anxiously awaiting a glimpse of the shining star in our lives. When the congregation rose to join the choir in a joyous hymn, Carolyn and I quietly slipped through the door and ran across the street, and into my grandmother's room where the television was kept.

We both lay on the carpeted floor and watched Elvis nervously begin his performance, but to our eyes he was perfect. I said to Carolyn, "He's the best-looking guy to come along since Eddie Fisher."

Carolyn agreed with my observation and so did all the kids in Fulton High the next day. Elvis was the topic of discussion during lunch and every other free minute we had.

Elvis was far beyond the physical reach of an everyday Knoxville girl, but I liked him anyway. I watched him perform, I bought his records and I saw his movies. Elvis was a dream man, but some of the dreams turned to nightmares.

I met Marty in early 1959, through some mutual friends, and we began seeing each other often. He was working in Knoxville at the time for a radio station, and I was with a department store. The months of seeing each other and seriously dating turned into an engagement before I had any idea Marty even knew who Elvis Presley was. We rented an apartment shortly before the wedding and one day we were moving in some non-essential clothing and odd pieces of furniture in anticipation of the time when we would live together.

As Marty was taking some clothes out of a box I noticed he had a white sweatshirt-like jacket with the name *Elvis* written in black script letters on the back. I picked it up and saw the initials *EP* on the front. There was only one Elvis so I looked at Marty and said, "Where did you get this? What are you doing with a jacket with Elvis' name on it?"

Marty said, "I know Elvis. We went to school together and we go skating a lot when we're both in Memphis. He bought some of us jackets to wear when we're at the rink."

"Oh sure," I said, not trying to hide that I thought he was making up a story to impress me.

Marty said, "Well, I do know him. I'm not joking."

"Really? Then why don't you take me to meet him?"

"I will," Marty said, "if he's in Memphis when we get there over Labor Day."

There have been times during the years that followed when I've felt I would have been a lot better off had I said *goodbye* to Marty on the spot, but I didn't. We went to Memphis to meet my future in-laws as planned and Elvis was out of town. Marty's sister did drive me to Graceland but I couldn't believe Elvis Presley really lived there. I couldn't see him and somehow I just didn't quite believe that was actually his home. I don't know where I thought he lived but I didn't think I was at his house, and I wasn't convinced Marty knew him all that well.

We were married shortly after we returned to Knoxville but Marty never liked living there and when the opportunity came, we moved to Memphis where he worked for another radio station. He did take me to Graceland then and I did meet Elvis.

It was evening when we walked into the spacious living room of Graceland. The white carpet and long white custom-made sofa, which spanned the length of one windowed wall, were stark against the red velvet drapes. Against the opposite wall was a great white marble fireplace with an enormous clock built in above the mantel. Smoke colored mirrors surrounded the clock and reflected the sparkle of every light in the room. I was impressed with the grandeur. There were several men sitting around and quite a few girls. Marty introduced me to those who were present but I was unable to concentrate on their names, faces or anything else which I normally use to associate and remember the people I meet. My mind was filled with the awesomeness of the occasion and the belief that none of it was really happening.

We sat there making small talk for about thirty minutes before Elvis came down the long red carpeted stairs which led from his private suite. He was wearing black pants and a red shirt, with his collar turned up, and his favorite navy blue yacht cap.

Marty introduced me by saying, "Elvis, this is my wife, Patsy."

Elvis got a big grin on his face and said, "Yeah, Marty, this is your wife Patsy."

He was obviously kidding me and being friendly and he impressed me at the time as being a very fun-loving person.

I'm certain that Elvis was accustomed to people behaving like complete ninnies when they first met him and he was absolutely marvelous at pretending not to notice. Before long I was actually beginning to feel at ease, at least enough to sneak a quick look at those incredible eyes. Without a doubt, his eyes were the most unique attribute Elvis Presley possessed.

I didn't meet Elvis again until Marty began working for him, and even then I didn't see Elvis that much at first. None of the other guys around Elvis were married in those days and I felt very uncomfortable not knowing if I was going to be the only girl at the house if I happened to go there with Marty. I was also very shy at the time and generally felt out of place in those surroundings.

When Marty went to work for Elvis in 1961 and traveled to California, I stayed with Marty's parents. His mother and father are great people but the addition of a daughter-in-law and a granddaughter to a settled household creates problems for all concerned. It was hard on me and hard on them, and when Marty returned from California we decided it wasn't going to work. He left Elvis' payroll and went back into radio, but by then the excitement of the life with Elvis was in Marty's blood and it wasn't long before he was back as a part of the group.

We moved to Graceland so Marty would be available when Elvis needed him. He was *on call* twenty-four hours a day even when they were in Memphis and, of course, they were all together twenty-four hours a day when Elvis was making motion pictures. That was his job, to be available when Elvis needed him, and Marty was devoted to his job and to Elvis. By then we had a son and Marty and I shared two rooms at Graceland with our two children. The surroundings were plush, but trying. Either there were so many people in the house it resembled an airport terminal, or it was like a morgue when the guys were on the road.

Elvis did his best to make me feel at ease when he was at home and he seemed to love my little daughter, Sheri. Often she would climb up onto his lap and hug him and then climb down again, and then back up and down again until one night Elvis picked her up and said, "Look little baby, you can sit in my lap if you want to but either stay there or stay down, you're wearing me out."

While living at Graceland, and even when we were not, it was like being in a wealthy commune with Elvis as our leader. Marty and I had no outside social life and no outside friends. Every evening the commune gathered and waited for Elvis to appear. All eyes lit up the instant he came down the stairs and went into the dining room where he would turn on the television and eat breakfast.

When Elvis ate he usually liked to have people around, especially in the early days when he would sit at the head of the table and the guys would all join him. Elvis didn't like to hear bad news or problems when he was eating breakfast, he said that was the wrong way to begin the day.

Dinner was different when he was at Graceland. He liked to eat at the large oval dining room table with as many of the guys and girls as possible joining him. Often Elvis would begin talking about music or religion or another of his pet subjects and get so engrossed in the conversation his food would get cold before he ate it.

Priscilla never liked to see that happen because she knew he would then just nibble on the cold dinner and later fill himself up with junk food which would add to his weight problems. There were times when Priscilla would arrange it so the two of them would be able to have dinner alone. We always understood and even welcomed the opportunity to have some time to ourselves.

After eating breakfast, Elvis usually joined the group which always consisted of the men on one side of the room and the girls on the other. Depending on his mood, Elvis would control the behavior of the women when our conversation became too loud by saying, "You're making too much noise."

These were not parties as I understand parties to be. It was impossible to enjoy the company of my husband, he might just as well have been on the road. Elvis owned him one hundred percent, regardless of whether they were in California or Memphis.

I needed Marty more than Elvis needed him. There were always plenty of people around to take care of Elvis' needs but I had no one, not even for companionship. If it had been another woman I could have coped with the problem, but who can compete with an Elvis Presley?

My life became one big resentment. I resented Elvis for taking Marty away from me so often, and I had nothing in common with most of the wives and girlfriends, but mostly at the time I just didn't really like them. They were, to me, strange people. I couldn't understand the guys' devotion to Elvis or working for him the way they did. I couldn't understand their taking the abuse which, regardless of what they now say, they did take. I felt my husband was becoming less and less a man and I was losing all respect for him. They were earning very little money, as far as salaries were concerned, and yet they all seemed to love the life they were leading. I felt cut off from everyone and spent most of my time with my two children. I was also pregnant again with our second daughter which, of course, made life more trying than it would have been otherwise. My reputation within the group finally became *grouch* and *smart-ass. "Don't say anything to Pat Lacker because she will tell you off."*

I feel Elvis hated to see me come in the door. He must have disliked me as much as I had come to dislike him. I had a chip on my shoulder and was always rebellious. He didn't like to be around people like that.

As the years passed Elvis and the people around him became like family. It was not necessarily a happy family but it was more than an employer and employee relationship. It was a way of life for us and life, unfortunately, is not all good. There were, of course, many happy times when I felt very close to the others. When we decided to build our own house Elvis was there to help every step of the way. He paid for the land, and during the time we were building the house he often came by to see how it was progressing.

After the house was completed, and we moved in, we invited Elvis and all the guys over to see it. We could tell Elvis was happy for us and it made us even happier to know he really cared.

The first time I saw Elvis perform live was in Las Vegas in August of 1969. All the guys and girls had gone to Vegas earlier except Barbara Klein and me. We flew out there a week after the opening night of the show and we didn't see Elvis prior to the performance. We were sitting near the stage and when Elvis finished his first song he said, "Hello Patsy and Barbara," in his warm laughing way, to us from the stage.

It made us feel very important because we knew he wanted us to know he was glad we were there. His performance that night was one of the best shows I have ever seen him do, and I felt very proud of him.

As happy as some of the times could be, there could be those as unhappy. If Elvis was in a bad mood and anyone voiced an opinion about anything, he was likely to snap, "What the hell do you know about it?"

Marty was always afraid I would make Elvis mad by saying or doing something which would offend him. One night the telephone rang and I answered it. I thought it was Elvis' father on the phone when the voice said, "Let me speak to Marty."

I said, "Just a minute, Mr. Presley," and called Marty to the phone.

Marty came to the phone and talked for a few minutes while I was watching television. When he finished he came over to me and said, "What were you so smart to him for?"

"What are you talking about?" I asked.

"Elvis wanted to know why you were calling him Mr. Presley."

"Marty," I said, "I didn't know it was Elvis. I thought it was his father and I always call him Mr. Presley. If he thought I was being smart I'll call him and say I'm sorry, but I didn't know it was Elvis."

Marty said he would take care of it. I guess he didn't want me to call because he knew I was being very rebellious at the time about everything. I was miserable and, as I look back now, I guess I set out to make everybody else the same way. I disagreed with Marty about everything.

If we were in a movie and everyone laughed at something I didn't laugh. When something serious would happen on the screen I would laugh at it. I was becoming a hateful person even to myself. In defense of my own attitudes I have to say it wasn't an easy life. Elvis kept everybody off balance. In a minute he would turn from being the most lovable person in the world to being the most hateful. He seemed to enjoy getting under my skin sometimes by saying, "Where's Marty, Patsy? Where's that fat little sonofabitch?"

In contrast to that behavior, Elvis could show so much concern for my health that I couldn't help but love him. There was a time when I had been alone all day and late into the night. Marty and I were living in the garage apartment next to Graceland and I wasn't feeling well. I called the house and told one of the maids to ask Marty if he could come over, and to tell him I wasn't feeling very well. Within minutes the door burst open and there was Marty with Elvis and the other guys. Elvis almost shouted, "What's the matter, Patsy? Are you all right?"

I could see the concern on his face and knew he really cared about me. A few days later, when Elvis, Marty, Jo Smith, Priscilla and a few others were going to Tupelo, I asked Marty if I could go along. He said he would ask Elvis, and when he did I heard Elvis say to a group who was there at the time, "I guess she can go, she's afraid Marty will shake in his boots if she's not around to protect him."

Despite all the different moods and actions I know now I loved Elvis like a brother even while I felt I hated him. He was a complex person who could make you happy or make you sad, according to his own mood.

Being a girlfriend was good, being a wife was not. Elvis, before he was married and to some degree even after, had a *no wives* policy when he was on the road. Whenever I heard Elvis say, "Let's roll," I knew Marty would be gone for weeks or months at a time.

Once we were separated for eight months while Elvis was making motion pictures. The girlfriends, and there were lots of girlfriends, were always welcome, but the wives were expected to stay at home and wait for their men to return.

Elvis often became upset with me because I wouldn't go along with just anything he wanted to do; such as the time in later years when he wanted to take everyone for a ride in his airplane. I did go on the plane but balked when he wanted to fly to Dallas to see his new airplane, the Lisa Marie, which was being renovated.

"No, I'm not going to Dallas," I said.

Elvis asked, "Why not? We'll be gone only thirty minutes."

"I'm not going, I have to go to work in the morning; besides I have three kids."

"Thirty minutes is all we'll be gone!"

"Yeah, like the time you took Barbara and a bunch of people and were gone three days without even a change of clothes."

He was becoming really upset so Marty broke in and told Elvis he would handle me. Marty was afraid I'd get mad and tell Elvis to go to hell.

Chapter Two

The Family Way

During those early years while we lived at Graceland, I came to know Elvis' family quite well. Grandma Presley was a fine lady, and she and I spent many hours together talking about everything and everybody.

Grandma, as most of us called her, is a very tall lady who wears sunglasses day and night. She always dressed very neatly and kept her dark hair sparkling. Her sense of humor was great and she endured the constant teasing of all the guys in good spirits until they finished, and then she would tell them exactly what she thought of each. No one ever accused Grandma of being bashful.

I grew to love her dearly over the years and she seemed to love me and my family. She stayed in her room most of the time when Elvis and the guys were at Graceland but when they were on the road she would be out and about the house. To get her out of her room for some exercise I often visited and told her how I needed to go for a walk and asked her to join me.

Grandma loved my little boy and for a long time she would call me every morning and ask me to bring Marc in to have breakfast with her. Marc, who was two years old at the time, welcomed a second breakfast of biscuits and bacon with Grandma about ten o'clock in the morning. I never told her he had eaten his regular breakfast several hours earlier. Needless to say, Marc became a little butterball before too many months went by. All three of my children loved Grandma and were in and out of her room all day.

When I was ready to make my first trip to California I was very excited about seeing the West Coast, but I felt very bad about leaving Grandma. Of course, she was never alone in the house but I thought I knew how she would feel being there with just the maids for company.

Elvis' father, Vernon, was polite but never friendly, and he appeared to resent our presence in the house.

Vernon was as tight as Elvis was generous. We all expected to see him drop dead some day at the sight of Elvis giving a stranger a new car. Had Vernon had his way, they would still have the first dollar Elvis ever made.

Vernon seemed to be afraid of Elvis in the same way I felt all the guys were afraid. They would laugh and joke and carry on but they were all careful about what they said to Elvis. I used to have black-and-blue marks on my ribs from Marty punching me with his elbow if I was laughing or saying something at the wrong time. There was never a question of who was the boss and who was the employee, even when they were having fun together.

Even though Mr. Presley wasn't friendly he was never unpleasant to me when I was living at Graceland and the guys were on the road. When my mother died he came to the garage apartment and told me to make any long distance calls necessary and he would take care of them. He also told me to let him know if I needed anything.

A lot of things have been said about Mr. Presley, but I don't want to forget the good things he did for me. My mother's death came at the lowest point in my life, when I felt I was faced with more problems than I thought I could handle and Mr. Presley couldn't have been nicer.

Some of Elvis' other relatives were a lot worse and really resented the guys and their wives. Elvis' Uncle Johnny once tried to break into my room when Marty was away with Elvis. Johnny was drunk, as was often the case, and in the middle of the night he started beating on my bedroom door. I told him to go away and leave me alone but he wouldn't stop. I was frightened. I called Vernon on the telephone and asked him to come over and make Johnny leave but Vernon said, "There ain't nothing I can do."

I finally told Johnny I was going to call the police if he

didn't leave, and eventually he gave up. I don't like to think about what would have happened if he had managed to break the lock.

That same uncle once tried to get Marty with a knife. He was drunk then, too. It was about two in the morning and we had just come back to the house after one of Elvis' nightly rides around Memphis and the surrounding country. Elvis went upstairs and Jerry Schilling and Marty were getting ready to leave when one of the maids told us that shortly before we arrived the front door bell had rung. She opened it thinking we were back and didn't have a key.

The maid said there was a strange looking man standing there demanding to see Elvis. She was scared and slammed the door, and called the gate guard. The guard wasn't able to find anyone when he got up to the house but Marty and Jerry were afraid he might be hiding on the grounds and try to get in after they left. They decided they better stay at the house, and were in the kitchen when Johnny came to the back door. He was holding his hand over a bloody wound on his side. He looked at Marty and said, "You sonofabitch, you did this to me. I'm gonna get you for cutting me."

Marty said, "Oh hell, Johnny, what's the matter with you now?"

Johnny staggered toward Marty and we saw he had a knife in his hand. He was so drunk he could hardly talk, but he could be dangerous, and Marty was in no mood to start fighting with him over a knife. Marty stepped back and put his hand on the gun he always had in his coat. "Now Johnny," he said, "I haven't done anything to you. You gotta get to a hospital and get fixed-up, but if you keep coming at me with that knife, I'm going to blow your head off."

That stopped Johnny long enough for Marty to call Elvis on the intercom and tell him what was happening. They were all afraid of Elvis, he was the meal ticket, and when Johnny heard Elvis say, "Get that sonofabitch out of here. I don't want to see his face in this house again," he sobered up enough to put the knife away.

Marty got a cab, paid the driver the fare, gave him a good tip and had him drive Johnny to the emergency room of the hospital.

One of Elvis' aunts once tried to stab Marty with a butcher knife. She was drunk at the time and, I'm sure, her resentment toward Marty and the other guys came out. Some of the family would see Elvis give gifts of new automobiles or jewelry to the guys and they would resent outsiders getting more than they got.

Marty was downstairs in the basement den doing some work on the books, and checking the list of Elvis' awards which were kept in glass cases on the walls, when Elvis' aunt came into the room. She was standing by the only doorway leading out and looked like she had really had too much to drink.

When she saw Marty at the other end of the room she screamed, "You son-of-a-bitch! I don't like you or none of your buddies."

She reached into her bag and brought out a big kitchen knife. Marty started talking with her and telling her how he had always liked her and had never done her any harm. He told her to put the knife away, but she kept cursing at him and began to come toward him.

Marty said he began to look around for something he could use to defend himself but kept trying to get her to calm down. She was getting very close when they heard Elvis shouting for Marty and his footsteps coming down the stairs.

The aunt got scared and put the knife away and, I think, Marty said a prayer of thanks. Elvis, of course, didn't know what had happened and when he came into the room he greeted his aunt and then started talking with Marty.

Marty didn't say anything to Elvis about it at the time, but a week or so later he told Elvis what had happened. Elvis just laughed and said, "She wouldn't have done nothing, she was probably just trying to scare you."

Marty said, "She succeeded."

In all fairness, I never saw Elvis' father drink to excess, and Elvis seldom touched alcohol. Perhaps he had seen too much with some of his relatives.

I can't even remember the first time I met Dee Presley, Elvis' stepmother. That's the kind of impression she left with me. I didn't care one way or another about her until we had a run-in in California.

Elvis wasn't feeling well and he and all the guys were in the den watching television. I was at my usual station, which was in the dining room with my three children. Jo Smith was in there with me and Dee had put her three boys in Jerry

Schilling's room to watch television. My daughter, who was four at the time, kept going into the room with the boys. I told her a number of times to stay in the dining room and leave the boys to themselves; the last time I told her very firmly and then went into the kitchen to warm some milk for the baby.

Dee came storming up behind me and told me she thought I had a real problem. I asked her what she was talking about and she said I had been cursing her three boys. I hadn't spoken to her boys but the way she said it made me so mad I could have choked her tongue out without blinking an eye. It's fortunate I didn't have a free hand, but I told her what I thought of her.

Dee rushed back into the den and told Vernon she thought they should leave because she had gotten me upset, which was putting it mildly. I was so angry by then I was crying and screaming at her at the top of my voice.

Everyone, including Elvis, came running out of the den asking what was wrong. I told Elvis I was sorry that something so petty had happened in his house, especially since he wasn't feeling well. Elvis told me I didn't owe him any apologies. He told me he knew how Dee acted. "I've gotten more publicity from her than I have from Colonel Parker," he said.

I still felt very bad about the whole thing but I wasn't going to take any abuse from Dee Presley, or anyone else.

Dee met Elvis' father in Germany when Elvis was in the army and stationed there. She was married to an army sergeant named Stanley, with whom she had three sons, Ricky, Billy and David. Vernon Presley became friendly with Sergeant Stanley and his wife Dee and before long the sergeant was out of the picture and Vernon and Dee were married.

Elvis didn't attend the wedding and acted like he resented her presence at Graceland. He became especially upset when Vernon and Dee moved into the room Elvis had kept locked for two years, the room which had belonged to his mother. Eventually Elvis did tell Mr. Presley to buy a house for the two of them and the three boys. Elvis used the excuse that he wanted to move his grandmother into the room Vernon and Dee were using, but he wasn't shy about telling the guys he really wanted Dee out of the house.

To the guys, Dee was the laughing stock of the household. She took great pride in ordering the maids around and generally being the lady of the house while Elvis was traveling. When Elvis was home, she seemed to be following him around most of the time or leaving him notes addressed to *My Little Prince.* I remember once when he came downstairs with one of her notes and said, "I've got her little prince, and you know where it is."

We were never sure what to expect from Dee next. She dressed like a teenager, wore enough make-up for a chorus line and told us every month she just knew she was pregnant.

Dee's favorite subject was religion. She talked constantly about sin and the necessity for everyone to lead a good life. She gave the impression that no member of her family would have touched a drop of alcohol if his life depended on taking it, but I've often met her in the supermarket with a basketful of beer and her son Ricky was constantly in and out of trouble for drug abuse. Obviously, Dee cannot be blamed for her son's shortcomings, only for her hypocritical attitude.

Actually, I really felt sorry for Dee because she seemed to be so terrified of growing older, but my pity lasted only as long as it took me to read the reports of the wealth she acquired as the price for giving Vernon a divorce; wealth which, one way or another, came from Elvis.

Chapter Three

The Flip-Side of Elvis

I eventually came to like Priscilla after she matured, and after she was no longer a source of my resentment, but when she was younger she was not my favorite person. When Priscilla was sixteen, she came to Memphis from Germany. The cover story for her parents and the public was that she would live with Elvis' father and Dee, but in fact she lived with Elvis. I resented the way Marty would do anything for her while ignoring me. That, of course, wasn't Priscilla's fault, but she seemed to enjoy it. She was the little princess to whom all the guys catered.

There was a time when I was pregnant and due for a checkup. I asked Marty to take me to the doctor but he said he was too tired to go out, he needed some sleep. No sooner was he in bed than Elvis called on the intercom and told Marty that Priscilla was having cramps, she needed something from the drugstore. Marty was dressed and on his way in minutes without so much as a grumble.

This type of thing happened constantly and with each instance, my bitterness grew. It culminated one day when I went into the kitchen where Marty was fixing himself a pizza. I said, "That looks good, give me some."

"There's more in the freezer," Marty answered. "Fix yourself one."

"Okay, I will," I told him and went and put one in the oven.

Priscilla came into the kitchen, saw Marty eating his pizza and said, "That looks good."

Marty said, "Have some."

I began to fume. Priscilla was standing in front of the oven and I snapped at her, "Move!"

"Don't you say please?"

"To whom I please, when I please, but I don't say please to the likes of you!"

"Well, gol-ly," Priscilla responded.

"Oh, you women," Marty interrupted. "If you're not fighting with your husbands you're fighting with each other."

I had a big kitchen knife in my hand to cut the pizza, and when he said that I completely lost control and turned and threw the knife on the counter toward Priscilla. Fortunately it did not hit her. "You two can both go to hell!" I screamed and ran out of the room.

"Patsy!" Marty yelled, but I didn't stop.

Priscilla followed me and said, "I'm sorry, Patsy, I didn't mean to upset you."

"Just go away and leave me alone. It's better if we don't discuss it."

Marty came out as Priscilla returned to the kitchen. "What's got into you?" he asked.

"I'm just tired of catering to the little queen. You give her more consideration than you give me, Marty, and I'm just tired of it."

The resentment had built to where I was beginning to be an ugly person. I didn't like what was happening to me and I wanted to get away to a normal life.

Priscilla was also a problem with my daughter. The two of them argued every minute of the day until, at times, I thought I had four children rather than three. Priscilla was, of course, a very young girl at the time and when Elvis and the guys were away she had little to keep her occupied.

Often when the guys were traveling Priscilla would stay in the garage apartment with me and she and my daughter, Sheri, would have arguments over what they were going to watch on television and everything else they could think to argue about.

One night they got into an argument over a television program and began screaming at each other. Sheri told Priscilla to go to her own room and watch whatever she wanted. Priscilla called her a brat and stormed out of the apartment. She was gone about thirty minutes when the intercom rang. Priscilla was on the other end of the intercom and asked to speak to Sheri. She told Sheri she was sorry about the argument and asked if she could come back to our place to watch television with us. Sheri told her she could, but she would have to watch what she wanted to see.

Another evening Priscilla and I were talking and Sheri was on the floor playing with some of her toys. Sheri had a rubber spider which she had left on the table next to where Priscilla was sitting, and without thinking Priscilla picked it up and began chewing on one of the spider's legs. She wasn't paying too much attention to what she was doing and while she was talking she bit the spider's leg off. Sheri saw it and really had a fit since it was one of her favorite toys. She told Priscilla she wished she would get her own toys and leave hers alone. Priscilla got mad again and ran to her own room.

Priscilla was a very petite and pretty girl with very long black hair, but in the early days she hid her natural beauty with far too much make-up. Elvis liked it, especially the heavy eye make-up and, I guess, that's why she wore it, but she is far more beautiful today.

Priscilla, along with a few of the other girls, made the empty days and nights a lot more bearable and after she matured I really grew to like her. When I needed someone she was always there to help. One incident stands out vividly in my mind. Elvis and the guys were in Los Angeles and Priscilla and Larry Geller's wife were with me in my bedroom.

I became very ill and Priscilla drove me to the hospital and called the babysitter to stay with my children. I don't know what I would have done without her that night.

Joan Esposito, Joe's wife, was the company drill sergeant. She seemed to love to give orders to all the women, except Priscilla of course. Most of the time when she and Priscilla were together, anyone seeing them would have mistaken her for Priscilla's personal maid. It was a joke among some of the wives. We thought she was trying to get to Elvis by being attentive to Priscilla. Joan was an ex-showgirl who took great pleasure in telling each of the women where they were to sit, or how they should hurry, or dress, or whatever, when we were going to a movie or anyplace. Often she would stand at the door of the theater and say, "Come along now, girls. Patsy, you sit over there. Now come on, we don't want to keep everybody waiting."

Her husband Joe, together with Marty, was foreman of the guys. Joan wanted everyone to know how close she and Joe were to Elvis. Most of us thought she was a very funny pain in the neck.

Joan was very much a part of my first trip to California, and it was some experience. While I was there Elvis had to go to Hawaii for one of the movies and, of course, Marty was with him. Marty and I had our own apartment in Hollywood, but fortunately, I had decided to stay at Elvis' home in Bel-Air while they were away. The Watts riots began shortly after they left.

Priscilla, Jo Smith and Joan Esposito were also staying at the big house and before the riots began we had a good time. Billy and Jo Smith always did the grocery shopping for the house, so before Marty left for Hawaii he gave Jo a check to cover all our expenses during their absence. Jo and I planned the menus and bought the food, but that didn't go over too well with Joan and Priscilla. Jo and I were southern girls and our tastes ran toward good old home cooking while Joan wanted things like spaghetti and lasagne. I guess she had adapted to her husband's food preferences since Joe had an Italian background.

Since Jo and I were buying the food that was one time Joan didn't get her way and most of the time Jo and I had the dining room to ourselves, which was fine with us.

When the riots started we were scared stiff. Five per cent of the city was burning and we were stuck in the middle of Bel-Air with no way to get out. The riots didn't come close to us, of course, but I still couldn't wait to get back to Memphis.

George Klein's wife, Barbara, was often sick. She had some unusual disease which made us think she was near death most of the time. She had trouble going up and down the stairs, and we were afraid she was going to faint and fall down them whenever we saw her hesitate.

Elvis decided one night that he would cure her. I think Billy, Jo, Marty and I were in his room when he called

Barbara and told her to come up. Elvis had a big, green ring which had a special significance to him and he held it in front of her face while he placed his hand on her head and spoke some solemn words to cure her. It was a riot, seeing Elvis sitting on the bed, legs crossed, performing a voodoo-like cure. I started to laugh because it *was* funny, and I really thought he was doing it as a joke, but then Marty punched me with his elbow and I knew Elvis was serious.

Elvis was high on the pills and when he was like that he really thought he was a faith healer. Anyway, when that cure didn't work, he bought Barbara a shiny new car which, if nothing else, certainly made her more cheerful.

Elvis was always into something strange like that, and he often convinced some of the others to believe and try the same weird things. Once, several of the girls were gathered at Graceland, waiting for Elvis and the guys to come home from a trip to the West Coast, when they decided to try to communicate through ESP.

It was late at night and since the guys were driving we didn't know exactly when they would arrive. Jo and I were looking out the window to see if we could catch sight of the headlights turning into the driveway, when Joan and Priscilla announced they were going upstairs to try to communicate with Elvis.

Stevi Geller, former wife of Larry Geller, one of Elvis' hair dressers, was also at the house and she decided to join them, but Jo and I were told to stay downstairs and not disturb their thought transmission. Jo and I were sitting there laughing about it when the guys arrived. Elvis, after he had greeted us, said, "Where's Priscilla?"

I told him she was upstairs trying to reach them by ESP. Marty went to the intercom and called upstairs and told Priscilla, "I hear you were trying to reach us on the road through ESP."

When Priscilla said they were trying, Marty said, "You must have been calling the wrong number because we didn't get the message, we're home."

Billy Smith's wife, Jo, and I became good friends. We had a lot in common and spent much of our free time together. Jo has long, beautiful dark hair and a lot of people thought she had a striking resemblance to Priscilla. As pretty as she is, personality and compassion are her two strong points. I could talk with her about any problem and she would understand and try to help. Jo and I had similar backgrounds and became friends the first time we met. We developed our own doubletalk which sounded funny to some people who didn't know us, and they probably thought we were crazy, but it always put us in a better frame of mind. Sometimes our doubletalk even allowed us to say things before the others which we otherwise would not have been able to say.

Patsy Presley Gambill is a nice person. She was Elvis' cousin and worked in the office at Graceland for a number of years before she married Marvin (Gee Gee) Gambill. Patsy and I spent many hours together while the guys were traveling. She would come to the house when she finished working and we would talk until all hours of the night. We liked each other and had it not been for Patsy's and Jo's company, I'm not sure I would have made it through those lonely days.

When our husbands were out of town, Jo and Patsy and I would see each other for lunch and go shopping together, or we would talk for hours on the telephone. They were often as lonely as I was and when it was time for the guys to come home we would go to Graceland to wait with other wives and girlfriends. The three of us always ended up waiting by ourselves away from the rest of the group. Regardless of the occasion Jo, Patsy and I seemed to gravitate toward each other and spend our evenings together.

When we attended the Man of The Year awards dinner for Elvis in 1970, Jo and I were seated next to each other. We were proud of Elvis but in our usual manner we made light of the occasion and laughed throughout the dinner and generally acted liked two country bumpkins.

Throughout the dinner, Jo and I picked at the delicious food, pretended we didn't know what we were eating and finally asked Marty if they were going to serve any pinto beans and corn bread. Marty finally gave up trying to make us behave and began pretending he didn't even know us.

At one point, when we were really giggling, Marty looked over to a distinguished man who was seated across the table from us and told him not to pay any attention. Marty said, "These poor girls haven't been out of the sticks too long."

Linda Thompson was a lot of fun. Most of us liked her and felt she was good for Elvis and that she really loved him. I don't know why they did not marry, but even after their affair ended they remained friends and Linda's brother, Sam, continued to work for Elvis. Linda also loved Elvis' daughter Lisa, and Lisa loved her. Lisa was at Graceland when Elvis died and she was the one who called Linda in California to tell her.

Linda told me of the conversation and how she tried to console Lisa. She said that Sam must have dialed the number but it was Lisa on the line and she said, "Linda, my daddy's dead."

"No, baby, your daddy's going to be all right. He's sick, that's all," Linda answered. She thought Lisa was mistaken, that Elvis had simply been taken to the hospital for an illness.

Lisa cried, "No, he's dead, my daddy's dead, Linda."

Linda asked Lisa to put Sam on the line and then learned the truth from her brother. He suggested that she might want to fly to Memphis for the funeral. Elvis' airplane, the Lisa Marie, was flying to California to bring back Priscilla, so Linda called to ask for a ride. Priscilla, however, refused the request. She told Linda she wasn't going to make a show of the funeral, that it was for family, not girlfriends.

Linda flew to Memphis on a commercial airline and Priscilla apologized after the funeral for the way she had behaved. Linda said that Priscilla told her she really believed Elvis would be alive had he and Linda remained together. Most of us believe that too.

Linda is a beautiful, tall woman with long brown hair and brown eyes. She was, at the time, very down to earth and fun to be around. There was never a time when Linda tried to make any of us feel inferior or make herself out as anything special because she was Elvis' girlfriend. Most of us appreciated her attitude and genuinely liked her. Linda would speak the same crazy talk when Jo and I did, and when the three of us were together we acted like little girls.

There were times when we would sing and dance and

pretend we were putting on a stage show, and when we were together at one of Elvis' rehearsals we would sing along with him. Elvis called us crazy but always laughed at our antics.

One year Elvis bought Linda a fur coat for Christmas and shortly thereafter we were together in one of the automobiles when Elvis accidentally knocked the ashes off a cigar he was smoking and they fell on the seat next to Linda. She told him if he burned up her new coat there would be fur flying. Elvis picked up on the fur coat and fur flying idea and laughed about it for a solid hour.

Somehow the conversation got on clothing and how clothes looked without a bra. Elvis said to Linda, "You and Patsy don't have to worry about that, neither of you has anything to put into a bra, so why wear one?"

During one of our trips to Las Vegas, I think it was in 1974, some of us were in Elvis' suite at the Hilton talking with him when Linda came out of the bedroom and said, "I'm going shopping, why don't you girls come with me?"

Elvis said, "Yeah, all of you go with Linda and I want each of you to buy yourself an outfit. I'll pay for it, and don't spare the expense, you know I'm a rich sonofabitch."

He was laughing but we knew he wanted us to buy ourselves something nice. We went to one of Las Vegas' exclusive stores and bought new outfits. That night I wore mine to his show and afterward told him how much I appreciated his gift. Elvis smiled at me and said, "That's okay, honey, you're welcome."

Linda and I, during that same visit to Las Vegas, walked through one of the big casinos singing religious songs at the top of our voices, while all the gamblers looked at us like we were really kooks. I think it was because of Linda that I became more comfortable around Elvis. I know the ice began to melt one night when Elvis and Linda and Marty and I were in the automobile together.

Elvis said to me. "Pat, I just don't know what else to do. I've tried all these years to get you to talk to me."

"Okay," I answered, "talk you want, talk you'll get," and I let loose with my feelings about the whole thing. He must have been sorry he ever asked. After listening to my tirade, Elvis said, "I realize that I have taken Marty away from you and the kids, but, Patsy, I never held a gun to his head and told him he had to come with me."

I weakly tried to explain the strange hold he had on people but by that time I was emotionally exhausted and my thought simply trailed off. To this day it's impossible for me to explain this *strange hold,* and I don't believe he ever fully realized the impact he had on so many people's lives. Marty loved Elvis. He would have done anything for him, there was a time when he would have given his life for Elvis. No one was immune, even me. A girl I worked with once said, "Elvis must really be a dumb person," and I was ready to kill.

His death had a funny effect on me. I didn't realize that I cared. I couldn't accept it, I couldn't even function. My nerves were shot, I went completely beserk. I couldn't understand my reaction, why I was unable to pick myself up. Marty told me, "Maybe you now understand a little better how I felt."

After that outburst in the car we talked about everything together. Religion was one of Elvis' favorite subjects and part of almost every conversation. He would tell us about the far eastern religions he was studying and what he thought about each of them. I don't remember too much about them but Elvis was deeply involved for a long time.

We would sit and have long talks with Elvis or sometimes he would play records and Linda and I would sing along with him to the music. We didn't have the greatest voices in the world but with Elvis' help perhaps we didn't sound too bad.

Elvis would say and do really crazy things sometimes. I remember one night when Marty, Billy, Jo, Patsy, Gee Gee and I were in Elvis' suite talking with him and all of a sudden he walked over to a mirror, looked at himself and said, "I'm pretty, look at that profile."

Then he looked over at me and said, "Pat's pretty too. I don't know what it is but it's something about her face."

Everyone was laughing when Linda said, "It's her eyes."

"No," Elvis said, "it's not her eyes. I don't know what it is, but it's not her eyes. She's got eyes like those kids in the movie, *Village of the Damned,* they can make you do anything."

The last live-in girlfriend, Ginger Alden, was very different from Linda. I've never met the girl so I have no first-hand observations, but no one with whom I've talked has anything good to say about her, and no one believes one word of what she tells the newspapers and magazines about her *engagement* to Elvis. Elvis didn't keep secrets. If he were going to be married, he would have told his father or Billy and Jo Smith; there is just no way in the world they would not have known.

Priscilla said that during the funeral service Ginger sat with a mirror in her hand fixing her eyelashes and hair. Michelle, Priscilla's sister, was outside of the mausoleum following the services and observed Ginger's mother pointing out celebrities to Ginger. Priscilla's feelings were that Ginger did not care one thing about Elvis and that she and her mother were simply there to see and be seen.

Elvis' uncle Vester reportedly told the newspapers that Ginger is no longer welcome at Graceland. Vester denies having said it, but Ginger is now required to call Vernon for permission to enter the grounds. Her mother is suing the estate because she says Elvis promised to pay the mortgage on her house but never did. Elvis probably did say he would pay it, that's the kind of person he was, but there is no way that lady is going to get a dime out of Vernon Presley.

Chapter Four

The Macho Syndrome

If some of the women were strange, some of the *guys*, as they called themselves, were downright weird. I know I must come-off as sounding like a miserable, unhappy, complaining woman, and I guess I was. Had I met any of these people under different circumstances, I probably would have liked them, but I was asked to give my opinions and impressions of the years with Elvis and I intend to do exactly that.

Even though Marty was able to control my actions by punching me in the ribs, he was never able to control my mind. In most instances, it will come as a shock to Marty to learn my feelings about the people with whom he worked and the people with whom he lived, because we seldom discussed them. I knew Marty would not approve of my feelings so I usually kept my opinions to myself, or discussed them with only the few friends I had within Elvis' entourage.

Most of us thought Joe Esposito and Charlie Hodge were the direct pipelines to Colonel Tom Parker from Elvis' household. We didn't care because we knew little of Colonel Parker but, nevertheless, we were careful not to say anything in front of Joe or Charlie which we might not want the Colonel to know.

Charlie thought he was a real celebrity. His mind must have increased the importance of handing scarves to Elvis during a performance, because, if you heard Charlie tell it, the show was built around him.

Charlie was once a member of the *Foggy River Boys* singing group before he began working for Elvis. He and Elvis met in the army and after they were discharged Charlie visited Elvis whenever he wasn't working. He was always one of the guys, even before he started working for Elvis, as I understand it.

Charlie was a loner most of the time. He stayed away from the group and often seemed envious of anything the other guys would get. I've heard about the time when Elvis gave Sonny West a Cadillac and all the guys, except Charlie, went outside to see it. They were all happy for Sonny and tried to share his joy with Elvis, but Charlie wouldn't come out to see the new car. Elvis knew Charlie was sulking and said to Marty, "Charlie's inside mad because he didn't get anything."

Charlie did a necessary job for Elvis with the scarves and water on stage and there's no question there was a genuine fondness between the two. Charlie just felt too self-important for my tastes. There were times when one of the guys asked him to help do something and he would say, "My job's on stage."

When something had to be done all the guys pitched into the work and when Charlie used his stage excuse everyone would get after him. On stage Charlie wore a guitar but it wasn't connected to the sound system. He did, however, sing harmony with Elvis on some of the songs.

Charlie's life was devoted to Elvis and we were all concerned for him after Elvis' death. Most of the other guys were married and had families but Charlie remained single throughout the years. Charlie is a short, dark-haired man of medium weight who I never saw without a cigarette. He was a classic chain smoker and chain kisser. There was never a time when I would see Charlie that he didn't kiss me hello, tell me a joke then kiss me goodbye.

I couldn't help but like Charlie, and feel sorry for him when Elvis would get mad if Charlie made a suggestion, especially at a recording session, and scream at him, "Keep your mouth shut or get the hell out of here. You don't know what you're talking about."

Elvis could be cruel when he was in a bad mood and Charlie's biggest fault was that he didn't know how to keep his mouth shut for his own good.

Joe Esposito had a good head on his shoulders but he never seemed to have any feelings about anything. I always thought Joe was a cold person. He's a flashy guy who soon won the nickname Diamond Joe because of his affinity for those gems. Joe liked Cadillacs and always had a new one to drive, but he did have a good business brain and paid close attention to Elvis' affairs.

If Joe had acted more human toward all of us I probably would have liked him rather than feeling indifferent. Joe also had the habit of being very smart with his mouth, and coming on like he was the final authority about everything, which didn't endear him to many of the others.

Elvis was good to Joe just like he was good to all of us. When Elvis bought the ranch in Mississippi he bought all of the guys house trailers so they could be there with him. The ranch was a fun place for all of us, and probably one of the most relaxed periods we ever had together.

Elvis had a habit of riding his horse around the ranch while he sat on its back eating hot dog buns. Cold, dry, hot dog buns! I'd die laughing whenever I saw him sitting on that beautiful horse with a package of hot dog buns on the saddle in front of him. He did some crazy things.

Often we cooked dinner outside and everyone came and had a great time. Elvis was the center of attraction, of course, and he could be very gracious when he was in a good mood. The ranch days are among the good memories I have.

When we were with Elvis everything was an adventure, and, to me, they were often dangerous adventures. He thrived on taking risks. I remember some of the nights when we went for rides. I was often sure they would be my last ride, he always drove so fast. Elvis loved fast cars and motorcycles, but I stayed away from the motorcycles, the automobiles were bad enough.

The thing I did enjoy was riding the golf carts. Jo Smith and I, with some of the other girls, went riding on a golf cart one night. I was driving around behind Graceland and decided I wanted to go out on the highway so we drove through the gate and went for a ride.

I don't know now whatever possessed me to do something like that. The cars were all honking at us to get off the road but we went on our merry way.

Lamar Fike was the happy fat guy of the group. He is six feet tall and, at that time, weighed over three hundred and fifty pounds. He now weighs 155. Lamar had a lot of good sense, but, unfortunately, he liked to tell all of us often how smart he was. He was overbearing in size and attitude.

Lamar was often the brunt of Elvis' anger and sarcasm, and when Lamar didn't resist, his wife was included in the insults. I often felt sorry for both of them. Lamar seemed to take it all with good humor but it had to be painful for his wife, even if it didn't bother him. The guys thought the remarks were funny because Elvis said them and, at times, they joined in, what was to them, the merriment.

I heard Elvis, when he was in a bad mood, say to Lamar, "Cool it, fatty, you're nothing but a joke," and Lamar would just laugh along with the rest of the guys.

Alan Fortas, like Elvis, could be sharp with his mouth when he wanted to hurt someone. I remember a time when the guys were getting ready to go on a trip. I was pretty far along in my pregnancy and as big as a house. This is enough to depress anyone, but I was also feeling low at the prospect of being alone again. Alan came into the house, looked at me and said, "If I had a wife that looked like that I'd trade her in for a new one."

The guys thought it was funny. I didn't.

There were times when Elvis seemed to want to keep his real feelings from the guys. Once, about a week before Christmas, I was in the downstairs den talking with Elvis while he picked at his breakfast of bacon and eggs. Elvis was usually a hearty eater but on that day he seemed distracted and depressed.

This was after Elvis' divorce from Priscilla, and he had asked Linda Thompson to go shopping for Christmas gifts for his daughter Lisa. Marty was in the kitchen with some of the other guys and they sounded like they were having their usual good time.

I asked Elvis if something was wrong and he said, "Boy, this is some Christmas. Priscilla is in Hawaii, Linda is out shopping and here I sit. Life can be really funny."

I knew he was saying that here he was with money, fame, the love of millions of people but somehow with all of it he was very much alone. His family was broken, and he felt the loneliness which can come only with the loss of the person most important in one's life.

I choked back my own emotions and tried to say something to cheer him up, but I was interrupted by the entrance of some of the guys and Elvis instantly became a different person. He never wanted anyone, especially the guys, to see what they could interpret as being a human weakness.

Jerry Schilling was married to a sweet little girl named Sandy. After their separation Jerry told me he loved Sandy but his *career* kept him from being married. I never did find out what Jerry thought his career really was, but he had a real ego. When Jerry first came to work he was a shy young man who blushed if Elvis asked him the time of day, but as the months went by he became more and more confident.

Jerry was a good looking young man and the best educated of the guys. I understand he had only a half year or so to go to complete college when he quit and started to work for Elvis. Jerry expressed his opinions around Elvis and, because he did, there were many hours of friction between the two. He was, however, loyal to Elvis and I think Elvis cared deeply for him. The two of them would get into very serious discussions which often ended in a disagreement, but the disagreement was temporary.

Jerry was one of the few guys who was able to get away and make a name for himself, and still stay within the group.

There was a time when he really upset me over a silly incident. It happened one year when Elvis ended a road tour with a performance in Memphis. I had become friendly with Kathy Westmoreland, a singer who worked with Elvis. Kathy and my daughter had also grown to like each other so I invited her to stay at our house while she was in Memphis.

Kathy and Jerry Schilling had been seeing each other prior to this time but had split up and, as far as I knew, were now just friends. One of the guys told me that Jerry didn't think it would be a very good idea for Kathy to stay at my house. I was told that he said Elvis would not approve.

I didn't know what possible difference it would make to Elvis and, frankly, I was sick and tired of having to have everyone's approval before I could do anything. Elvis had a homecoming party at Graceland and while we were there I asked Jerry why he thought it was any of his business who I had at my house. Jerry denied the statements attributed to him.

That was one of those days when I wished I'd never heard of Elvis Presley or anyone connected with him. I ended the day with a bang by walking into a glass door and raising a big knot on my head. Fortunately, I was walking up the steps instead of down but it still didn't help my mood very much.

Billy Smith was one male relative of Elvis who turned out to be a responsible, nice person. Elvis almost raised Billy and as devoted as he was to Elvis, Billy was one of the few who would say *no* when he thought he should say *no*. Billy got a dirty deal at the end. Elvis often told us how he was going to take care of everyone in his will. Most of us didn't expect anything, if we outlived him, but as much as we heard him tell Billy how he didn't have anything to worry about, we were shocked to find he was left nothing.

Elvis gave Billy a house trailer, in which Billy and Jo lived at Graceland, but when Elvis died, the ownership papers were still in his name and Vernon refused to let Billy keep the trailer, even though we all had heard Elvis tell Billy and Jo the trailer belonged to them.

Even with that happening, Billy remains devoted to Elvis and his memory. He tries to protect Elvis' name and flatly refuses to admit to anything which might tarnish Elvis' image.

There were others, of course, whom I did like and with whom I shared times of great pleasure and feelings of being very much a part of a family. Whenever I see snow I'm reminded of a time when we visited the snowbound hills of Idlewild and almost stayed longer than we had planned.

It was in 1967, when Marty was in Los Angeles with Elvis. I was no longer able to go to California because our oldest daughter had started school, and we didn't want to move her from school to school every few months.

Marty called and told me to fly out for the weekend, which they were going to spend in the resort area of Palm Springs, California. It sounded like fun since I had heard all the guys talk about Palm Springs, but I had never been there.

Before I left I had my hair cut quite short and styled, and I thought it looked good until I arrived in Los Angeles and met Elvis at the house. He looked at me and said, "Patsy, you look like a chicken."

Of course he was joking. Elvis was constantly teasing and when things were going well his sense of humor was terrific, and, at those times, he never meant to hurt anyone, but it was necessary to know that not to be offended.

We drove to Palm Springs on Friday night and on Saturday morning Elvis decided he wanted to show us Idlewild, which had been the location for one of his movies. We all piled into the big limousine and drove from the warm sun of Palm Springs desert to the snow of Idlewild. That in itself was strange, just experiencing the sudden change from summer warmth to winter cold in such a short time, but it was a fun drive.

We left the highway to ride around in the woods and soon became stuck in the snow. All the guys, except Jerry Schilling, worked to free the car. He was busy taking photographs throughout the entire episode. Finally Elvis called a halt to the ineffectual attempts to move the limousine by ordering everyone out of the car. He would drive while the others pushed. Like magic, the big car glided out of its imprisonment.

I asked Elvis how he had managed to succeed when everyone else had failed. His eyes twinkled as he answered, "I used to be a truck driver."

It had been a fun experience and we were all delighted that Jerry had captured the sequence with photographs. When he discovered there was no film in the camera, we bombarded him with snowballs and came close to burying him under a ton of snow.

Chapter Five

According to Placidyl

Against the background of this cast of characters, Marty began the pill religion with the amphetamines, or diet pills. I had never been around anyone who took drugs and honestly didn't know what was going on. He was behaving strangely, doing crazy things such as staying up for forty-eight hours or more, and painting the apartment in weird colors. At times he even forgot I was there, which really made me feel good. Thank God he, for some reason, didn't stay on amphetamines too long, because from what I hear they're even worse than the ones he did get hooked on. And hooked he was. Our life became a horror.

Marty became a total stranger to our children and to me. He was so strung out on the Placidyls that when he was home he spent all of his time in the bedroom. There were months on end when he would come home on Friday night, go into the bedroom and not come out until Monday morning. Or he would be with Elvis. When they were on the movie kick they went to the movies every night. I begged him to stay home with me and the children but he would say, "I'm going to the movies, I don't care what you say, I'm going to the movies."

There was no reasoning with him. I'd say, "Look what you're doing to yourself. You're going to kill yourself. Don't you care anything about me or your children? Why don't you stop taking those things?"

Marty's answer was, "You know I love you and the kids.

I know what I'm doing. I'm not going to take anything that'll harm me."

It went on and on for a period of more than ten years. Placidyl was the god that made him feel good. He couldn't walk without staggering, and he fell down more than any human being I've ever seen, but he kept it up until we were so broke he could no longer pay for the pills. Placidyl is a sleeping pill or tranquilizer which, when taken in large quantities, makes the user feel high. The Placidyl was supported by Valmid, Dalmane, Valium, Darvon, Darvocett, Empirin, Codeine No. 3 and other assorted pills.

There were so many pills that one closet shelf was filled with empty bottles which, for some strange reason, Marty saved. He saved the empty bottles until one night when the wife of one of the guys called. She was fed up with the drugs, she had had enough. She told Marty she was calling the authorities and sending them to our house as well as to Graceland and their own place. Marty was so scared he made me take all the empty pill bottles, put them in paper bags and throw the bags out of the car alongside the road. It didn't make Marty stop with the pills, he just quit keeping the empty bottles, and he developed a paranoia about keeping the doors bolted when I was away. He was afraid someone would come to the house. However, she never carried out her threat.

One night I woke to the firing of a gun. Marty was outside the house with his pistol shooting at something. I was sure he would come in and kill himself or all of us, so I grabbed the children, ran to the car and drove around all night. I was too afraid to go back to the house.

I don't know who was taking what or how much, but I wasn't going to be a part of it. My only first-hand experience with the drug culture came one night when we were in California. Elvis brought a plate of brownies out of the kitchen and gave me one. I ate it and shortly began to feel ill so I asked Marty to take me home. In the car Marty started laughing at the way I was acting and told me the brownies had been laced with marijuana. I was furious and wanted to go back and raise hell, but Marty talked me out of it.

After Marty quit working for Elvis he started two separate music businesses in Memphis which failed, at least partly, because of the drugs. There was just no way he could have run a business in his condition. Things were no better at

Graceland. Elvis was making a shambles of his life, Marty was doing the same and I suspect some of the other guys were just as bad off. Marty, however, was my concern. I loved my husband and didn't want to leave him, and I was sure he would be quickly dead if I were not around. I threatened divorce, told him he would never see me or the children again if he didn't stop, threatened to turn them all in to the authorities, and I might as well have been talking to the wall.

The children were completely my responsibility. They had one parent and a man who scarcely spoke to them, and yet they, too, loved him. My daughter often said to me, "You better do something to help daddy. He's going to die."

She once said, "I'd give everything I have, even my guitar, if daddy would just be like other daddys."

I knew something had to be done. The source of the pills was Elvis' great friend and physician, Dr. George Nichopoulos. I absolutely hated what that man had done to my husband under the guise of medicine. My husband was addicted to drugs, our lives were being ruined and Nichopoulos kept the pills coming as fast as Marty wanted them.

I went to Graceland to see Nichopoulos and told him to stop the drugs. I told him I was going to report them all if anything happened to Marty, I begged and threatened, and Dr. Nichopoulos laughed at me. I'm only sorry now that I was too afraid to carry out the threats.

I considered going to Elvis, the only person who had any influence with Marty, but did not because of his frame of mind. Elvis was also taking pills and I was sure he would kick me out of the house, and tell me not to come back. I was afraid that he would also be angry with Marty because of me and that he would stop seeing Marty. Undoubtedly, this would have been the best thing for Marty, but my real fear was that it would cause an irreparable split between Marty and me. I did not have the courage to force upon Marty a choice between Elvis and me, I was afraid I would lose.

There were thousands of pills, and I mean *thousands.* I don't know how many Elvis took a day, or if they led to his death, but I do know that he went downhill just as Marty did. The drugs may or may not have been the direct cause of his death, there seems to be some doubt among the medical authorities, but the pills were ruining his life. He was very overweight, bloated and he slurred his words to such an extent that anyone around him had to know what was going on.

Priscilla told me Elvis' father said to her after the funeral that he didn't know Elvis was on drugs. Her reply to him was that he had to know. We all knew, but failed to do anything about it.

It was a nightmare life that ended for me when we finally ran out of money, and Marty found the strength to kick the pills. It was a living hell when it was going on, and a dying hell when he was trying to quit. There were nights when he was in so much pain, I offered to buy him some of the Placidyls. I couldn't watch him suffer the way he was. Marty was strong enough to say *no* and somehow we got through it alive.

At least we did get through it alive, which was a better fate than Elvis', and for that I am grateful. Not being strong enough to help Elvis is a burden of guilt we'll all have to carry for the rest of our lives. Had he been different and had we been different, our lives could have been full of the joy of love and friendship because we did love him and he loved us. From the first awe of meeting through the resentment of loneliness there was always love. I blame Elvis for starting Marty on the pills just as I blamed him for taking Marty away from me so much. I know Elvis didn't twist his arm, but Elvis didn't know the devotion that Marty and some of the other guys had for him.

Toward the end he seemed to have become completely confused about who cared for him and who didn't. I think all of the guys loved him in their own way. I know Marty did, and Billy did and Sonny and Richard and Red did. I've seen them and lived too close to them, before and after Elvis' death, to believe anything else.

Their love was genuine and I believe Elvis knew it, at least during the better years. They took expensive gifts from him, we all did, and things would probably have been better had none of us taken anything, but Elvis was a giver. He enjoyed giving and we were none rich enough to refuse, but in the end some of us may have been able to help had we not taken so much. If any of us had been able to say we gave more than we received, perhaps we could have generated enough respect in his mind to, at least, have been able to talk with him about how his life was going.

PART THREE

View From the Outside

Leslie S. Smith

Chapter One

Nobody's Diamonds Shine Like Mr. Levitch's

The people who populated the life of Elvis Presley are as diverse as those found at any of his concerts. Some are sharp, some are dull, some are educated, some are ignorant, some are funny and some are sad. All, however, speak of Elvis in tones of love and devotion. He was the one great thing which happened to them, his glory was their glory and his fame their fame. They were the chosen few who were allowed to be a part of his life. They *knew* Elvis Presley.

Harry Levitch is a Memphis jeweler who supplied Elvis with many of the rings and watches which he loved so well. Mr. Levitch radiates refinement, honesty and an affection for Elvis beyond that of merchant for client. Elvis was a friend, the merchandise was of secondary importance. His memories of Elvis go back to the days when the young man was neither wealthy nor famous, and his stories are stories of tenderness and love.

"There was a time," Harry Levitch recalls, "when we were in Las Vegas with Elvis. We had seen one of his performances and were sitting with him as part of a large group of people, including a number of celebrities. Elvis looked over to me and said to the whole group, 'I haven't introduced my friend and jeweler, Mr. Harry Levitch from Memphis. Nobody's diamonds shine like Mr. Levitch's.' "

"He always called me Mr. Levitch. I'd say, 'Elvis, call me Harry,' but he never would. It was always Mr. Levitch.

"Elvis was a beautiful young man. We loved him like a son and suffered when we began to see what was happening to him. I remember when we were last at Graceland. My wife and I stayed only a few minutes because we could tell Elvis didn't want us to see him in that condition. Afterward, Frances and I talked about Elvis and worried about what we could do to help. One day, another of Elvis' friends, Paul Shafer, came to the store. Paul was vice-president of Malco Theater Corporation and arranged the private movie showings for Elvis.

"Paul said to me, 'Harry, I'm worried about Elvis. We've got to do something to help. We're older than he is and I think he's always thought of both of us in a fatherly way. Maybe if we went to Graceland and talked to him we could get him into Mayo clinic and off the stuff he's taking, and get him away from the people who are giving it to him.'

" 'I'm worried too, Paul,' I told him, 'and I'll go with you, but we probably should see if Vernon would be there with us. He's Elvis' father and maybe the three of us could make him see what's happening.'

"Paul said he would call Vernon and get back to me. A few days later Paul did call. He told me he had talked with Vernon, but Vernon told him he didn't want to get involved."

Frances Levitch loved Elvis in much the same way her husband did. She speaks of Elvis as she would probably speak of a lost son. She talks about how polite he was, and how happy he always seemed when they were together.

" 'Elvis," she once said, when he was looking for a new ring, "you try this one on, it's right for you.

"He laughed and said, 'I don't know if I like that one or not, Mrs. Levitch.'

"Elvis, now you listen to me. That's the ring for you," I told him, and sure enough he bought the one I liked best. He was such a sweet, young man you couldn't help loving him.

"I'm not a great cook, Harry will tell you that if I'm not around, but I do make good cheesecake. Once I made one especially for Elvis and carried it to Graceland. When I gave it to him Joe Esposito was there. He said something about Elvis being on a diet and not eating cheesecake, but Elvis just laughed and ate two big pieces while I was sitting there talking with him. He seemed to enjoy it so much that, diet or not, I'm glad I made it for him."

Richard Davis is a young-looking, middle-aged man who still seems to live the happy-go-lucky life of the years with Elvis. He laughs about the happy days of the past, jokes with pretty girls and pokes fun at those around him, but he also conveys a sadness which reflects his deeper feelings about his friend.

A likable man, Richard talks easily of the good times and the bad. He remembers the gifts, the friendship and the love and he tries to share his memories with those about him.

"Vernon was some old dude," Richard says. "I remember the time he fired me. I'd been hurt while working with Elvis. I had pinched a nerve in my neck which was so uncomfortable I had to have an operation. When I got out of the hospital the doctors told me to take it easy for a couple of months or I'd be right back in. Well, of course, I didn't pay too much attention and went back to work. But they were right. It bothered me so much I had to lie down every few minutes just to get through the day.

"Elvis saw the pain I was in and told me to take a few weeks off, and rest up, until I was well. We were in California and Elvis and the guys were getting ready to come back to Memphis. I stayed in California and began to feel better after a few days rest. I was looking forward to getting back to Memphis, but the first paycheck I received from Vernon, after Elvis left, included a pink slip, he had fired me.

"Elvis and I were the two crooks in the group. At least, that's what the other guys used to say to say about us. We could get into anyplace, anytime. Once when we were in California, Elvis wanted to see a house which he was thinking of leasing. I forget now exactly what happened, but I think we called the real estate agent and he was out.

"Elvis drove up to the house anyway, and when we arrived we tried all the doors to see if we could get in, but they were locked of course. Elvis wanted to see the inside again so I jimmied the lock on a sliding glass door in the back. The minute I slid the door back I saw the tripper for the alarm system and grabbed it.

"I thought I had kept it from going off and we all went

inside to look over the house. Elvis was upstairs when I knew we had been caught. There were police cars in front when I looked out the window, and the doorbell began ringing.

"I went to the door and smiled at the policeman who obviously thought I was a burglar who was going to try to talk his way out of a tight spot. He asked who I was and what I was doing there. I told him Elvis wanted to see the house again and when we couldn't reach the real estate agent we decided to have a look on our own. The back door, I told him, was unlocked so we came on in.

"He didn't believe me for a minute and kept his hand resting on the gun he was wearing. His partners were backing him to the hilt and ready for me to make a break. 'Okay,' he said, 'if Elvis is here, where is he?'

" 'He's upstairs,' I told the policeman.

"He looked at me and said, 'Then you better call him down here so we can see him.'

"I called Elvis and after what seemed like forever he came down. The policemen were relieved, I was relieved and all of us had a good laugh over it. Elvis, of course, charmed them completely. He could have talked them out of their guns and badges if he had wanted to.

"Sure, I was part of the drug scene. Day in and day out there were pills. They were a part of our way of life, easy to get and easy to take.

"But the important things to remember are the good things. We loved Elvis and he loved us. We may all have been a little strange, and done things which hurt us, but the important part, the part which people should know and understand, is also the part which is easy to overlook when we're talking about the drugs. Elvis was a beautiful man. He did more for people than anyone will ever know. Not just us, the guys, but people he didn't even know. He was a generous, beautiful man."

George Klein refuses to discuss Elvis with anyone who is connected with the publishing media. It's impossible to blame him. So much is taken and twisted and contorted to make it sensational for the weekly newspapers that it's a wonder sometimes why anyone is willing to talk with anyone else. George is polite on the telephone, but firm in his resolve not to talk. His feeling seems to be that he will be disloyal to Elvis by discussing their life together. An offer to include *whatever* he wants to say falls on deaf ears. His world with Elvis is not to be shared.

Elvis was George's friend. He did much for George, and, in his own way, George is now repaying that debt. Reason may say that there is a lot for all of us to learn from the life of Elvis Presley; but for George Klein loyalty dictates silence, and even though I don't agree with his thinking, I have to respect his feelings. Since then George has entered into an agreement to write the script for the new movie about Elvis, "King of Rock 'n' Roll."

Billy Smith, Elvis' cousin and constant companion for years, now works for the railroad.

Billy, a short man with blonde hair, has been described by some of the guys as being a good athlete and very fast on his feet. He is a down-home type of guy who avoids the flash of some of the others who were a part of Elvis' life.

Billy has said to Marty that some of the guys would be shocked if they really knew how Elvis felt about them. A statement which prompted Marty so say, "Deep down inside, I sometimes wonder if he ever really liked any of us."

When Marty became foreman of the group of guys Elvis told him, "Leave Billy to me."

Elvis was protective of Billy, perhaps because Billy was a relative, or perhaps because he was the youngest member of the group, a situation which annoyed Billy from time to time and possibly made him more independent than he would otherwise have been.

Billy speaks freely of Elvis to the fans who come to view the collection of memorabilia which Billy owns. He is, however, cautious about what he says for publication and warns that there may be subjects he will not discuss. When asked about Elvis' death, Billy said, "I'm satisfied with the medical reports I read. I have to believe them. I'm not a doctor, I don't know what caused Elvis' death so I have to believe what the doctors say. The only drugs I know about were those prescribed for Elvis by his doctor.

"I don't believe Elvis was going to marry Ginger, at least not in the foreseeable future, but I also don't blame her for saying they were going to marry. I think it's natural for her to say what she has said.

"Yes, Elvis told me many times I was in his will, but I can honestly tell you neither my wife nor I wanted anything from him except the memories we have. If anyone changed the will, or led Elvis to believe there were things in it which were not there, then they have to live with themselves. We didn't want it, but I also don't believe Elvis would have told us we were in the will if he hadn't believed we were.

"We had him for a lot of years and that's what I want to remember, the years together and how much he loved us."

Jerry Schilling, eight years younger than Elvis Presley, is obviously a fan as well as having been a close friend and associate of the late entertainer. Jerry is certainly the best-looking, and probably the best-educated member of the Presley entourage. His easy-going, friendly and relaxed manner seem a part of his pleasantly casual Hollywood Hills bachelor home. Jerry, who now manages the Beach Boys as well as the Sweet Inspirations, a group which worked with Elvis for many years, speaks freely of his feelings and thoughts about his life with his friend.

When I commented about the spectacular view from his home, Jerry quickly said, "Elvis bought this house for me."

Jerry has the reputation among the other guys as being the most outspoken of the group. His comparatively liberal attitudes were the basis of many arguments with Elvis and, according to the other guys, Jerry never hesitated to express his opinion, or to tell Elvis he was wrong. This was a quality not shared by too many of the guys who generally seem to have preferred peace and security to forthrightness.

When asked about the use of drugs, Jerry expressed the view that enough has been written and said about them. He feels they have been blown out of all proper perspective and deserve no further comments. Jerry says Red, Sonny and Dave "exaggerated and took things completely out of context," in their book, *Elvis: What Happened.*

"What did Elvis think about the book?" I asked.

"He told me," Jerry said, "that everything that could be written about him had already been written anyway, at one time or another, so it didn't upset him that much personally.

What really bothered him was that this one came from inside, from friends. That hurt him personally, it hurt his pride. It came from people he had been good to, and he had been good to all of us. To have something like that done by his friends hurt him. Also, he thought a lot of other people could be hurt. He said, 'I've got a seven-year-old daughter, who I think about. There's my father and the people who have worked with me and been friends and helped me, who could be hurt by a book like this.'

"Then I think it was extremely embarrassing for him, extremely," Schilling continued. "In the conversation I had with Sonny West after they had begun the book, Sonny told me, 'Well, maybe this will shake him up.'

"I said, 'Sonny, you're writing the book because you're writing the book. You want to make some money.'

" 'Yes, I do,' he told me.

" 'If you think this book is going to shake him up, you're wrong. As insensitive as you're saying Elvis is, you know he's really that sensitive. You're telling me one thing you think this book could do, I'm telling you I think it could do the other.'

"It's easy for me to say this now," Schilling continued, "but I also said it before the fact when I talked with Sonny on the phone while Elvis was still alive, and before the book was put out."

"Do you know if Elvis read the book?" I asked.

"No, that's always been a puzzle. I know he was aware of certain things in the book but I don't honestly know if he read it. I don't know if anybody does know."

"Billy Smith says no."

"I don't think he did. Knowing Elvis and his career, and how many movies he wouldn't see of himself, I wouldn't think he had. It wasn't his type of thing, that there was a book coming out and he would tell somebody to get it. But he did know of most of the things that were going to be in the book."

"How long, prior to his death, had it been since you had talked to him or seen him?"

"The conversation I'm talking about was when the book was just finished, and of course it was about a year before it came out. Elvis never believed it was coming out. I don't know if it was John O'Grady who told him that or not but he always thought, he told me many times he was very confident when he said, 'The book's not going to come out.'

"He dropped it for a long time during the period when they were writing it. When we heard that it was going to come out I told him, 'Elvis, I ran across a lawyer in Beverly Hills who's working on this thing, and the book is going to come out.' He didn't want to believe they would do it, but when he realized it was going to come out he was really angry. I don't know if it was John O'Grady or someone else who made him think there was going to be some kind of compromise."

"Other than the apparent attempt by O'Grady to talk to Red and Sonny to try to convince them not to release the book, Elvis never made any effort, that you know of, to stop it, in the sense of calling Sonny or Red?"

"Yes, he called Red."

"I know he called Red the one time, but according to the book he said to go ahead with whatever they were doing."

"Well, that was after he thought he could not convince them to hold up on the book. Elvis was never the type of person to ask somebody to do something they didn't want to do. The mere fact that he was calling Red was, if you knew Elvis and I'm sure Red knew, to say, 'Hey, this has gone on too long,' but he was not going to come out and say, 'Red, please don't write this book.'

"He would have been lowering himself. But the mere fact that he called and talked to Red, Elvis apologized in that way. He apologized by telling you something else, or taking you on a trip or whatever, but you knew it was because you had an argument the night before, and he felt bad about it. It could have been your fault as well as his. He couldn't stand anger or arguments. He was so sensitive he couldn't stand to have bad feelings going on. The maddest I've ever seen Elvis was when the guys would get into an argument, or look like they were going to fight. One time Marty and Red had an argument over the slot cars and Elvis got so mad he looked like a wild panther. He couldn't stand for the guys to argue.

"It was a brand new slot car track. It had just been hooked up and we had sat down to use it for the first time. The room was built for that, it wasn't built as a trophy room.

Elvis took the control and smashed it down on the track. He split the track open. He couldn't stand it, he wouldn't have arguments in his house."

"Why do you feel that Sonny, Dave and Red were actually fired?"

"I think there were probably several different reasons that happened all at the same time. I don't know exactly why, but I do know a couple of things which Elvis told me, he said they just grew apart. He said they didn't have anything in common anymore, and I think that was a big part of it. The other part of it was the lawsuits. I think Elvis was also getting tired of the over-protection, even though there were times when he certainly needed it.

"The firings happened at a time when we hadn't worked for two or three months so you have a lot of protection and no reason for it. The next month when he went out on tour he would need it. Maybe I should just leave it at that, there are a lot of details but basically it was because they grew apart, and because of the lawsuits. I don't know, everybody keyed on Elvis' life so much, especially those who worked for him."

"I've heard it said that the guys, and I guess this includes you, were hangers-on."

"I'm not sensitive about it," Schilling answered.

"You split away, and went out and did your own thing."

"For periods of time, but I always came back. That was my thing. In fact I was talking to Lamar once and said, 'Let's face it. Elvis is a big part of our lives and always will be.' "

"I guess what I'm asking is, was there a genuine feeling or was Elvis a security blanket?"

"How I felt about it personally, I had a lot of admiration for Elvis, even from his image before I ever knew him and I gained more from knowing him personally. There is a lot of time for boredom in jobs like we had, a lot of time when you had to have an inner strength to cope with that type of life. You say to yourself, 'I'm leading this type of life, it's all I know, what will I do if I am fired?'

"You have a great amount of insecurity. I knew Elvis prior to going to work for him, and I had known some of the guys who worked for him before me. Some people worked for him because it was a job and some people were there because of their liking for Elvis. I think almost everybody started working for Elvis because of a friendship type of feeling.

"All of the original people mostly came to work because of friendship. It wasn't a situation where Elvis said, 'Okay, I need an accountant and a security man.'

"Everybody was kind of multi-functional. I sort of helped with security when I first started working for Elvis when I was twenty-one years old. I stood-in for him in the movies for a few years. I worked as a personal aide, I got into the editing of his films and then I was personal public relations for the last five years. That was the job he offered me when we went to Washington to meet the President. I went with him on that trip.

"I was working on a film at the time and I was just doing the weekends with him, he decided he wanted me to work for him full time again. He offered me a job but I never accepted it. It was really funny, we talked about it and I told him how I felt about it. I told him I couldn't sit around with all that time off in Memphis because I'd go crazy until time for a movie. I said, 'How do you think I feel, we'd come back to Memphis and I sit there for three months and we go to the movies all night.'

"He was so great he just said, 'How do you think I feel, I do the same thing.'

"I said, 'But Elvis, it's different. You're doing it by your choice, you've gone out and set records around the world, and this is your way to relax. This is my job. It's different when we're working doing things.'

"So he said, 'You don't have to come back to Memphis. Come back part of the time. Stay out in California.'

"He asked me what I needed financially. We talked about everything but never made a decision. About two weeks later he sent me some cards that said *Jerry Schilling, Personal Public Relations to Elvis Presley* and pay checks started coming in so I was hired back. I thought of the situation with all the guys around, I made a little secret agreement with myself, and this really was the reason I left a couple of times. I said, 'The day that the work becomes a job, I'll quit because I don't want it to ever interfere with this friendship.' The job was a work-friendship situation, there's no way it could be just one or the other. Not only did we work together, we lived together. I think that the group who worked with Elvis was set up, not consciously, but it was set up out of necessity so that Elvis could live the type of life he needed to live, and wanted to live, and I think this group provided him with that."

"Why do you suppose Elvis sort of created his own community and never really did anything, as you say, the big thing was to go to the movies? He paid the people that he wanted to be around, to be around him. To me it's almost unreal."

"First of all, the people around him, overall, were sort of a special breed of people. I think basically, the group was a reflection of Elvis. Here's a guy who was a well-known big entertainer who was a nice guy. Also, he was pretty sharp, no dummy could have entranced the world like this man did. If you didn't know Elvis, you could think he was an average guy, but this man was so sensitive, so quick and so deep that I really feel like he had to go to the movies, and the amusement park, just to get thoughts off his mind. We knew that, we did childish things when we were grown men. It was a way for release. Elvis came out of pure poverty. I'll always remember the first night they were playing a record of his over the radio in Memphis, he tried to borrow money that night or had borrowed money that night, to get into the movies. So here's a guy that can rent his own theater and invite all his friends, he loved it. He wasn't a guy who would go to a gourmet restaurant, but the movies were a big thing to him, and that became his way of life. And during the first part, he couldn't do anything else, he couldn't go anywhere in those first years. So what began out of necessity, became life. It was like you going to a good restaurant with friends, this was his way of enjoying himself.

"He was pretty close to Memphis, and to the people and a lot of the simple things in life. I used to say, 'Jesus Christ, let's go to Europe,' and one time we planned to go to Europe for a vacation.

"We got all set and Elvis wanted to go. He told me he was going to go this time. He said, 'I guarantee you we're going to go.'

"The Colonel had a meeting with him and said if you go to Europe on vacation you're going to insult the fans, and there was some truth to it. The Colonel said you've got to at least have a press conference in each country you go to. Elvis wanted a vacation so we wound up going to the Bahamas, which was nice but it wasn't Europe. But, you ask why he didn't do a lot of things that people in his position would have done, that's a perfect example. There was always somebody to throw a wrench into the works."

"What are your feelings about the will? Particularly in relation to Billy, why wasn't he in the will?"

"First of all, I'm surprised that Elvis made a will, that one was made. Even though it's like the world knew that this man was going to die young, but Elvis wasn't thinking of dying, why would he think he would be leaving something to his peers? I think this is a very big point. I remember a relative one time came to him, this was about ten years ago, and this relative had had an argument with her husband. She said, 'Elvis, don't you leave him anything, I just want what's mine.'

"Elvis came to see me and said, 'What's she talking about leaving him anything?'

"It really made him think, the relative was at least twenty years older than Elvis. It seems the world thought of Elvis as almost destined to die young. I've heard this brought up about a few of the guys. I personally think it's bullshit. That's like I'm leaving my money to Joe, or Charlie, or to Marty. Why should Elvis be leaving anything to me or Billy? Looking at it as history now it makes sense, but in actuality, put it in a real-life situation, it doesn't make a bit of sense. Not at all."

"Do you think things would have been different with Sonny, Dave and Red had their firing been handled somewhat differently?"

"Yes, I think the dismissal was not handled right. I understand their being upset, I understand their anger and I agree. That would have been a situation had Elvis ever asked me about it where we would have disagreed. I would have probably said, 'Elvis, you could at least have talked to the guys and said things are not working right now, you should have said here's two weeks, here's a month or, six months pay and told them to go out and get something else.'

"I don't mind the guys being upset, it was handled totally wrong, but at the same time, if you knew the nature of Elvis, he sensitively could not handle it. He couldn't look at them and say, 'Hey guys, you're fired.'

"At the same time, I'm thoroughly convinced that at least one and probably two, and possibly three of them would be working for him today."

"You feel he would have asked them to come back?"

"Oh sure, but it was handled wrong and my feeling is that they could have complained, did whatever they wanted to, but I still don't think it gave them the right to go to a publisher and to degrade the man's image."

"Is there anything that you would like to add?"

"I talked about being a kid, looking up to him and all and then becoming, so to speak, a peer. In friendship he just became another guy, but a very special friend, you could always depend on him. At the same time, he was a very special man, but he was also a human being and like any human being he might do something wrong. Judge the man by what he did. He was a man who made a lot of people in the world happy, he brought a lot of joy to the world and gave the world a lot of freedom. He dared to be different. Here also was a man who never really hurt anybody. He did a lot of good and if he hurt anybody, he hurt himself, and that wasn't intentional. But I think he had a right to do that. I think the world lost a lot of magic when Elvis died, and I know it will never be the same for me."

Chapter Two

The Authorities

Jerry Francisco is the Shelby County Medical Examiner. Dr. Francisco, a highly respected member of his community, released, on October 21, 1977, the following report concerning the death of Elvis Presley:

The investigation of the death of Elvis Presley by the Office of the Shelby County Medical Examiner has been completed. The death certificate has been signed and filed with the Memphis and Shelby County Health Department. The cause of death has been ascribed to Hypertensive Heart Disease with Coronary Artery Heart Disease as a contributing factor.

The autopsy report from the Pathology Department of Baptist Memorial Hospital, which includes the toxicology results, was completed October 18, 1977 and has been reviewed.

All of the findings have been discussed by the staff of the Section of Forensic Pathology at the University of Tennessee Center for the Health Sciences. This includes 3 Forensic Pathologists and 1 Toxicologist. The toxicology findings have also been discussed with 2 other Toxicologists in the United States. It is the considered opinion of all the Forensic Pathologists and 2 of the 3 Toxicologists that there is no evidence the medication present in the body of Elvis Presley caused or made any significant contribution to his death. The third Toxicologist was of the opinion that all medications were in the therapeutic range and individually did not represent an overdose. All the Toxicologists agreed that the decision of whether those medications played any role in death causation should be left to the Forensic Pathologist.

All of the medications present had been prescribed by his doctors. There was an extensive search for illicit drugs and they were not found to be present.

The report of Medical Investigation has been completed and will be filed in the Office of the Chief Medical Examiner at 858 Madison Avenue, Memphis, Tennessee 38163. According to TCA 38-710 this report is a public document and can be obtained from the above office. The report of Medical Investigation contains no significant information that is not contained in this press release. The autopsy was not ordered by the District Attorney General and thus is not a part of the file of the Medical Examiner. The autopsy results and opinions were considered in arriving at the conclusions contained within the Report of Medical Investigation and the Death Certificate.

Signed/J.T. Francisco, M.D.
Shelby County Medical Examiner
Professor of Pathology—UTCHS

Signed/J.S. Bell, M.D.
Chief Deputy Shelby County Medical Examiner
Associate Professor of Pathology—UTCHS

Signed/D.T. Stafford, Ph.D.
Toxicologist—Shelby County Medical Examiner Office
Assistant Professor of Pathology—UTCHS

Signed/C.W. Harlan, M.D.
Deputy Shelby County Medical Examiner
Instructor of Pathology—UTCHS

A certified copy of the report of Medical Investigation, referred to in the above press release, does not reveal any significant information not included in the release. If anything, the information contained on the single sheet is notable for its scantiness. Most of the printed questions such as body weight and temperature are not completed, as one would expect them to be on a report of investigation of death. A consent of autopsy was signed by the family and the autopsy was performed at Baptist Memorial Hospital.

Dr. Francisco is an impressive man. He makes a visitor feel comfortable and confident he is hearing the absolute truth. There is no question about the doctor's ability or sincerity, he is a pillar of the Memphis medical profession.

"Doctor," I said, "I'm having some trouble with the conflicting reports. I understand the autopsy is a private document and I'm not asking you to reveal anything which may be a part of it, but your press release has stated that drugs were not the cause of death, and, in fact, there were no drugs present other than those prescribed by Elvis' physician, and those were in therapeutic levels."

"That is correct. We found no heavy, or illegal drugs."

"I've talked with friends of Elvis' who have said there were drugs, including cocaine.

"The former bodyguards said in their book that drugs were a major part of Elvis' life. The conflict doesn't make sense. I could understand the bodyguards making it up for revenge or to sell books, but to my knowledge the other people have absolutely no reason to lie. None are saying, 'I was the hero, I tried to get him off the drugs, I tried to save him.'

"As a matter of fact, they say just the opposite. What I'm trying to convey is that these people have nothing to gain by lying. My question, then, is how do you reconcile their statements in the light of your findings?"

"I can't reconcile them," Dr. Francisco replied, "I suppose you have to consider the credibility of the witnesses. I know of a case where six prominent citizens said they saw a man shot in the back. They were prepared to go on the witness stand and swear they were telling the truth, but the autopsy proved the man was shot in the chest. People sometimes see what they want to see, or honestly are mistaken in their beliefs."

"Doctor," I said, "there is no way these people could be honestly mistaken. It's just not possible. There are too many saying the same thing. Now, are you telling me that Elvis was not using any drugs other than those which you said were present? Are you saying there is absolutely no question about that fact?"

"No, no," Dr. Francisco answered. "That's not what I'm saying, nor have I ever said that. What I said, and am saying now, is that we found no evidence of drugs beyond those reported. I have no way of knowing what Elvis Presley did. I'm only saying that, in my opinion, diet was a lot more likely a cause of death than drugs. I found no evidence of drug abuse. Let me explain that a little more. If someone were using hard drugs by injecting them there would be evidence in the body of those drugs. The drug itself would be assimilated into the blood but the filler used with the drug would pass on to the lungs and be there when the autopsy was performed. If cocaine were taken to any extent by sniffing, then the nostrils would become ulcerated and that would be easy to see. There are hundreds of types of drugs, some are easy to find, some are difficult, if not impossible, unless they have been taken shortly before death. All I'm saying is I found no evidence of drugs beyond those we reported finding."

Maurice Elliott is vice-president of Baptist Memorial Hospital in Memphis, Tennessee. He is a good-looking young man who seems well-qualified to do his job as official spokesman for the hospital.

"Mr. Elliott," I said, "do you mind if I record what we say?"

"After what happened with the *National Enquirer*, I'd just as soon have somebody record the conversation."

"That's the first thing I was going to ask you. Is there any truth at all in the *Enquirer*'s reported interview?"

"No, there is no truth to the article that was in the *National Enquirer*," Elliott replied. "It was very embarrassing to us. We talked to them and that was our mistake, because they totally misconstrued or took out of context what was said, and it was not an accurate portrayal of what we talked about to them at all."

"They generally do. I'm surprised they even bothered to talk to you before they wrote the account of the interview."

"Well, live and learn. Next time we'll know better."

"Does that hold true also for some of the accounts that have been in the newspapers, even Memphis papers?"

"If you're talking about the Memphis papers," Elliott said, "shortly after Elvis' death they, particularly the *Com-*

mercial Appeal, had a rather detailed account of what was found and so forth. They had a source somewhere. They never attributed it to anyone. If you go back and look, you'll see they never said a Baptist Hospital source. We suspect that the information did not come from Baptist Hospital, and we suspect that because we were so very careful to make sure the information wasn't available to anyone.

"I'll tell you my speculation, we let the Medical Examiner's office have a copy of the autopsy report for their review, and when we did that we particularly asked them not to make a copy and they agreed not to. Then they returned it to us. Well, it was shortly after the Medical Examiner's news conference, where he attributed the death to heart disease and mentioned there were a certain number of prescribed drugs found in the blood stream, that this started to come out in the paper. I have no basis other than my own speculation to believe this, but I think somewhere in his office is the source the newspapers were using for their articles, and again, I really can't comment on the accuracy of the articles one way or the other. We never confirmed, or for that matter denied, the findings of the Medical Examiner. From his news release, from that point on, it was primarily speculation."

"Is there any truth to the disagreement, or supposed disagreement, between Dr. Muirhead or other doctors at Baptist Memorial and the Medical Examiner?"

"I guess the assumption that is somewhat obvious is that if we did not confirm it there's some disagreement, and I guess that's what has led to a lot of speculation. There was no disagreement on our part that the drugs found were prescribed. I don't think there's any question that hard drugs were not involved, or not found during the autopsy. We did not discuss their findings before they had their news conference. Well, we discussed it before they had their news conference but we didn't discuss it before they released the information.

"There is," Elliott continued, "I think, room for professional people to differ on results in a case like this. What I'm saying is, in Elvis' case an attempt was made, after the fact, to determine the cause of death. There really, and I think the Medical Examiner would agree with this, there really was nothing found that a person could point to and say this was absolutely the cause of death, that it was a stroke, that it was a coronary or what. So taking the same facts that were found there is some difference, there is room for a difference of medical opinion and I think that's what has created the continued speculation."

"Did Dr. Francisco actually view the body?"

"Yes, Dr. Francisco was here as a consultant to us. He was called in and I'm quite sure he was present during the autopsy. Of course, the gross autopsy doesn't tell you that much. Being present is not that important, other than confirming things from visual observation, such as the presence or absence of needle tracks in the arm. The critical information comes from the chemical and toxocological studies, the microscopic studies which take some time.

"I think," Elliott continued, "again not based on what our pathology department found, but based on speculation on what Dr. Francisco said, there was some coronary artery disease. Now that doesn't mean there was a heart attack. We could determine that, so the question is was there enough coronary artery disease to cause death, and that is a very subjective thing. You can have different doctors look at the same results and come to different conclusions. The other thing, obviously, he said there were ten medications in Elvis' blood stream, I think most of them were sedatives. Okay, assuming that they were prescribed and within prescribed levels then the other subjective thing is, taken in total were they enough to suppress his nervous system to the extent to cause death. I don't know that an answer will ever be found, or definitely agreed upon between those two possibilities. Now it was the Medical Examiner's opinion that the coronary artery disease was enough advanced to explain death."

"You're not expressing an opinion?"

"No, I'm just saying that based on his news release those are two obvious possibilities in the medical community. Any medical doctor you talk to who reviewed the Medical Examiner's news release will, I think, agree those would be the possibilities."

"Are you totally satisfied that there was no violation of any existing federal or state law concerning the abuse of drugs? You can say with a clear conscience that nothing further should be done on this?"

"Yes, and I say that for this reason. We turned over our detailed toxicological studies to Dr. Francisco. We had one of the best labs in the country do these studies. Dr. Francisco independently did toxicological studies so he had his own to compare. Neither one indicated any non-prescribed drug use and the reason we turned the autopsy report over to the Medical Examiner to review was to specifically tell us whether this was a coroner's case. You see, if it was a coroner's case, if he found that there was reason to think that there were drugs involved, then it would be turned over to him, the records would be public information and there would be no question about it."

"Now you're speaking only of illicit drugs?"

"Right."

"Speculating, and I'm not asking you to divulge any secrets or anything that might not be ethical for you to talk about, but if I take two aspirin and two Bufferin as an example, you might say that I've taken the proper number of aspirin and the proper number of Bufferin."

"Together they might cause a problem for you," Elliott interjected.

"Were that the case are we not getting into the realm where we're dealing with something that is illegal?"

"No, there's no federal statute, or as I understand it, there's no law involved. For instance, if some doctor prescribes a sleeping pill for you and they say take one every three hours and you take one every two hours, that may not be wise and it may cause you problems but there's not necessarily, as far as I know, any law being broken."

"If in fact," I asked further, "the doctor said take two aspirin every hour and take two Bufferin every hour, just using those as an example again, would you now be involved in a situation where there may be a federal or state law involved?"

"I don't know, I'm not really a good person to speak about this. I can say I don't know if there would be a law involved, but there would possibly be grounds for a malpractice suit and review by the state licensing authority. You know, as to how that doctor is practicing medicine. If a doctor prescribes drugs out of keeping with a patient's condition or to where they would be harmful to the patient, then obviously it gets into the question of malpractice and the fellow's competency to practice medicine. Let me add, I don't know that all these medications were prescribed by one doctor. I do know that was reviewed and the people reviewing it seemed satisfied that there was nothing out of sorts about what occurred."

"I understand that Dr. Muirhead has been advised not to say anything."

"Well, I guess you could say that. We met with him and we asked our hospital attorney what legally are we required to give out or what should remain confidential, and we decided it would be best if I act as spokesman for the press rather than to get a bunch of people involved. From that standpoint, he has been advised not to say anything."

"A statement that has been attributed to you, did you once say that you wish you could release the autopsy and settle the whole thing once and for all?"

"Yes, I think I probably did because what I was trying to convey was that it's not the hospital's desire to suppress the information, but we're required by law to maintain the confidentiality of any patient and the fact that it was Elvis doesn't change that. It's up to Vernon Presley. He's got a copy of it, it's not for us to speak for him. That's all I was saying, if it was up to us, I'd give it to you in a minute. I have no desire to maintain the confidentiality of it, other than conforming with the law."

"Can you tell me what other doctors were called in when Elvis was in the hospital prior to his death? Or is that confidential information?"

"You mean when he was in here on prior occasions?"

"Yes."

"Of course Dr. Nichopoulos was his attending physician and Dr. David Meyer, the eye specialist, was in."

"Was the drug abuse specialist, Dr. David Knott, in attendance?"

"I just don't know whether he was or not. It's possible he was, but I just don't know for sure."

"Is Dr. Nichopoulos associated with the hospital?"

"Yes, he's on our staff."

"Are you still being bothered often with questions like these?"

"Not really. On the occasion of the anniversary of Elvis' death, we had a number of calls but other than that it has pretty well subsided."

"Is there anything else you can tell us?"

"Well, I can tell you basically what occurred at the time of his death. I don't know if that's of any interest to you. His medical record, I can say, we've got in a safe-deposit box at the bank and it's sort of a hot potato now. We don't really know exactly what to do with it. We hate the idea of having to keep it in a safe-deposit box forever but we don't see any other possibility.

"We had the *Rolling Stones* magazine call a few weeks ago. They had somebody they said had a copy of the autopsy report who wanted to sell it to them for something like ninety thousand dollars. And the thing that surprised me was they sounded like they were willing to buy it, if we could confirm that it was a real one. There were a number of offers made shortly after Elvis' death to try to get a copy of the autopsy report.

"I first met Elvis here at the hospital when he came in at the time his wife was having their baby, and then he was in several times after that of course. I really admired the fellow and the people with him, the Memphis Mafia. He was a very polite, undemanding, down-to-earth type person, especially when you consider the sort of fame that he garnered. We were overwhelmed when he first came in, we just got calls from all over the world, and everytime he came in it was just unbelievable the interest people had in him. I mean all night long there were calls from Wales, London, South America, Canada, all around the world.

"We've had others, not of his stature in terms of fame, but others in the entertainment business, and some of them can be rather hard to take, but he was always very much a gentleman. For that reason people did develop a real fondness for him. Whenever he was in here there was always all sorts of speculation. It was hard on the hospital from the standpoint that Elvis had no one to speak to the press. We had to sort of act as the intermediary and we really could never say anything. I don't think we ever really gave Elvis' diagnosis when he was here, it was always he was here to recuperate or for a rest or something like that, and you know the kind of questions you get from the press on that. There was always speculation that he was dying or dead, and it seemed so ridiculous, he was such a young fellow and robust.

"Around three o'clock, the day of his death, I got a call

from our emergency room supervisor and she said, 'We're Harvey-teaming Elvis and it doesn't look good.' Those were her exact words."

"What's Harvey-teaming?"

"Harvey-teaming, that's our emergency resuscitation team and, well, it shocked me no end to get that from her, because that was just the most remote thing I could think of. I went down there immediately and into the room where they were working on him. It appeared to me right away that he was dead.

"His face was blue and, after you've seen a few people in that condition it's kind of obvious. But I think Dr. Nichopoulos felt there might be some reason to believe he could be resuscitated, I think he said his eyes weren't totally dilated or something. He was obviously making every effort. About half a dozen of Elvis' associates were in the room next door, Charlie Hodge, Joe Esposito, Al Strada, Dick Grob and one or two other fellows, and I believe his cousin Billy Smith was there.

"In about thirty minutes, Dr. Nick came through the door and he said, 'It's all over, he's gone.' And after he said that he just started crying.

"He put his head in his hands and tears started rolling down his cheeks, and everybody else in the room started crying. I remember Charlie Hodge was going to go out in the hall but Joe Esposito stopped him and said, 'No, don't go out there like that.'

"He wanted him to be composed first. So they waited awhile and then Joe came up to my office to make some calls. I think the first person he called was Colonel Parker. He was concerned about a date they had set up. Dr. Nick was going to go back to Graceland to tell Vernon, to confirm it, and to get an autopsy release. He didn't want us to announce the death to the press until he called us after he had talked to Vernon. We waited for about thirty minutes, and again, that was very difficult because the word had already gotten out. Dr. Nick called back in about thirty minutes, and Joe said he was ready, so we came back to the library to tell the press. Joe and Charlie Hodge were there and there were cameras and microphones all over the place. I left them there and then Charlie came and got me and wanted me to be there, he said, with them. I thought he was just being polite and after they fiddled around a bit, I moved off again but Charlie came and got me. The cameramen said they were ready so I told Joe to make the announcement. He stood up and started to talk, but he got choked up and said, 'I can't do it, you go ahead and do it.'

"I hadn't given any thought to the situation and here were all those cameras, and television, and all of a sudden without giving any thought I realized I was going to have to announce to the world that Elvis had died."

Chapter Three

Take A Lesson

Dave Hebler is an intelligent man who looks more like a banker than a bodyguard and karate expert. Hebler lives in a pleasant southern California community where he conducts seminars on personal self-defense and spends much of his free time writing. He conveys a certain amount of anger toward those who knew Elvis and who deny the reports of drug abuse and strange behavior.

"Did Steve Dunleavy, the writer who worked with you on *Elvis, What Happened,* work for the *National Star?*" I asked.

"Yes," Hebler replied, "he was a staff writer for the *Star.*"

"Are the facts in the book true?"

"Not only are they true, we can document every damn bit of it."

"Are they exaggerated?"

"If anything they're underplayed. As a matter of fact, to go on with that, we deliberately watered down a tremendous portion of the book so that the names of innocent people, or people we didn't think deserved being slammed, would be concealed. If you notice in the book we don't name people. We talk about incidents and in those areas where we have to give a name we give a fake name."

"I made up a list of questions concerning some of those events and names. One that comes to mind right now is the

Fetchum Bill Story. Marty said he doesn't know who it was about."

"Marty knows. Actually that guy, Fetchum Bill, is kind of a pitiful guy. He's not too bright, and we didn't want to put him in the light that would subject him to ridicule, so we tried to disguise his identity as much as possible without losing the essence of the thing. Funny dude, which is why we put him in the book. He was hilarious."

"Some of the other things may not be as innocent. I remember, for instance, there was a comment about a doctor in Palm Springs."

"Oh God, they were all over, doctors everywhere. All I can tell you is that of all the doctors and medical people Elvis was involved with, that I have knowledge of, the only one who was worth a damn, who cared, and tried to do something for Elvis, the right thing for Elvis, is George Nichopoulos. Doctor Nick is the only doctor who didn't give Elvis crap."

"Did you, Red or Sonny have anything to say about the book after it was finished as far as the editing of the content was concerned?"

"Yeah."

"So the final edition met with your approval?"

"Yes. Right, as a matter of fact, I think there was only one mistake in the book which we didn't catch. That was the date when something happened during one of Elvis' films."

"Tell me about the drugs for a second."

"Okay."

"What kind, how many and how often? The thrust of what I'm driving at here, Dave, is, was it an everyday situation? Did Elvis get high once a month or once every six months or how often?"

"All the time I was with Elvis, it was daily. Every day, oh yeah, let me speak at length about the drugs, okay? There are a couple of points, maybe a number of points I'd like to make about that. Since Elvis' death, there's been a lot of people talking about him and about his involvement with drugs, and all of them have stated, among other things, 'Oh sure, Elvis took a sleeping pill and he had other medications, but all his drugs were prescription, he never touched the hard stuff.'

"It really gets to me," Hebler continued, "you don't think Quaaludes are hard stuff? You don't think Demerol is hard stuff? You don't think Hycodan is hard stuff? Oh Christ, you can go on and on and on. The truth of the matter is that pill addiction is ten times worse than heroin. And I'll tell you something truthfully, if Elvis had done just coke, cocaine, and none of those pills, I'd have gone and got it for him.

"So in the first place, my intelligence is insulted when I hear people talk in that manner, but I'll agree with them on one point, all of that stuff was prescribed. They were prescription drugs. He got them at a drugstore and they were prescribed by a doctor, how about a hundred doctors!

"Now, if Elvis didn't die from a drug overdose, and I wasn't there, and I'm not a doctor, so all I can talk about is what I think, based on the information I've gotten from other people, and my personal observations of him while I was with him and the kinds of drugs he took and the quantity. If it didn't kill him, it sure as hell contributed to his decline. People were making remarks about him being on stage and stumbling and mumbling and being grossly overweight and puffy. It's obvious everybody saw it, and everybody says it was because he was sick.

"All right, bull shit! Sick, sick my ass. He had a ton of drugs in him, that's why he was like that. It would take us four hours sometimes to wake him up to do a show. Come on! He abused medication. I'm not saying Elvis was a dope addict, we never did in the book as a matter of fact. Furthermore, when I tell you that Elvis took drugs and he took a tremendous amount of drugs, I don't tell you that because I want to run his reputation down. I'm talking about a man with whom, at one time, we were very close, I mean really close. Man, I cared for him, a man I cared for, a man I loved, and I had to stand there and watch him commit slow suicide, and was totally helpless to do anything about it. So, you know I don't really give a damn what the public thinks. I don't care what they think. It doesn't matter to me, not a whit. What I would like them to do though is take a lesson and realize that if you don't think Quaaludes are bad, take a look at Freddie Prinze. You know what happened to him. Look at Judy Garland. The list is endless, look at Elvis Presley. You think diet pills are good, take a lesson, you know what they are, they're horrible, they're monstrous.

"Everytime I see one of those damned ads for *Sominex*, I want to blow the damned thing up. You take a look at Elvis at the end and what he became as a result of those drugs. You've got to know that his bizarre behavior, his wild rages, his mumbling, his incoherency, his slobbering, his whole grossness, his appearance, everything about him was directly related to drugs. Name a disease that makes you look like that. Name me a disease that causes you to be that way. You can't name it, because there isn't any. Let me go on a little further.

"After he died, they did an autopsy, which was not made public by the way, but they did admit they found eleven different drugs in his bloodstream. Let's leave that point for a minute and jump ahead to another point and then come back to that one. Not long ago, Dick Grob, Ed Parker and Gerald Peters were on the *Tomorrow Show*. Tom Snyder asked Dick Grob about the drugs. Dick, who still works for the estate, pooh-poohed them, he only took prescription drugs, and all that. He works for the estate, of course, and doesn't want to get fired. Then Tom asked him, I guess he was curious, 'Was he sick before he died, was there any indication that this was going to happen?'

"Dick's comment was this, just a few hours prior to Elvis' death, he talked to Elvis personally, Elvis was alert, he was in good spirits, he was looking forward to going out on the tour the next day, healthy, just finished playing racquetball.

"Well, if he was so healthy and feeling so good, why in the hell did he have eleven drugs in him? That's kind of inconsistent, isn't it? On the one hand they say it's all medication, he was sick, man, and he took all those drugs because he was sick, and on the other hand they say just the opposite. Who the hell are they trying to kid? Are we all morons or something?

"Back to my point, they found eleven drugs, and they went on to say that all of those drugs were within prescribed limits or therapeutic levels. He didn't die, they say, from a drug overdose, he died from heart failure. A couple of things are funny about that. The first one is, here is a man who had constant medical attention for the last ten years of his life, didn't they know he had a heart condition? Here's a man who had doctors around him all the time, and yet he weighed some two hundred and sixty pounds, I understand, when he died. Do you know what kind of a disease causes that? What was he doing playing racquetball? No, no, no, I suggest to you that the reason he was like that was because of the drugs. That's my opinion.

"There are other things about it, things that just don't jibe to me. About this business with drugs, you know I really understand why he did do the drugs. I really do, and it was pitiful. That's what it was, it was pitiful. I feel it's important to talk about the drugs and Elvis' involvement with drugs, because I really honestly feel that it was because of drugs that Elvis went into a decline and eventually died. When he was straight, he was the greatest guy in the world, he really was, he was a super guy. We would rough-house, fool around, kick each other in the ass. He was just a super great guy when he was straight. He popped those uppers and downers and he was like a ping-pong ball whipping down the hall. You didn't know if he was going to say good morning to you or shoot you.

"Another thing I want to say about the *Tomorrow Show*. Gerald Peters owns London Town Livery service, he was Elvis' driver. Tom Snyder asked the three of them to recall their favorite funny story about Elvis. Gerald's funny story was about the night he and Elvis and another guy were in the limousine and some teenagers peeled off down the street, which incensed Elvis no end. He ordered Gerald to 'Catch them damned guys,' and off they went after them, with Elvis firing his gun.

"Firing the gun, okay? Now Gerald said he fired it in the air, I suspect that really isn't true because I know the person that was there in the car, and he tells me that he fired at the other car. Now does that sound like the actions of a rational man? Now is that highjinks, just funsees? I can recall a time coming into Graceland. I was driving, cars were parked outside of Graceland, like they always were and sitting on top of one of the cars was a tin can. Elvis popped up out of the sun roof, took the gun and, boom, fired at it. It was amazing to me that no one noticed. No one noticed! Does that sound like the actions of a rational man? It sure doesn't to me. And we can go on and on, with incidents like that, and all of them, I believe, are because of the drugs. I've seen him both ways, I've seen him when he was straight and I've been with him when he was straight, and I've been with him when he was blown out of his mind and I can tell you there's a real difference. So I'm pissed off about the drugs and I'm pissed off about the people who just relegate them to unimportance, just put them aside. Damn, that's the reason why he's no longer here. He's not here anymore, man. He's dead. And that's why he's dead."

"Dave, if I'm understanding correctly, what you're saying is, that this was more than an occasional thing, more than you or me or any of the rest of us going out, getting drunk and having a big time on New Year's Eve, or three times a year, or six times a year, or whatever, and making a fool of ourselves. What you're saying is that this was damn near a daily situation?"

"Not damn near, it was."

"It was a daily thing?"

"Oh yes. You know Red made the comment in the book that Elvis was a walking drugstore. The man was. For instance, to document what we're talking about, we could if we wanted to produce for you one hundred and fifty prescription bottles, over a very short period of time. One hundred and fifty of them, we can produce that."

"Let me ask you, you talked about some of the drugs, the cocaine?"

"I never saw him take it. I saw some coke that was supposedly his. And we broke the toe of the guy that was bringing it in. But I never saw him personally take coke. I know it was there, everybody said it was his. As a matter of fact, one of the guys cut it with aspirin frequently, and threw some of it away. But I personally never saw him take coke. I never saw him smoke marijuana and he never touched heroin. But he took pills, oh boy did he take pills."

"What was the source? Where did they come from?"

"Doctors."

"Doctors all over the country?"

"Elvis had a clever way of doing it. He knew the *Physicians Desk Reference* backward and forward. What he would do, we would be in Las Vegas, and he'd have a problem, and go see a doctor and he'd get a prescription for pill X, and he knew how to mix pills. He knew what pills went with what other pills to give the kind of whatever he was looking for. Then he'd call another doctor, an eye, ear, nose and throat doctor, and he'd get a prescription for that. Whatever, an ingrown toenail, he'd get something for it. Or dental work, he had perfect teeth. I don't know what the hell they were working on his teeth for, but he would have dental work and get pain pills for it. I went to a hospital with him one time when he had a prescription for some Dilaudid. It was about two o'clock in the morning, it was in Memphis, Baptist Hospital, and I went in there because they had an all-night drugstore to get the prescription filled. The guy took the prescription, came back a minute later and said, 'I can't fill this.'

"It was for fifty pills, and I mean super-strong too. I said, 'Why not?'

"He said, 'Because I just filled one a day or two ago for a hundred of them from another doctor.'

"So, the cumulative effect was enormous. An isolated incident, in and of itself, wouldn't be that bad, but I can't believe that the doctors didn't know. I know that most of these doctors knew. Come on, I knew. These are medical people. But for them to issue a prescription for one single thing that really wasn't quite that bad, they would do it, and they did it."

"The drug store in Memphis would not fill it?"

"Yes, that was the Baptist hospital."

"It was the pharmacy at the hospital?"

"Yes."

"So obviously that prescription was in Elvis' name?"

"Yes. He didn't always do it that way though."

"Were there times when pills were picked up when the prescription was written for you or someone else?"

"Not for me, not to my knowledge anyway, there were none in my name. I know there were some in Sonny's name, and Red's name."

"You did in fact pick up pills at the drug store that were in Elvis' name?"

"Yes."

"Just for background here, when did you begin with Elvis, what was the date?"

"I don't know, I was only on the payroll for the last two years but I was around two years before that on a friendship basis. I traveled with him and that kind of thing."

"You mentioned a little while ago about standing by watching and not being able to do anything. One of the big things that keeps bothering me, and I keep getting back to it, was why didn't somebody put their foot down? Why didn't somebody say, enough of this nonsense?"

"Well, maybe it's as simple as this. In order to put your foot down with somebody, you've got to have enough power to make it work. I don't know too many people who can go to their boss and say, I don't like what you're doing, and get him to stop it without being fired."

"There's no question you would have been fired."

"I don't think so, we were pretty well of a mind about that. We would say things, and what we would try to do was to get him to do things instead of drugs. I think Doctor Nick was instrumental in getting Elvis involved in racquetball, and was instrumental in getting him to build the racquetball courts behind Graceland so that he could get some physical activity, you know, work it out naturally. We would try to do things of the sports and activity nature that didn't require drugs, but what the hell, what do you do with a forty-two year old man?"

"Did you, Sonny or Red or any of you, the other guys in the group, Billy or anybody, ever sit down when Elvis was up in his room and say, 'Damn it, we've got to do something about this? The man's killing himself and he's ruining our lives too.' "

"Oh yeah, we talked about it all the time. As a matter of fact, it was the general opinion of everybody there that he was lucky to be alive, he should have been dead ten years ago."

"You never reached the conclusion that you had to say, 'Okay, we're all going to confront him tomorrow morning when he walks down the steps and say, 'Hey, this is it, you either stop it or we're going to all take a hike.' "

"It wouldn't have worked. It would not have worked. He would have said, 'All right, take a hike.' "

"Did you ever discuss it with Nick?"

"Doctor Nick?"

"Yes."

"I can't recall any specific conversations with Doctor Nick about it, although he was there when conversations were going on. He was privy to what we were talking about but Doctor Nick, you know, had, really had, some ethics about his doctor-patient relationship. There was no way Doctor Nick was going to reveal to us anything of a private nature or anything of a medical nature concerning Elvis, I mean he wouldn't do it."

"How about Vernon?"

"Aw shit, Vernon. The man's an enigma. I can't quite figure out his motivations at all. I don't know what to think of him. He obviously saw what was happening, you would have to be a total moron not to. But he never, to my knowledge, attempted to do anything about it or say anything. I don't know, maybe he did."

"He never said to you, to your own certain knowledge, 'My son's going to hell, we've got to help him get off of it.' "

"No, no, I suspect that Vernon probably thought that everybody was trying to jump into Elvis' pocketbook. That was their only concern, I think that's the way he felt about everybody. The strange thing about it is, I don't think he really knew who his friends were. You take a guy like Red, he worked for Elvis for four years with no pay. It's come down to this now, that I'm the materialistic one. I've been accused of being the one who saw Elvis as a dollar sign, all I cared about was ripping him off. The plain fact of the matter is, and I can show you my income tax returns, I made a hell of a lot more money in my studio than I did working for Elvis. There were occasions when he offered me money that I didn't take, that doesn't make me the good guy and I'm not trying to promote myself that way. He gave me a car and he gave me jewelry and I took it, sure, I took it. I never asked for it, and I never tried to promote it. As a matter of fact, when he gave me the last car, he stuck a gun in my face to make me take the damn car, I didn't want to take it. I'm not trying to give the impression that I'm a wonderful person, I've got my bad points too, but I can honestly tell you that I never, ever, did anything to harm him, in any way. I never did, I defended him all the way down the line. I'd have jumped out and took the bullet for him."

"The phone conversation at the end of the book. Elvis was talking to Red, he says, 'They're trying to prove us all insane.' Who was he talking about, who was trying to prove him insane?"

"I don't know, probably the attorneys for the guy who had the lawsuit against Elvis in the Tahoe incident. I suspect that was it, you know he was bugged about that, and the thing about it was he was totally in the right. The guy who brought the suit was totally in the wrong, he really was. Clearly he was wrong. If you look at it, I think there were two lawsuits altogether, maybe three, involving incidents with Red and Sonny over a twenty-four-year period of time. That's not a bad record, when you consider you're dealing with mobs of people everyday. That's pretty damn good. We all make mistakes, if it was a mistake, but it wasn't a mistake. It was clear. I think the guys handled themselves with remarkable restraint. You never saw us get thrown in jail for busting up places or anything. It never happened. We never did that. But you know that was bugging him, plus in my case he was told some negatives about me by a guy who was supposedly a good friend of mine, a guy that I supported for fifteen years and the guy vigorously denies it now. He's got his own book out now, Ed Parker. He told Elvis that I was sneaky, underhanded, that I was very, very clever, very materialistic and to keep me at arm's length, don't let me get too close. Now the guy denies it, he doesn't talk to me but he denies the hell out of it, but we've got a tape recording when Elvis called Red and he names him. It's coming right out of Elvis' mouth. Plus, and probably Ed Parker doesn't know to this day, that when he said that to Elvis there were other people there. Those other people came forward and told me. Now I hold no rancor toward the man, the man's his own worst enemy, and I don't really care, but the point is that I think, I don't know for sure, but I think that was the reason for my demise."

"Why Sonny and Red?"

"I don't know, the problem with the thing is, and the thing that hurts more than anything else and hurt at the time, is that none of us had the opportunity to give our side of whatever the beef was. I found out about this afterwards and never had an opportunity to say, 'That's wrong, that's not true and here's why, because I really didn't do that.'

"Red, even worse than that. How could there be any question about Red's loyalty, about Red's abilities, how could there be any question, here was a man who devoted his entire life to this man. And Sonny, typically the same thing, sixteen years. All of a sudden he became incompetent? It doesn't wash, it doesn't. Plus, we were lied to when we were let go, Vernon lied to us all over the damn place. That bothered us as well, why couldn't you just be honest about it and straight up. No, he couldn't do that. So I think it was our treatment more than anything else which bothered us, plus obviously nobody could call us or anything else. Anybody who uttered our name was fired."

"What are your feelings about the will? I find it somewhat hard to believe that Elvis, given what facts I know about Elvis, I find it awfully hard to believe that Elvis didn't mention anybody in the will, even to the extent of saying, 'I'm not leaving a dime to any of these rotten bastards,' if in fact that's what he thought. I'm talking specifically now about Billy," I continued my question, "I can see it with the other guys, they're not related, but I find it hard to believe he didn't leave Billy something, and perhaps a token to the rest."

"Let's talk a little bit about what my feelings are. In the first place, Ed Parker has his book out now and he's going around telling the world that he was Elvis' second daddy and he was closer to him than anyone else. The truth of the matter is that the closest person to Elvis was Billy Smith. No one was closer. Secondly, I sat there one day with Elvis in Graceland and he was telling me about the circumstances around how he met Charlie Hodge. It was after Elvis' mom passed away and Charlie was on the ship with him going to Germany. Charlie comforted him, was a companion to him, helped him, joked with him during a very traumatic period in Elvis' life. Elvis really felt strong about that and told me, 'Because of that, Charlie will never want again, I'll see to it.'

"I thought, fantastic, you know that's pretty great. Well now, Elvis has been dead a year and Charlie's out in the cold. He wasn't left anything and he's not going to get anything. Not from Vernon he isn't. Billy, who was closer to Elvis than anyone could possibly be, he's back working on the railroad."

"So why didn't Elvis do that in his will, the will was filed not that long ago?"

"Interesting, isn't it? I wonder if he really wrote the will. The will is inconsistent with his attitude, and the attitude that he professed not only to me but to everybody else. Do you know, for instance, there was a time during 1974, when we had a meeting in Las Vegas in his room. All of us were there, all of the guys, and Elvis told us at the time that he was going to do something he had never done before. He was going to make sure that if anything happened to him, our futures were assured. He said he was going to do a couple of things. Number one, he was going to do a movie, and in that movie he was going to give each one of us a percentage of the film. Retirement, if you will. Furthermore, he was going to give each one of us fifty thousand dollars. He was going to do that.

"Elvis always indicated, not only by his words but by his actions as well, that he cared for his people and wanted to protect them and take care of them. He wanted to make sure that if anything happened to him they would have something to fall back on. And then he dies and this will surfaces and nobody gets anything.

"There are a certain number of people who like to characterize all those who worked for Elvis as hangers-on, like they were some kind of blood-sucking leeches, but nothing could be further from the truth. They're loyal guys, every damn one of them, they cared for that man, everyone of us did. We loved him. That's why we worked for him. Almost everybody had their home life screwed-up as a result of it, that was the extent of their dedication to the man. To just blithely characterize these people as something that crawled out from under a rock, really disturbs me. They earned everything, every damn thing they got. That was no easy job."

"Would your speculation on the will then be that Elvis simply neglected to do these things, obviously you have no way of knowing, but you can speculate."

"I would think that probably what happened is that he just left it to his father to draw up something and he just signed it. Elvis never read things, not to my knowledge he didn't, he just said, 'Hey, do it,' he didn't want to be concerned with the fine print.

"I don't want to interject a note of, like I think there's a conspiracy, because I really don't think there is, but it's certainly incongruous, and furthermore, it's a damned shame.

"Particularly with Billy. It strikes me as not being in character. You know I love Billy and Jo, I really like those two. I have heard from people that after we did our book, Red, Sonny and I, that Billy had a lot of hard feelings toward us, as a result of doing the book. It bothers me quite a bit. I really didn't care what anybody else thought but that kind of bothered me. I think it's a shame. I really do. I didn't want to hear that, but that's the way it came down.

"But I would think that if anybody should have gotten something, and they all should have, it should have been Billy. It's a damn shame, all of them should have gotten something, and they still should. I wish Priscilla could have been the executor. I've got a lot of admiration for that lady. She's together and I think she would have done the right thing. I have no such feelings as far as Vernon is concerned. I think Vernon will keep every dime he can possibly keep."

"What about Doctor Nick? You speak highly of him."

"Heck yeah. I love him. He really, really and truly tried the best he could to protect Elvis and save his life. The man, I used to call him my daddy, I really liked him. He is a man of integrity and he's a hell of a doctor. When it comes to the business of being a doctor, he's got his thing together. And furthermore, he does it with a measure of humanity. He's really not the cold, callous M.D. He does care. I've seen him go non-stop, around the clock trying to save the life of a friend of his who collapsed at a racquetball tournament. I was there. I watched the torment in Doctor Nick when he was trying to save this guy's life and when the man died.

"This man who was a life-long friend of his; he collapsed with a heart attack while playing a game on the court. And from that minute on Nick did everything and anything he could possibly do to save that man's life. And I really truly believe he would have done the same thing for Elvis, done the same thing for me, or the same thing for you. I'm sure he was aware of Elvis' problem and I think he tried to approach it in such a way where he would at least have some semblance of effectiveness. There was no way he could walk up to Elvis and say, 'Hey, you damned junkie, you're going to die you son of a bitch and you're not going to get this anymore.' It wouldn't have worked. No way it would have worked."

"Why couldn't he have said that?"

"Because it wouldn't have worked. Maybe he did. Obviously, neither one of us knows. Elvis would have closed off, would have just shut up. Now, since Elvis' death, Doctor Nick is no longer welcome at Graceland. He's no longer Grandma's physician. He's been asked to leave. That's what I understand. But I think Nick really tried, tried to do the best job he could possibly do. I admire and respect him for that."

"Are you saying that Doctor Nick was not writing the prescriptions?"

"No, I'll tell you a story. I think it was in 1974, Elvis was hospitalized, he had to interrupt an engagement and from Vegas went to the Baptist Hospital in Memphis. While he was there, a package arrived for him. We opened up the package and it contained hundreds of damn pills, from another doctor."

"What other doctor?"

"It doesn't matter, but this same doctor's been interviewed since then about Elvis and he denied that Elvis ever took any drugs; however, we have that same doctor on tape admitting the drugs. We've got a nice little tape recording of him. Two or three of them. Okay, one of the guys took the bottle of pills and gave it to Doctor Nick and said, 'Look what just arrived in the mail.'

"Doctor Nick took it and had it analyzed, and they were the same old pills Elvis had been taking all along. That will give you an indication of what was going on. There were a lot of things, like for instance, how did Doctor Nick know, or any other doctor know, that his patient had just received a prescription from Doctor Joe Blow somewhere, of prescription X, and he had downed three or four of them. The man's not superman, not divine by any means, now how could he deal with that? Maybe you're dealing with a specific medical problem and it's compounded by all these other activities going on that you know nothing about. It would be a herculean task. I don't know how a man could solve it."

"To your own certain knowledge, none of the prescriptions you ever had filled were prescriptions which were authorized by Doctor Nichopoulos?"

"That's true. That's right. I never did. Not that he didn't prescribe medicine for Elvis. He obviously did."

"I'm talking about the excessive prescriptions."

"Well, no, but his prescriptions could be considered excessive in light of the other prescriptions that Elvis got from other doctors. But he didn't know of those others."

"What I'm asking is, take the Placidyls or any of them, did he prescribe, for example, one hundred of them on the first of July and ten days later prescribe another hundred of them?"

"No, Doctor Nick didn't do that. Yeah, I know what you're saying, other doctors did."

"You specifically do not want to name the doctor you were talking about?"

"No, I don't want to name him. Why?"

"The only why being Dave, is that if all this is the result of the excessive use of prescriptions and the abuse of drugs, my feeling is that somebody contributed to this. That being the case, I think there is a certain amount of responsibility, and I think our responsibility is to say who it was."

"Well, I could do that. Except that I'm already secure in the knowledge that that doctor is rueing the day, and will continue to rue the day, and my little contribution will have nothing to do with it. I promise you the man is paying. He is."

"Okay, I'm doing all of this by the grace of your good will, so obviously I'm not going to push you."

"All you'd get is a lawsuit and you don't want that," Hebler replied.

"Well, I think we're going to have to live with that, if they come. I've come to the conclusion that we're not going to pull any punches, we're going to call it as we see it."

"The problem is, one of the reasons why I don't want to name the man is because I can't document it. In other cases, we can document everything. So if there's no documentation behind it, the only thing it does is cause a big brouhaha and does nobody any good."

"Is there anything you would like to add?"

"There are a couple of thoughts, one of the things I would like to be put across is that with Elvis I really think the good far outweighed the bad. The man obviously is a legend, always will be. One hundred years from now no one will know your name or my name but they will remember his. He made a contribution which was enormous. He was capable of tremendous generosities, tremendous feelings, he was also capable of tremendous negatives and in a way, Elvis was his own victim. Because, and it's all intertwined with his fans. Take a man, any man, I don't care who he is, and subject him to inputs on an hourly basis for twenty-two years, and the inputs tell him that he is God incarnate, it's going to affect him. He's going to start believing it. The man could do no wrong, he could literally do anything he wanted to do, anything, and get away with it.

"Now, that's got to tell you that you have some kind of power. That's easy to abuse. Elvis' fans, they didn't just like him, they didn't just care for him, they adored him, they deified him. Man, it's tough being Jesus. Can you possibly conceive the incredible loneliness that man suffered? Who the hell's he going to talk to? Jesus doesn't talk to just anyone. Who's he going to talk to, where's his peer? Where's his contemporary? The sad part of Elvis' life was that he always wanted to be one of the boys and never quite made it. He had an enormous ego. Obviously, he would have to have in that business to be the kind of success he was, and he never ever did anything in moderation. Nothing, he didn't do anything in moderation, his successes weren't moderate so how can you expect his failures to be moderate? I think there's a plaintive side to Elvis that's sad, the sadness that he had, the loneliness that was there and I know he felt it. I do, and it was constantly perpetrated. It was constantly thrust on him, he could never escape it. He was a victim of his own fame, a victim of his own public relations, a victim of his own tremendous, outlandish popularity. Outlandish, beyond all reason.

"It makes you wonder, What did it take, what kind of integrity did it take to be able to live all those years under that kind of pressure. No wonder he took some pills. No wonder, really. I think it's important that when you talk about Elvis or something that's published about Elvis, that that particular point be brought forth because I think it's an elementary part of his total makeup. How in the hell can you make a definitive comment about anybody, let alone Elvis. You're talking about an extremely complex intelligence, the man was an intelligent human being, who was subjected to tremendous pressures all his adult life, all of his life. For the most part, he handled it pretty damn well, so I don't want anybody to get the opinion that when I talk about the negative aspects of Elvis, that I'm trying to put him down or that I'm bitter, or trying to get even, because I'm really not. I think it's important that people realize a total picture of a man of that stature, if we're going to talk about a man of that stature, let's talk about the total man as much as we can. And let's understand that he wasn't Jesus Christ. He wasn't God, he was a man just like you and I. A man who had some incredible talents in an area that caused him to be the legend he became. I don't know too many people who could have been in Elvis' shoes and carried it off as well as he did."

Chapter Four

I've Tried Them All

Sonny West is a big, friendly man who seems comfortable talking about Elvis and the years they spent together. He expresses a preference for the changing seasons of Tennessee to the eternal summer of southern California, and speaks of being pleased about living again in his home state where he is working in the motion picture industry.

"Is your book, *Elvis, What Happened,* true?" I asked.

"Yes, it's true."

"Is it exaggerated?"

"No. I've noticed some people have said that, but that was their way of trying to avoid saying it's true. Saying there were things blown out of proportion, which they are not. Linda Thompson has said that. That time over the Mike Stone thing, she was crying, she did not know what was going on in his mind, what he was going to do. She did not think that Elvis was acting. She made the silliest damn statement I ever heard when she said, 'Evidently they didn't know him very well because he always liked to be an actor, he was a frustrated actor.'

"I thought it was damn silly for her to say something like that. I've been around him a lot more than Linda Thompson and Red has also, for sixteen years and over twenty years respectively, and I've seen him act and I've seen him pull things, and I guarantee you Red and I both had tears and were crying because we thought Elvis had snapped. We thought he had had a mental breakdown."

"Did you, Red and Dave have the right to approve the final manuscript and say, 'Yes, that's what we want to say?' "

"Yes."

"Let's tackle the drug problem right off. What kind, how much and how often?"

"Boy, it started off with uppers way back in 1960, then went to sleeping pills to counteract them, then went to pain medication. Percodan, things like that, that he would eat, I mean really, almost like candy. Then he graduated to things like Demerol, morphine and Dilaudid. At the end he was taking that pain pill for terminally ill cancer patients, Dilaudid. In fact, he made a statement to Pat, Red's wife, down in Palm Springs, in 1976. 'Pat,' he said, 'I've tried them all, honey, and believe me Dilaudid is the best.'

"Certainly there were times he had pain, he had an ingrown toenail that came back once in awhile on him and he had work done on his teeth. We all have and maybe they do give us ten or twelve Percodan or Empirin Codeine to take, but I guarantee you that ninety percent of the people do not use the whole load. But Elvis would get them by the hundreds. I don't know why it continued to go the way it did with him, I really don't know.

"He got heavier and heavier into them," West continued, "and even Doctor Nick has been quoted as saying he had to go in once in awhile and clean him out. He'd find bottles of the stuff and throw them away. I don't know what it was. Perhaps it was his life style that was hurting him at the last, those last two or three years. The drugs were keeping him in sort of a limbo rather than hemmed in like he was. It really got bad that last year-and-a-half or so."

"You're saying that it got progressively worse?"

"Oh yes, and I've got to say it got progressively worse after his divorce. Latter part of seventy-three, seventy-four and seventy-five it was getting worse and in seventy-six it was bad and, of course, in seventy-seven it continued. Fans don't want to believe our book, there are some of them who will never believe it. Even if Elvis told them himself, they wouldn't believe it. There are some that don't want to hear it because they're afraid it might be true. I have a good friend down in Memphis, his wife loves me, thinks the world of me, but she will not read our book. She doesn't want to know. She has no doubt that whatever's in there is true because she knows me, but she won't read it. There are people like that. I don't blame them, if they are weak enough to turn their heads against him, then that's their thing they have to deal with. When I hear his records, I just miss the man, I hear him and I wish I was going to hear him for many more years. I don't think back about the bad times."

"How often, Sonny, were the drugs a daily thing, once a week, how often?"

"It was daily."

"Are you saying he was pretty much high every day?"

"Yes, that was no exaggeration when we said he takes pills to go to sleep, to get up, during the day, it was a continual thing."

"There were times though that you would say for a week at a time, a month or whatever that he was not on them?"

"Oh yes. The last time I remember him being straight for an extended period of time was in seventy-two when we were getting ready to go to Hawaii. We went on a diet together, that shot thing, five hundred or one thousand calories a day, prepared frozen meals, terrible stuff. I had already been on one when we were in Vegas in August and I had lost about twenty-five or thirty pounds. Lamar was on it and he lost weight, Joe Esposito lost, we were on it together then. Then Elvis decided he wanted to go on it for the Satellite show, we were off work during December, then in January we were going to Hawaii, so Elvis and I went on the diet again. I went all the way down to 195 pounds and he came down from about 195 to 175 or 170. He looked great. During that time he did real good. He probably was taking appetite suppressants to keep from being hungry. You get awful hungry on that diet, but he got down.

"It was possible he was taking sleeping pills and maybe a tranquilizer during the day and the suppressants, but he wasn't into the heavy stuff like pain pills and getting out of it. Then the night after the Satellite show, he was totally wiped out."

"He started right back again?"

"Started right back, but kept his weight looking real good for our stay in Vegas, and he looked pretty good during the summer right up to our next August show in Vegas, maybe even more, it's hard to remember when the weight started getting itself established where he didn't take it off. He'd put a little bit on between tours, but not a whole lot, maybe fifteen pounds and take off maybe six or seven. So it was a gradual thing to where he was putting on twenty-five pounds and only taking off ten, so he slowly built back up to over two hundred pounds."

"What would you guess, how heavy was he?"

"Well, in July of 1976, he probably weighed 210 or so. He shouldn't have weighed over 170. The next year he put on another 25 or 30. I understand at his death that there have been estimates of weight up to 240, between 230 and 240 at the time of his death."

"What was the source of the drugs?"

"Doctors around the country. Many of them not knowing that Elvis was getting them from other doctors. He had doctors in Vegas, Los Angeles and Memphis. Dentists, doctors, podiatrists. They had no idea Elvis was getting pain pills and stuff like that somewhere else. The cocaine and stuff that came in, came in with some people who were actually working for him. They got it from a dealer and they would get it in to him. Those are the ones we stopped at times, threatened them until Elvis found out about it and threatened jobs on our part. He said he needed the stuff because he was just taking cocaine to get him awake and alert over and above the medication he was taking to knock himself out."

"Let's talk about the cocaine for a little bit. To your own certain knowledge, he was using cocaine?"

"Yes. No question about it."

"You've actually seen him do it."

"Yes. Now when I saw him do it, it was in later seventy-five, and I don't think he was using it at that time. I saw him with a comedian up there on the thirtieth floor, outside on the balcony in Vegas, the Hilton. First time I ever saw him do it."

"You actually saw him do it, he was sniffing it?"

"Yes. And after that, Elvis used to take these cotton balls and soak them and put them in his nose, and we were told it was liquid coke. He used to do that, but I actually saw him sniff it that time in seventy-five and after that it was Red and Joe Esposito and these guys that were breaking the coke down, actual coke that he was going to use, breaking it down and putting BC powder or something in there so he was getting a little bit of coke but mostly BC powder or whatever it is they put in."

"Did you ever pick up prescription drugs for Elvis?"

"Yes I have, but I don't know what was in them. I would just be told go get the prescription. Marty and I went once to Vegas and we got some prescriptions filled at various drug stores."

"They were things like pain pills?"

"Yeah, pain pills and things like that."

"Were they in Elvis' name?"

"Well, that's going back so far, back in the sixties, somewhere in there Elvis started getting drugs in other peoples' names without our knowing about it. We'd come across a prescription that would have Charlie Hodge, Joe Esposito or my name or Marty's on it and we'd never even seen them. So that's the reason I don't know when he started doing that. I don't know if it's because he wanted to get that narcotics badge but he did start getting them in other names."

"He never said, 'Sonny, I'm going to get a hundred of these but I'm going to put them in your name'?"

"He knew better because I had told doctors not to do that. When I lived with him in 1972, or around there, a full bottle of liquid Demerol was delivered to the house in my name, and I intercepted it. I took it back to Schwab's Pharmacy on Sunset Boulevard, at Laurel Canyon, and I told them to tear up those forms and never again send anything up there in my name unless I called and told them that the doctor is ordering something in my name, my son's name or my wife's name. That was some doctor, I guess, who had influence with the drug store and they could call and order just about anything, and put it in someone else's name."

"What do you think is the real reason why you, Dave and Red were fired?"

"I think there were several things, or any combination of things. Vernon Presley didn't like some of us guys. I also know I did have a lawsuit, one in sixteen years, from a guy up in Tahoe. He had tried to come in the back-exit door, and had drawn back on Elvis' step-brother and I hit him one time. He filed in Federal court against me and Elvis. I was a resident of California and this guy was also, so when the time came up, the statute of limitations, and he didn't refile against me in the state I was dropped from it. This upset Elvis even though he didn't like the guy and told me later he wished I had broke his head wide open. He also made the comment, 'Damn, Sonny hits the guy and he's not even being sued anymore, I'm the one being sued.'

"Well the guy wasn't going to get anything from Elvis either, because the guy was saying that Elvis had hit him twenty karate chops and Elvis never hit him. Now, I'm out of the lawsuit and I think that upset him. Plus, I think there were some other lawsuits, but not against me. There were some people, probably Mr. Presley or Mr. Presley's lawyers, who were intimidating Elvis, telling him he might lose some money, or we were going to continue to get lawsuits or something like that. Things like that were being said to Elvis.

"I had had a discussion with him about eight or nine days before I was fired, down in Fort Worth, Texas. I'd asked Elvis about bringing my wife Judy and my son Bryan down. Judy and I had separated and had problems in seventy-five for about nine or ten months. So I asked Elvis about bringing my family. While I was at the hotel waiting for Elvis, I called Judy and she was crying. There were no prepaid tickets for her to come out. She'd gone to the trouble to find out why and talked to the supervisor of American Airlines in Memphis. He said Mr. Presley, Vernon, had said, 'No, she is not on Elvis' expense account.'

"This was the first time she had been to Memphis in over a year. It hurt me and I got very flushed, but I calmed down. Elvis came in and got out of his traveling clothes and into his pajamas. I told him what had happened. Elvis began protecting his father by saying, 'Well, it could have been a crank call.'

"I said, 'No, Wally said that your father said no a couple of weeks ago when I made those reservations.'

"I know Wally had checked with Vernon Presley before the day Judy called. Then Elvis said, 'There have been some guys abusing it, so Daddy and I set it up where he or I have to okay it.'

" 'I know that Elvis,' I said, 'that's what I'm talking about, but he didn't okay it.'

" 'Well,' he said, 'I haven't talked to him for two or three days.'

" 'Elvis,' I said, 'I did this two weeks ago. Your dad turned it down then because Wally turns right around before he prepays a ticket and checks, he doesn't wait until two days before she's supposed to come in.'

"He knew I was telling him that his father had done this. He said, 'You tell Judy to come on in and I'll talk to Daddy. Tell her not to worry. I'll set it up. It's just a mistake.'

"I said, 'Okay Elvis, I appreciate it,' and I left.

"He never raised his voice, I never raised my voice, nothing, but I found out from a couple of guys later that he was calling me every name in the book after I left. I guess that's what they meant when some of the guys said that we were intimidating Elvis about too many things there at the end. He didn't feel like he had the hold over us anymore. He didn't feel like he could threaten us in any way. And all of the intimidation part was only for his own good. We weren't scared of him saying, 'You're going to be fired.'

"If he was going to fire us he was going to do it. We had turned from young kids that he used into grown men. Back to the separation thing. During my separation I was very confused, lonely, and hurt. I did see other women now and then, and when I did, I didn't care to be around the other guys and their wives because the wives were close to my wife. They thought that I was the ass because of what I was doing, and I couldn't blame them. Some of them had had their husbands go through the same thing. I just didn't care to be around.

"Elvis got jealous of my relationship in seventy-five with John Bassett, the guy that brought WFL into Memphis, the professional football team with the World Football League. I just think there were a lot of contributing things."

"You say there was only one lawsuit against you in sixteen years, but there were others. Were those others against Red or Dave?"

"I'll let you talk to them. I don't want to say anything about that. I just had the one and I do know that the one was enough to upset Elvis with the influence he was getting from the other people, his lawyers and Vernon. There were various people putting pressure on him about us guys. Suspicions were being cast upon the group as being insane."

"What are your feelings about the will?"

"It's hard for me to believe it. That's all there is to it, it's hard for me to believe it. I heard that Elvis told his cousin

Billy Smith, 'You are in the will, you never have to worry anymore if something happens to me.'

"It's hard for me to believe that the guys who were still with him, Joe Esposito, Charlie Hodge, the ones who were with him at the end were not mentioned. It's hard to believe he didn't leave them a year's salary to help them get something else established. Forget the guys that were gone, he was mad at us. I'm talking about the ones that were still with him after all those years. How come they weren't left something? I don't know if we'll ever know about that because the only one who could tell us is gone. I do know that Elvis was terrible about reading legal things. I don't know if he was led to think there were other things in the will. Why would he go to his cousin who I know he loved very much and was very close to and tell him he was in the will? Billy was around him more than anyone, and for Elvis to make a point of telling him that, and then he's not in there at all, it's just confusing to me."

"You mentioned some Denver men in the book who were very concerned with Elvis."

"Yes, that was mainly with Red when they went back there for Captain Kennedy's brother's funeral. That was also when one of the police surgeons saw a prescription for Dilaudid and said, 'What the hell's he doing with that?'

"I didn't even know what Dilaudid was. I'd never heard of it. And he said, 'That's a pain pill for cancer patients, they use it a lot for them.'

"The doctor was even wondering if Elvis had cancer or something, without letting it be known. That's when they became aware of it. I think quite possibly they had noticed at different times he was under some sort of medication, they may not have known what. I hear there's one or two of them that denied it in the press. I don't know if they did or not but we thought that these were the guys that were really committed. Evidently they feel that nothing's to be gained by telling the truth about Elvis. I think they are stupid if they think that way, because I think a lot of the youth in this country, if they knew that Elvis Presley could accidentally get hooked on overabuse of prescribed medicines, that anyone could be hooked. There's no telling what would have happened if he had done what Betty Ford did, said, 'I've got a problem, it's bigger than me and I need help.'

"There's no telling what kind of influence Elvis would have had on the youth, and families, of America. But, that's those guys, maybe they didn't want too much said because it would sound kind of bad for them to be narcotics agents and having a guy around them for two or three years who was taking the stuff. I sure would like to take a lie detector test with them.

"I admire the Captain very much. He has kept his mouth shut, was never quoted and I believe he's one who would say I don't want to discuss it, but he would not say I don't believe anything negative or positive. He would just say I don't want to discuss it, that's my personal business with a friend, but I don't think he would say, no, I never noticed anything."

"He's the one in Denver?"

"All of them are in Denver, but he's the Captain."

"Of the Narcotics Division?"

"No, Captain on the police force. In fact, he may be Assistant Chief now. The other guys were the narcotics boys. I think Jerry Kennedy had, at one time, been in narcotics or something, but then he moved up to administration. Sharp man."

"He hasn't said anything about it?"

"Not in print, that I know of, but I saw the others. One that upsets me is the guy Cantrell. Do you know why he dedicated his life to drug enforcement? His father was a musician and he overdosed. This is the guy who has a new Seville that Elvis gave him. He has not only seen his father overdose from the drugs, but here's Elvis with a bad problem, not overdosing from it, but just in a bad way and he's going to deny it. That's a hypocritical son-of-a-bitch to me. Elvis told us that Bob told him that he had dedicated his life to drug enforcement because of his father overdosing. He was going to stop it any way he could, and then he turns around and says that Elvis didn't take the stuff."

"There was a prescription once in your son's name?"

"Yes, but I can't remember what it was. It was a prescription in the name of Bryan West. It had to be something other than an antibiotic because why would he get an antibiotic in my son's name? Amphetamine or barbituate or something like that."

"Do you know who wrote the prescription?"

"No, it was when we were in California and my son was

only a year old. It was one of those doctors in Los Angeles. He had two or three there."

"Why do you suppose some of the other people are now saying all this never happened?"

"I don't know, because they all know it's true. They all know it. Esposito, all of them. There's been some who have kept their mouth shut. Jerry Schilling for one. Jerry I admire, but Esposito started lying right from the very start. He said he found Elvis in bed. Elvis was on the floor in the bathroom and Esposito didn't find him, the girl found him, so Joe lied from the start. I don't know why people want to believe him on everything else when he was already caught lying. He's been on television news saying 'I found him.'

"He was asked if he found him in bed and Joe said, 'Yes.' "

"I understand there was a time when Elvis was in the hospital in Memphis and he received a package of prescription drugs in the mail from a doctor. They were intercepted by you?"

"Several of us intercepted them, they were addressed to Elvis' aunt, Delta. That's what Elvis had told the doctor to do. We took out some of the capsules. We started suspecting because this doctor had said he was breaking the stuff down. Elvis knew what the capsules were supposed to look like. These were some sort of pain pills and the doctor said he was breaking these things down taking half of the medication out and putting aspirin in. We gave some of them to Doctor Nick and Nick ran tests on them and they were one hundred per cent strength."

"Do you know who the doctor was?"

"Yes."

"Will you say who the doctor was?"

"Just say he was in Las Vegas. A Las Vegas doctor."

"Why would you not want to name him?"

"Well, I'll tell you the truth. This person has some tremendous influence even as far as out of this country. Even when we wrote our book, we turned over a list of names to our lawyer, in a sealed envelope, to be opened upon the death of the three of us."

"Tell me about Doctor Nichopoulos, was he involved in this at all?"

"Let me tell you something, I felt, and in our book we

indicated that Nick had tried to control what Elvis was getting, but I've heard things to the contrary since. I heard stories, different things about what went on that last year so I don't know. I think it would be wrong for me to make a comment about Nick because I don't know, but while I was there Nick was refusing him different things."

"You know that Nick was refusing to give him what he wanted?"

"Yes. When I say I know it, I know that Elvis got mad at Nick sometimes, and that he didn't take him one time on tour. He took another doctor. Elvis was putting Nick down for a few months and then he went back to Nick. So I can't imagine that if Nick was giving him everything he wanted why would there have been a problem?"

"Was there ever a time when you or the group of guys, including Nick, said, 'This has got to stop, we'll sit down with Elvis and tell him.' "

"Yes, and the one person who should have been there wasn't there, and that was Elvis' father."

"Why wasn't he?"

"I don't know. His father could have come to us, several of us in the group, and said, 'I've made arrangements to commit Elvis to such and such sanitarium. I want to take him when he's asleep at night, roll him up in a blanket and take him, and no one's going to know about it. We're going to say he's gone out of town.'

"We would have done it. Elvis would have fired us the next day when he woke up in that place, but he may have hired us back. In fact we heard that he intended hiring us back, and he only wanted us fired for two or three months the time he did fire us, but you can't play with peoples' lives like that. I've seen Elvis do it over the years, he liked to teach people lessons."

"You say that Vernon wasn't there, he wouldn't join in on it?"

"He should have come to us. That's his son."

"But did you guys and that's again including Nick, did you ever say, 'This has gotten out of hand completely, we've just got to do something'?"

"It was not so much saying that it was out of hand, we just sat down and talked several times about what was going on and what we were going to do. Nick knew he was getting this stuff in and he said, 'We have to keep cleaning him out, we have to keep getting that stuff wherever we can find it and get it.' "

"Nobody ever thought of a direct confrontation? All of you saying you would leave if it didn't stop?"

"No, there was never anything like that. Number one, you couldn't get everyone to leave, some of the guys as I told you earlier were getting the stuff to him so you couldn't get everyone to leave."

"Some of the guys, part of the group, were getting things to him?"

"Yes. That's what I mean, some of the people were getting stuff to him around us and through us without letting us know anything, and at the same time talking with us and saying, 'Yeah, it's bad.'

"There were times, like with Esposito one time, Elvis was really getting paranoid and raising hell. He picked up an ashtray and threatened to break Joe's head with it. And Joe was actually on the phone after that trying to find someone to hire him, because he was going to quit."

"You never said anything directly to Elvis yourself, like, 'Elvis, this has got to stop, you're really overdoing it.' "

"We've sat and talked and hinted that medicines taken in too large an amount can hurt the throat, the body, take away lung capacity, these things work on your nervous system and respiratory system and stuff like that, but you just didn't give Elvis, at least we couldn't, an ultimatum like, 'You got to stop or we're going to walk.'

"You couldn't get enough of them to walk. You saw us, three very key people he fired, just like that, and in fact, it worked in a way he liked for it to work. It psyched-out the other people, the others who were around. Several of them said, 'My God, if he'll fired Red, Sonny and Dave like that he'll fire any of us.'

"So it worked in a psychological way that Elvis liked. He liked to show people that he could be very unpredictable."

"You never talked about this with Mr. Presley?"

"No, you couldn't approach him. Everything you said to Vernon Presley he went to his son about. You couldn't ask Mr. Presley for a confidential conversation. He would go to Elvis and say, 'Son, you know Sonny came to me and he's concerned about you, saying that you're taking too many drugs.'

"Vernon didn't like us guys. He even made the statement one time when they had borrowed some money on the home, I think when Elvis had bought that plane and they were short, he said, 'If it was up to me, I'd fire you all, but Elvis wanted to keep you, so we borrowed the money to keep everybody on the payroll.'

"Elvis kind of laughed, you know that nervous laugh, and said, 'You know daddy's just kidding you.'

"But we knew he wasn't. Elvis knew he wasn't, otherwise he wouldn't have had to say it."

"I want to read you something," I said to Sonny West. "Quantities during a forty-six month period of time, that's two months less than four years: 6,464 Placidyls, 3,204 Darvon, 1,508 Hycomine, 708 Empirin Codeine #3, 500 Dalmane, 400 Valium, 216 Darvocet, 200 Valmid and assorted pills which are not important, total 13,291 pills, in roughly 1300 days. The average is ten per day."

"That's from one doctor?" Sonny asked.

"Yes."

"Nick?"

"Yes."

"God-a-mighty. Whew! And that's for Elvis?"

"No, this is for Marty," I answered.

"Whew!"

"I have certified copies in my brief case of these prescriptions from the pharmacy, issued by Dr. Nichopoulos for Marty Lacker."

"How many Placidyl?" Sonny asked.

"6,464."

"In four years? I'll bet you I didn't get more than 500 from Nick in four years. But I'll tell you, Marty was really hooked on them. But if he did that for Marty, if Marty used that many, you'll find out on Elvis that the volume will be much higher. The Placidyl and Darvon will be much higher. The Valium will be much higher, those are the things that I know Elvis used a lot of."

"Unfortunately, Kessler's Pharmacy only has records for that four-year period. They destroy them over the years but these are certified copies signed by Frank L. Kessler. Name of patient, Marty Lacker, name of physician, Nichopoulos, over and over, Nichopoulos throughout."

"Good gracious."

"Now, in light of that, are you saying you do not think that Nick was giving them to Elvis?"

"Oh no, I never said that Nick wasn't giving them to Elvis, I know that Nick was. What I said was that I didn't know how much Nick was giving Elvis compared to what the other doctors were. I will say this, if Nick was that free with Marty, then I sure would like to see what he gave Elvis. If he was that free with Marty and Marty wasn't giving him anything, what the hell was it that Elvis got? I had no idea on these things, it kind of boggles the mind."

"There are a lot of Elvis Presleys growing up today, and an awful lot of influence could have been exerted on the younger people while he was alive and even today with an honest approach to the whole thing. If all you guys were to say, 'He's dead, here's what the hell happened and it's time we all learned a lesson from it' instead of pretending there was no problem," I stated.

"Elvis had a tremendous ego, everyone will tell you. If nothing else, they'll tell you that. I just don't think his humility in that particular area was big enough for him to overcome the ego and admit he had a problem. He kept denying it to us over the years by saying, 'I know what I'm doing.' "

"Sonny, is there anything else you would like to add?"

"The excerpt of your book printed in *Ladies Home Journal* left the impression that Elvis did not get a narcotics badge."

"Yes, I know, that was an error in their editing. He definitely did get the badge."

"And he used it for his own reasons. He did say that agents don't bother other agents. I discussed this with the Colonel once, about the stuff and what would happen if he got caught with it. That was the reason we couldn't go to England and some other places. Because of the drugs. Colonel was scared to death of that."

"Are you saying that's one of the reasons why he didn't travel outside the United States?"

"Yes, Colonel Parker was very concerned about what Elvis was taking, and about how you get into England or the other countries without Elvis being checked out. How would it be, Elvis going into England and having one of those customs agents confiscate something that the doctor or someone's carrying which you're not supposed to have. It concerned him, that along with the language barrier, the security. How do you tell a bunch of people who don't speak English to stay where they are? They don't understand what you are saying. All security is a bluff. If you have 50 cops and 1,000 people and all 1,000 decide to charge, you can't stop them. So it's a bluff, and this country is very good on that bluff. We put 15 or 20 cops across a stage and there's 15,000 people, they keep them away because the people don't all decide to charge at one time. They come up there five, six or seven at a time and we can control them. We had twenty-five come up at one time and some of them got on stage. So it's just a bluff, and these are some of the things that concerned Colonel Parker about going. Elvis could have gone to the Palladium in England and played there, he would have liked to, but Colonel was very concerned about drugs."

"Then you are saying Colonel Parker was aware of the drug-abuse problem?"

"Yes, he was. He and I have had conversations about it, the Colonel was very concerned about Elvis' health. The Colonel didn't mind Elvis being overweight if it was from a legitimate reason and Elvis couldn't get it down, because he still sold out, people still loved him. The Colonel even joked, 'Well hell,' he said, 'Kate Smith was heavy.'

"What concerned him was when the drugs became obvious and shows had to be cancelled. A whole engagement in Vegas had to be cancelled and rescheduled for December of seventy-five, that's when it started getting to the Colonel."

"And this was all because of the drugs?"

"Yes. Drugs bringing on other complications like the time they were coming out in the jet commander and Elvis couldn't breathe. Everyone else was breathing fine but Elvis' respiratory system was messed up so they got him down on the ground, switched planes and a couple, three hours later he was fine. We worked one or two days on that engagement and we had to quit, cancel and go back to Memphis, and he went into the hospital for four or five weeks. He was all bloated up, they were trying to draw fluid off of him, they were punching him with needles, big syringes like they use to take fluid off the knee or something, but they couldn't get any fluid. It looked like he had fluid in him but they couldn't get anything. He had holes in him where they put those damn things in. The Colonel was concerned about him. He didn't know exactly what Elvis was taking, he probably figured it was pain medicine or something because Elvis was slurring his words, or he wouldn't wake up, or he would do half a show, and the Colonel would get upset about it. We'd talk. Colonel had his way of going to Elvis a few times and trying to make him think he was extremely upset and up-tight to make Elvis think he'd better straighten up. Colonel tried that a few times. Colonel never feared Elvis at all. Never feared being fired or anything else. It happened one time, Colonel said, 'Fine, I'll make up my bills and send them to you.'

"Elvis called him about two weeks later.

"Now, that was over the *maitre'd* who worked at the Las Vegas Hilton. He was fired. Elvis jumped up there and put down Mr. Hilton. He said big guys don't know, this man was having to do this and that to feed his family. He just put Hilton down, the Colonel went up to Elvis and said, 'You don't do that.'

"Elvis seldom did, he never did it in politics, never made public statements about his beliefs, only in our group. He normally didn't do something like that and I feel he did it due to what he was taking. Elvis fired the Colonel and the Colonel said, 'Fine, I'll call a news conference in the morning.'

"Elvis said, 'Fine, I'll call one tonight,' and walked out.

"I stayed with Elvis two and a half weeks after that and he was running me ragged. He wasn't sleeping. Dr. Ghanem would give him a shot to knock him out, and tell me to go to sleep and two hours later I'd be asleep and here Elvis would want me up. He finally had me call Colonel Parker. He said, 'We've got to call that old son-of-a-bitch, Sonny. He's not going to call us.'

"The only thing that hurts me about the Colonel is I had been working with him since we first went back on the road in sixty-nine and he didn't speak up for me when we were fired. At first, there was talk about some one alternating with me, but the Colonel was teaching me a lot on the road and he said, 'No, I don't want to break anyone else in, maybe once in a while but I don't want someone on a whole tour, I want Sonny.'

"Elvis sometimes even accused me of being too much like the Colonel. He knew Colonel wasn't scared of him and he used to say, 'We're going to have to get someone else to swap off with Sonny, he's getting too much like the Colonel.'

"He never did swap me off because the Colonel wanted me and it's the one thing that hurts my feelings, I don't feel like the Colonel spoke up for me like he could have. Colonel could have gotten me my job back. I was very influential with the Colonel getting a station wagon. I was influential on that airplane which Elvis was going to buy for him. I just don't feel that he stuck up for me like he could have. I'm not saying that he should have, only that he could have if he had wanted to, he could have got me my job back."

"Are you satisfied with the death reports?"

"No, I'm not really. We were told that he suffocated to death. That he fell asleep in the bathroom. We've all carried him into the bedrooms when he was completely, totally asleep, out of it. Like a limp ragdoll. The Placidyls always hit him hard. They told us they found him face down, his face buried in the carpet, with his tongue out and black, and they thought he'd broken his nose because it was mashed to the side from lying there. They first thought he had fallen in the bathroom and broken his nose. This came from one of the guys who worked for Elvis. He made this statement to a girl who knew us and then she told us. He fell asleep and suffocated, we also heard that they had to pry open his jaw to get his tongue back in his mouth. Esposito said he gave him mouth to mouth resuscitation. Hero Joe.

"I don't know if we'll ever get the truth from any of them. I wouldn't have been able to sleep in that house another night had I still been living there when he died. I would not have been able to sleep there, and I don't know if I'd have been able to be very cool at all."

Chapter Five

It Wasn't All Bad

Red West is a surprisingly quiet man considering the tough image he projected as a longtime Elvis bodyguard, and the parts he has played on television. He's not as outgoing as his cousin, Sonny, but anyone who doubted his ability to take care of himself would be making a serious mistake. West is now a firmly established actor who has completed one television series and is ready to begin a second. His home is southern California where he lives in a new, though somewhat modest, house in a subdivision where the lawn grass has not yet taken root.

"Red, are the facts in your book true?" I asked.

"They certainly are," West replied. "Every word is true."

"Are they exaggerated?"

"Not a bit, no. In fact, some of it was probably under-exaggerated."

"Did you, Sonny and Dave approve the final manuscript?"

"We sure did."

"Let's jump right on the damn drugs. That's obviously what most of the controversy is about."

"It was a small part of the book, but then that's sensationalism."

"That's the thing that everybody seems to be split about. What kind of drugs were used, how often and how much?"

"It started out with diet pills and then it built up into sleeping pills, how often was every day for the last five years. It was more and more and more, just unbelievable amounts. Unbelievable amounts, and before I left he was into cocaine. I don't know what happened the last year, but I heard from people that it was really unbearable. If it was any more bearable than when I was with him then it was hell."

"He was actually into cocaine while you were with him?"

"He certainly was."

"You have seen cocaine being used?"

"I used it with him."

"That's a pretty positive statement. What was the source of the drugs?"

"That's something we didn't say in our book. We didn't mention names, but I will say it was a singer and a relative that brought it in to him. One particular time we were on tour, I don't remember what city we were in but they were sent back to Nashville, Tennessee to get some more because he was out. When they got back we knew where they had gone and Joe Esposito intercepted the stuff, and he and Dr. Nichopoulos took it and emptied it out except for a small amount and crushed up aspirin or some powder and put it back in there. But it was a singer in a group that he had with him and one of his relatives by marriage."

"Did you ever pick up prescriptions for Placidyls or anything like that?"

"No way."

"Having had some time to kind of think about everything, have you given any thought to why you, Dave, and Sonny were actually fired?"

"Yes, I have thought about it. I think it boils down to pressures being put on him by his father because there were about three lawsuits at the last from people who tried to con their way into the suite. When we had to get them to leave they started something, and, of course, then when we had to do something about it there was a lawsuit. Vernon told us on the phone that it was because they were cutting down on expenses, but we knew that was bullshit. So, the only thing I can say is it was those three lawsuits. One was settled for a very small amount and the other two, I think, were just thrown out."

"As far as you know they were all settled?"

"Yes, now Dave Hebler, he wasn't involved, I don't know why he was released."

"Was there ever a time when you said directly to Elvis or to the other guys, about the drugs, 'This has gotten out of hand, this has got to stop.' "

"Well, that might have been another reason that I was released, because I talked to Elvis on at least three occasions about it. I said, 'Your personality has changed, it's bad.'

"On the tape, in our book, in our phone conversation I said, 'We were worried about your health,' I was going to get into it and then he came back and said, 'Yeah, I guess that's why you are writing a book.'

"I completely forgot about what I was going to say and said, 'Well, don't talk about me hurting you, look what you done to me.'

"I talked to him about it on three occasions. In Las Vegas twice and in Memphis once, then I said, 'Well, forget it.'

"One time on tour in Detroit or somewhere, when the stuff was being brought in, Ed Parker, who's put us down saying we're lying about the drugs, and I went down to this singer's room. I kicked in the door and broke his foot, and told him if he ever brought anymore drugs around it was going to be a lot worse. And then Elvis found out about it later and called us into his room and said, 'I don't like these bully tactics, I need that.'

"And I said, 'Man, if you need it, I'm not going to say anymore about it. You can have it.'

"That was about a year before we left, so I think all of this together, he wanted people around him at the last who would go along with the program and I didn't go along with it."

"Ed Parker went with you?"

"Ed Parker, and I believe Dick Grob. I'm pretty sure Dick Grob, and one other guy who was along for a short time. That was Dave Hebler's partner in a karate school. Dave got him a job with this singing group, and he was with us. I know for a fact Ed Parker was there."

"That leads me to a very obvious question. Why do you suppose some of the guys, like Ed Parker, are denying the drugs now?"

"That's what I would like to know. I guess it's just trying to keep his image clean, that's the only thing I can think of. Of course, Ed's got his own book out and he's going to try to do all he can to promote it, but that's what really bugs me, these people are coming right out and lying and why, I don't know. I'm glad Marty's coming out so maybe that will settle it. I think everybody knows now because there have been too many people who have come out and verified what we said, like the girl who almost died. Maybe it is to protect his image, I don't know."

"What are your feelings about the will?"

"That's another thing that I feel funny about. Why was the will pushed through and drawn up? It's kind of strange. Why was his father made the beneficiary? Elvis had talked about a will and joked around on the airplane and said he was going to leave everybody a certain amount of money, and we all joked and said, 'We won't worry about that because it's a long way off.'

"Then to see this will that's all drawn up and the date is scratched out from one year to the next at the top, I don't know. I think somebody had an idea that something was happening.

"You can see it with a lot of the guys," West continued, "but thinking particularly in terms of Billy Smith, who was not only close to him, but related to him, and yet cut out completely, it strikes me as being rather strange."

"There's a man in Denver, Kennedy?" I asked.

"Yes, Captain Kennedy, Bob Cantrell and Ron Pietrofesso."

"Have they said anything about Elvis and the drugs?"

"Since his death? No, I haven't heard anything; seen anything. I heard that one of them, I think it was Bob, said it wasn't true. I didn't read this, I just heard it from somebody else so I don't know exactly what he was talking about, but I know that Ron, Elvis told me this, that Ron almost broke down and said, 'Look, let's put you in the hospital, nobody will know about it, and get you dried out.'

"Elvis said, 'You think I'm not strong enough to beat this?' and right then, that's when we left Denver, suddenly.

"They were aware of it, there was no way they couldn't be. While they were there, they saw the pills in his bedroom. Kennedy and all three of them."

"Was Colonel Parker aware of the drugs?"

"Yes, very much. Because he used to call me and say, 'Do you think Elvis can go on stage tonight?'

"One time I said, 'No,' and he cancelled the show in Las Vegas.

"I caught the wrath of Vernon and Elvis after that, not really that much. Elvis knew I was right and he kind of just said, 'No, you shouldn't do that, I can get ready.'

"I said, 'Well, you were in your bedroom and the Colonel was down there, and it was almost show time and I didn't know what to do.'

"The Colonel would call me when he was on the road and ask, 'What kind of shape is he in?' and I would tell him."

"He never made any effort to stop it? It would seem to me that Colonel Parker, Doctor Nick, Vernon and all of you guys would have tried to stop it."

"I guess everybody was afraid. They knew how he would blow up."

"Colonel Parker wasn't really afraid of him. At least that's my understanding."

"I don't think he was afraid of him, but he almost got dropped once there in Las Vegas when they had an argument and as far as Elvis was concerned it was over with, but a couple of days later Elvis called and straightened it out. I've wondered about it, why in the hell Vernon, or the Colonel didn't, I mean Vernon was the only one who really had the authority to do anything. I don't know, it's a shame."

"You never discussed it privately with Vernon?"

"Not with Vernon, no."

"And he never mentioned it to you?"

"No. I just discussed it with Elvis and lightly with the Colonel."

"You did discuss it with the Colonel, straightforward, not just how is he tonight or like that?"

"He wanted to know who was bringing it in. He was suspicious of all the doctors. I remember one of the doctors was brought into his office in Las Vegas and was questioned about it and asked, 'Do you know where this is coming from?' "

"There was a time when a box of pills was delivered to Elvis while he was in the hospital in Memphis, and it was intercepted by you guys."

"No, I probably wasn't in on that."

"Tell me about Doctor Nick. Was he supplying Elvis with pills?"

"He gave him prescriptions. And then, other things that would come from outside. I saw him empty these things out and I guess he probably knew the amount he could take or whatever. But I did see him empty capsules and put in it whatever, sugar tablets or whatever they call them. I've seen him do that. But he did write a lot of prescriptions, a lot of prescriptions."

"What are your feelings about him in general, I guess what I'm really asking is, do you think he was helping Elvis or do you think he was creating problems?"

"Well, I thought with him there that he could keep it under control and I thought that's what he was doing. Undoubtedly something happened."

"Are you aware of the number of prescriptions he wrote for Marty?"

"Yes, Marty told me about it. Man, I've seen a fruit jar full of some kind of sleeping pills, they were blue and white. There were more pills around there than any fifteen people could take in a year."

"Did they come from Nick?"

"I don't know where those pills came from, but Nick was the doctor on call at that time."

"I assume that everything got progressively worse over the years. Am I right on that?"

"Yes. The early years were great. Just fun and man, we had a ball. Went everywhere and did everything. Then it went downhill. Especially the last five years."

"And you attribute that solely to the drugs?"

"Yes. Solely to it. I don't know what caused it or whether he just liked the feeling of being out of it. But why? I don't know why."

"Do you ever speculate on it?"

"Oh yeah. I have my own thoughts, maybe it was the break up with Priscilla, but he was out of it when she was there on the ranch. He was getting ready to start a movie at Universal and I went ahead to Nashville and told the producers and everybody that he had picked the songs. He hadn't even heard the songs for the movie, I picked them. Finally he flew in a couple of days later. He had this cowboy outfit on, chaps, like he'd just got off the ranch, way overweight, and this was when they were married, so that's why I say I don't know what to blame it on. Maybe he was insecure. Sometimes I had the feeling that he couldn't believe that this was all happening to him and wondering why and was a little embarrassed about it, and these things gave him a false sense of security.

"I know when he was acting, doing movies, he was very embarrassed about it and being an actor myself I know the feeling, but you take these diet pills and you get this false security and it's just a crutch, something to make you feel good and you don't really care whether you goof up or not."

"Do you know John O'Grady? There was an article in the *Enquirer* quoting him about Doctor Shapiro. Do you know if any of that's true?"

"I don't know. I know Max Shapiro. When you said intercepted some pills awhile ago I remembered Sonny intercepted something from Shapiro. I read the article and I know John O'Grady and he could dig pretty deep, and we know Shapiro was bringing stuff around so I think it was true. I heard that Shapiro was going to sue but I never heard anything else about it."

"I've been trying to contact O'Grady, but he's been out of town, to confirm that the *Enquirer* story is true, that they didn't make it up."

"No, I don't believe they could make something up like that."

"Do you have any further comments?"

"I hope that Marty covers the good times like we tried to do, too. It wasn't all bad. It's a shame that somebody of that magnitude could get hooked on this stuff and just kill himself. He had so much to live for. One thing that I'm proud of about our book is that I heard that two people, Rod Stewart, the English rock singer, and the Mexican boy from Cheech and Chong read the book after Elvis died and they put it together and straightened their act up. If we saved one life with that book, then it was worth it.

"That's what bugs me with these people who know damn well what we said was true, the people around him like Ed Parker who come out and say what they do. That is something they are going to have to live with. I don't worry about it because I know what we did, and I know that we wrote the book long before he died, hoping for money of course, but also hoping he would read it and say, 'Well, the truth's out, I'd better straighten my act up,' but I guess he was too far gone."

Chapter Six

The Price of Health Care

Doctor George Nichopoulos is a Memphis physician who became Elvis Presley's doctor some years prior to the singer's death. Doctor Nick, as the guys called him, was one of the group. He is a short, well-dressed, distinguished-looking man with silver-gray hair who often traveled with Elvis and became the family doctor for most of the guys and their wives. The doctor's wife, Edna, was a friend of many of the guys' wives, and his son, Dean, worked for Elvis during the later years.

Doctor Nichopoulos was a partner of Elvis, Joe Esposito and one Michael McMahon in a racquetball venture in Memphis which seems to have turned sour toward the end. The doctor is well-liked by many of the guys who feel he always had Elvis' best interest at heart.

Memphis public records reveal that George C. Nichopoulos and Edna S. Nichopoulos borrowed from Elvis A. Presley the sum of two hundred thousand dollars as evidenced by a non-interest bearing promissory note of either July 29, 1975 or July 29, 1976. The deed of trust, as recorded, carries both dates.

A second deed of trust is recorded which shows that on March 3, 1977, George C. Nichopoulos and Edna S. Nichopoulos became indebted to Elvis A. Presley for an additional fifty-five thousand dollars. This deed of trust states that the promissory note is interest bearing and payable in installments with a final maturity of March 1, 2002.

From these public records it appears that Doctor Nichopoulos was indebted to Elvis Presley for a total of two hundred and fifty-five thousand dollars. Two hundred thousand dollars of that amount was non-interest bearing.

An interesting side light of these financial dealings is that the Executor of the estate of Elvis Presley, Elvis' father Vernon, lists on the inventory of the assets belonging to the estate the following:

Promissory note dated March 3, 1977, in the face amount of $25,000.00, secured by Trust Deed on Lot 40, Section A, Eastwood Manor Subdivision, payable to the order of Elvis A. Presley and bearing interest in the amount of 7% per annum.

Lot 40, Section A, Eastwood Manor Subdivision is the home of George C. and Edna S. Nichopoulos. Either the trust deeds are filed incorrectly in regard to interest, or the executor's inventory report to the probate court is incorrect.

Repeated attempts were made to communicate with Doctor Nichopoulos regarding his association with Elvis Presley. Messages were left with his secretary requesting that he return the telephone calls, and explanations were given for the reason for the calls, but they were never answered. It is, therefore, impossible to include any comments by Doctor Nichopoulos in this manuscript.

Patsy Lacker speaks harshly of George Nichopoulos. She remembers the pain of the drugs and blames him for being the source. It would be difficult to find fault with her reasoning. During one forty-six month period, January 24, 1973, through October 28, 1976, Doctor Nichopoulos prescribed the following medication for Marty Lacker: 6,464 Placidyl, 3,204 Darvon, 1,508 Hycomine, 708 Empirin Codeine #3, 500 Dalmane, 400 Valium, 216 Darvocet, 200 Valmid and 91 other assorted pills which are not important.

The total number of pills prescribed by Doctor George Nichopoulos for Marty Lacker, and consumed by Marty Lacker, during that forty-six month period was thirteen thousand two hundred and ninety one (13,291). The average per day was ten.

Placidyl is an oral hypnotic used for insomnia. According to the *Physicians Desk Reference* the following warning is to be considered when prescribing Placidyl: *Prolonged use of Placidyl may result in tolerance and psychological and physical dependence. Prolonged administration of this drug is not recommended.*

Valmid is a sedative-hypnotic. Dalmane is a hypnotic for insomnia. Hycomine is a cough suppressant and respiratory tract decongestant. Valium is a tranquilizer. Empirin Codeine #3 is a narcotic analgesic pain killer. Darvon is an analgesic pain killer containing phenacetin which has been reported to damage the kidneys when taken in large amounts for a long period of time. Propoxyhene, also found in Darvon, has been known to cause cardiac arrhythmias.

The reason for isolating those forty-six months is that we have certified copies of the records from the pharmacy which filled the prescriptions. Unfortunately they did not preserve records prior to that period, and we have only Marty's and Patsy's word that the average amounts were approximately the same for the six years prior to January 24, 1973.

Marty Lacker has no anger against Doctor Nichopoulos. "There were times when he was very nice and tried to do everything possible for you, but there were other times, and his son was worse than he was, when you would ask him something and he would come out with a smart remark to try to show off.

"That's the only thing I feel toward Nick in a negative way. I don't have any grudge or feel bad toward him because of the pills or any of that. It may sound funny, or stupid, but I just don't have it.

"When Elvis wanted something, nothing was going to stop him from getting it. Nick used to come to the house just about every night to check Elvis and see if everything was all right. He would bring his medical bag along and when he was finished with Elvis he might set it down, and go into another room to talk with some of the guys. Well, the first time I remember this happening Nick had left the bag by one of the doors and Elvis saw it. He walked over to the bag and tried to open it, but Nick had locked it. Elvis started cursing under his breath and I started laughing. It happened again the next day. Elvis called Nick into the room, aimed a pistol at the bag and said, 'If you keep locking this thing I'm going to blow it open.'

"We all took it as a joke but I guess Nick realized what Elvis was saying to him, so, he later said, he began leaving a prescription drug bottle full of non-drug capsules in the bag and not locking it so Elvis would think he was getting something he wanted.

"There's no question Nick was writing prescriptions for what Elvis wanted. He was Elvis' doctor, he treated him, but the drug prescriptions came from other doctors too. Nick wasn't the only one. That's why I keep saying that Nick was the lesser of all evils, he tried to control it. He knew Elvis was getting it from other people, so he limited and controlled what he gave him. But he knew, he knew what Elvis was getting and he knew what Elvis was capable of doing. Everyone of us told Nick, especially Joe who was real close to him. Joe would tell Nick, 'Elvis will just go to another doctor to get what he wants if you don't give it to him or make him think he's getting it by giving him a limited amount, he'll go to another doctor.'

"We've all said it and Elvis would go to another doctor whether he knew him or not. He would have thought nothing of going to a doctor's house and knocking on his door. You know when a doctor saw Elvis Presley there he would be thrilled and either call his nurse or his wife to meet Elvis, and Elvis would sit there and con him into giving him exactly what he wanted. He was an actor, he could sit there and say, 'I'm having a problem sleeping, or 'I've got a pain here,' and the doctor would believe him.

"He would act like he didn't know anything about medicine and the doctor would believe him and tell him, 'I'll take care of you. There's nothing for you to worry about.'

"When Elvis left he would have exactly what he wanted, and the doctor would think he had done a real service for Elvis Presley.

"I picked up prescriptions for Elvis or had one of the other guys do it when that was part of my responsibility as foreman of the guys. We used a lot of different pharmacies to keep too many prescriptions from being on file at one place.

"We've often talked about the pills when Elvis wasn't around, all of us have. Mostly we joked about them and there was always the question of how he was going to be when he got up. That is, what kind of mood he was going to be in which really meant, was he going to be on the pills.

"If he stayed upstairs late and called down on the intercom you could tell if he was on the pills, and if he was, someone would say, 'Oh hell, he's out of it again.'

"Of course we used to say that about each other too. But I have to say this, most of the guys did not use anything during the day. I did, but most of them did not. I was the fool.

"Occasionally we had serious conversations about the pills but most of us thought it was futile, there was no way we could change things. There was also the thought which ran through my mind and, I'm sure, some of the others', and that was I didn't believe anything would harm Elvis. It didn't matter what he did, nothing would harm him. I know how scared I used to be about flying but when Elvis was along I never worried. I just didn't believe anything would happen.

"It's a strange thing to say, but I had the feeling that regardless of how many he took nothing was going to happen to him, I don't know what it was that made me feel that way.

"There were times when we talked about it as a group. Mostly after Elvis yelled at somebody or did something which we felt he wouldn't have done had it not been for the pills. Lamar used to say things, but he never did anything about it. Sometimes Red or Sonny or Joe would say something. Joe and I talked about it a lot, just the two of us but the conversation usually ended by one of us holding up our hands and saying, 'What the hell can we do about it?'

"There was no way we could really do anything about it. There were times when it was a real problem for me or Joe. We were in a position of responsibility and had to get things done, but sometimes we couldn't because Elvis wouldn't talk about something. If he was irritable because of something he was taking, or something he wanted to take, he would just cut you off. He would say, 'I don't want to talk about it,' and there was nothing you could do.

"Joe and I got mad many times when he would act like that, but the next minute he would come in with that smile on his face and wipe all the anger away, until the next time.

"There was never a real conference, as such, of all the

guys to talk about Elvis' problem. You didn't know Elvis. You had to know him to understand the situation. Elvis would get what he wanted. If Nick had said, 'No', to something Elvis wanted, he would have said, 'Get the hell out of here and don't come back.'

"He would have gotten another doctor who probably would have given him anything he wanted, and not cared what happened. Nick was able to control things by being there. I know of times, and Sonny says the same thing, that Nick would substitute sugar pills, or vitamin pills, for all the other junk. He cared about Elvis and I honestly think he knew that if he left, things would have been much worse than they were. He could, at least, partly control what happened, but if he wasn't there someone else would have been.

"It would not be right to lay all the blame on Nick. If he was wrong, we were all wrong, including the public. We all contributed to Elvis' life, and death. You had to know Elvis to understand. He was going to have his own way about what he wanted.

"The fault lies with all of us. Every single one of us, including the public who really didn't know him that well. They thought they did, but they didn't. I'm speaking of the people who met him once or twice and sat and talked with him, because that was his nature, but they didn't get to know him. We, who were around him all the time, really didn't know him. I don't know if he even knew himself.

"Elvis was so damn dynamic he would overpower anyone, and he wouldn't listen. If that was really what he wanted to do, we could sit and talk until we were blue in the face, but it wouldn't do any good.

"We knew that, at least some of us did. It would be like talking to a wall. Elvis did what he wanted to do. There had to be times when he knew he shouldn't be doing what he was doing, and there had to be times when Nick knew he shouldn't be giving him what he gave him, but most of the fault lies in Elvis' abusing, really abusing the prescription medications. At one time Nick tried to combat that by having someone hold the prescription drugs and giving Elvis only the right amount. It was easy to abuse the drugs, especially if he didn't fight it too much.

"Part of the fault was the pressure of his life, his life-style, the disappointment, the split with Priscilla, his mother's death. I know those kinds of things happen to a lot of people, but we're not talking about a lot of people, we're talking about one individual, and how it affected him.

"Elvis was a lonely person. That's why he had to have companionship all the time, female and the guys. He knew we loved him, he knew that even though natural doubts crept into his mind about all of us, but deep down he knew we loved him.

"Where the fault lies? You've got to put it on all of us, including him. He probably was his own worst enemy. Most of us are."

Chapter Seven

Prescription For Death

"Parker is a rude, crude, son of a bitch, and you can quote me on that."

John O'Grady, the man describing Colonel Tom Parker, is head of a private detective agency whose main office is located in Hollywood, California. O'Grady, a former sergeant with the Los Angeles Police Department where he was a narcotics expert, was a long-time associate of Elvis Presley.

"People put up with Parker because they had to, not because they liked him." He continued, "If you wanted Elvis you had to deal with Parker as far as the concerts and business were concerned, and everybody wanted Elvis. Parker couldn't get a free cup of coffee in Vegas today. The only thing he ever had in his life that was worth anything was his association with Elvis Presley. I remember once in one of the dressing rooms, Parker told Charlie Hodge to get down on all fours and bark like a dog, and poor, dumb Charlie did it.

"I looked at Parker and told him, 'If you ever said something like that to me, I'd push your damned head through the wall.'

"He walked out of the room. Elvis came over to me and said, 'Aw, John, leave him alone. We've got to keep the old fool happy.'

"Charlie Hodge was likeable, but he was Elvis' whipping boy most of the time. Charlie tried to avoid any controversy. He agreed with everybody about everything.

"All the guys were ignorant shit-kickers, except Joe Esposito. Nobody did their job, not one of them except Esposito. He was head and shoulders above the rest as far as brains were concerned. I recommended to Elvis that he get rid of all of them except Joe. I don't think Esposito had an emotional involvement with Elvis, it was a job for him and he did it well. You never saw Joe on the drugs or trying to get every broad he came into contact with. When there was work to do Joe took care of business, but the rest were worthless.

"We tried to get Sonny, Red and Dave to give up the book idea. I called them and said, 'We're not taking you back to work, both because of Elvis' feelings and my recommendations, but we'll pay to have you retrained to do another job and put up the money to get you started in business.'

"Well, they now say I was trying to bribe them, but the damn fools should know you can't bribe a private citizen, unless you try to get them to do something illegal. It's a business deal, not a bribe.

"Parker knew about the drugs and didn't care a bit as long as it didn't affect his pocketbook, and it's absurd for Vernon to say he didn't know. I delivered a copy of the investigation we did concerning the drugs to him. That was a long time before Elvis died.

"Elvis was his own man. He did what he wanted to do, he ran the show. It was the same thing with the doctors, Elvis told them what he wanted and they gave it to him. When we did the investigation we tried to scare the doctors off. The only one we didn't bother with was Nichopoulos and that was because of Esposito. I believed him when he told me Nichopoulos wasn't giving Elvis anything. I didn't know of the relationship between Esposito and Nichopoulos, their business deals in the racquetball thing.

"I tried to get Elvis interested in working against drug abuse and interested in police work, but as much as I would talk to him about doing television messages against drug abuse, and things like that, the guys around him would talk him out of it.

"I never saw Elvis once, or talked to him once after the Satellite Show that he wasn't strung out on drugs. He came to my office one day and walked into the wall he was so far gone. He would call in the middle of the night and talk for hours and you couldn't understand one tenth of what he was saying. I'd sit and watch television with the phone at my ear because he would just be mumbling or rambling on about a dozen different things at the same time.

"Elvis was a completely different person in the later years he was so heavily on the drugs. During the investigation we did we found that not only were the doctors giving Elvis what he wanted, they were also writing prescriptions for his friends who were giving the drugs to him.

"Shapiro, the dentist, admitted to the newspapers he was writing prescriptions for Elvis' associates when he knew they were giving the drugs to Elvis. He said he did it to protect Elvis' privacy. They all knew what was going on. Everyone of them knew, and they knew it was illegal."

"I talked with Elvis about the drugs a lot but it didn't do any good. I was sure he was going to die from them and I talked to his attorney, Gregory Hookstratten, about trying to have Elvis committed to a hospital. He asked me to talk with Priscilla about it and I did. She tried to get Elvis to go into a hospital but he wouldn't listen to her. Elvis always thought he could handle everything and I don't think he realized how bad off he was.

"Priscilla is a bright woman. She knew the guys were hangers-on and she resented them. Once she said to me, 'How would you like to get up and see that bunch of goons around your breakfast table every day?'

"She didn't like the guys being around. They were at least partly the cause of the marriage split-up.

"Linda Thompson was different. I had to throw her out of the house once. I don't mean physically, but I had to get her out of the house for Elvis. I got her an apartment, he didn't want her around anymore.

"Ghanem, the Pakistani doctor in Las Vegas, could tell you a lot, if he would. Ask him how he managed to get where he is today, where the money came from. Ask him about the drugs.

"Ed Parker, not the Colonel, was harmless. He didn't know Elvis that well, of course now he's saying he was Elvis' best friend to help sell his book, but he wasn't around that much.

"Vernon Presley had the will made up the way he wanted it, and then got Elvis to sign it when he was in the right mood. I've told Joe Esposito and Charlie Hodge to sue the estate. I know Elvis wanted to take care of them.

"Elvis had a great sense of humor. He was really a funny guy. When he was straight I could sit and talk with him for hours at a time. I tried to get him interested in politics, he was a natural leader and had the ability to be a senator or governor or even more. He could lead people. I once told him to give up singing, he had done everything he could ever do as a singer and get into politics but I couldn't get him interested.

"Elvis had a buzz in his head. There was something in his head that made him do the things he did, to be the way he was."

Marty Lacker conveys a somewhat different impression of Colonel Parker. In response to a question about Colonel Parker being concerned about going to England because of the drugs, Marty says, "I never heard that. Even when I've talked with Sonny, who was with the Colonel a lot, he never told me that. I always thought it was the security and the fact that the Colonel didn't have many contacts over there.

"But the Colonel would talk to you when you were alone with him sometimes, and maybe he did tell Sonny that. The Colonel could do and say some funny things.

"Once he called a meeting when we were in Hollywood, after Elvis had fallen down in the bathroom, and tried to change everybody's jobs. Elvis was heavy into reading about Oriental religions and mysticism at the time and the Colonel didn't think much of that. He was also pissed off because the fall caused a delay in starting production of one of the movies.

"He and Elvis met for a few minutes in Elvis' room and then called Joe in, I was told to wait outside. After about an hour they called me into the room and the Colonel did all the talking. He said, 'This is the way we're going to do it from now on. Mr. Presley's tired of reading all these damned books and he wants them all taken out of here and burned.'

"Elvis shook his head and said, 'Yeah, I'm tired of all that crap.'

"The Colonel went on to say, 'From now on we're going to have one chain of command. Mr. Esposito will be in charge now and Mr. Lacker, you will handle special projects, and there's one special project we all know about.'

"The special project he was talking about was Elvis' forthcoming wedding. I was relieved because I had been wanting to get back to Memphis and my family but I was still a little hurt by the way it was done. The Colonel then gathered all the other guys together outside and went through the whole thing again.

"The Colonel is a brilliant man in his own way. People make the mistake of underestimating him and when they do they come out on the short end of the stick. The Colonel kept things on the upbeat, he kept the atmosphere happy. He played his practical jokes and pranks but it was all for a good purpose and the guys knew it. He kept the Elvis machine going, he provided the opportunities for everyone and he made no false pretenses. He is the master at what he does, managing, promoting and putting deals together and his advice is greatly sought by many in the entertainment industry. I know I got one hell of a good education from just being around him."

Max Shapiro is a Beverly Hills dentist who also has an office in Las Vegas. There is an article in the *National Enquirer* wherein Doctor Shapiro is quoted as saying he wrote prescriptions for Elvis' friends knowing the prescribed drugs would be turned over to Elvis. Only the *Enquirer* and Shapiro know if he really admitted taking part in the affair.

Marty Lacker tells of at least one time when he and Sonny flew to Las Vegas and picked up drug prescriptions from Shapiro for Elvis. Marty says, "I had some business to take care of in Los Angeles and in Las Vegas, we were in Memphis at the time, so I called Shapiro and told him Elvis needed some pills, either Empirin Codeine or Demerol, and asked him if I could pick up the prescription when I got out there. He said 'yes,' so I flew to Los Angeles where I met Sonny and the two of us went on to Vegas. After completing our business there we went by Shapiro's office and picked up the prescription which I later had filled."

Shortly after Elvis' death, Max Shapiro filed a claim against the estate for almost $15,000 for dental work for which he said he had not been paid. The Memphis court denied the claim.

The name of a third doctor, one Elias Ghanem, creeps into the conversations with singular regularity. Marty says he only knew Ghanem casually, that he was a doctor in Las Vegas who treated Elvis on occasion. Dave Hebler refuses to confirm, or deny, that Ghanem is the doctor about whom he is speaking when he says, ". . . we have that same doctor on tape admitting the drugs."

Later in the same interview, Hebler says, ". . . one of the reasons why I don't want to name the man is because I can't document it."

Sonny West speaks of the doctor who sent drugs to Elvis when he was a patient at Baptist Memorial Hospital. When asked, "Will you say who the doctor was?" Sonny replies, "Just say he was in Las Vegas. A Las Vegas doctor."

To the same question, "Why would you not want to name him?" Sonny's comment is, "Well, I'll tell you the truth. This person has some tremendous influence even as far as out of this country. Even when we wrote our book, we turned over a list of names to our lawyer, in a sealed envelope, to be opened upon the death of the three of us."

Doctor Elias Ghanem did not respond to a telephone call to his office, even though a full explanation was given to his secretary regarding the reason for the call. Once again, therefore, it is not possible to include any comments by one of Elvis' physicians.

Doctor Max Shapiro, the Beverly Hills dentist, was not reluctant, however, to discuss his association with Elvis.

Doctor Shapiro said, "There is no truth to the *National Enquirer* story. It's an outright lie. I'm suing them. I never gave Elvis anything except what was called for medically. I have the original tape of the *National Enquirer* interview. They made it sound like I'm a drug pusher.

"I told the girl who did the interview that sometimes I would write a prescription for Elvis in the name of one of his friends but that was not an extra prescription, or a way for Elvis to get an extra amount. There would be one prescription for something Elvis needed medically and if it was say in Marty's name, then Marty knew it was for Elvis and Elvis knew it was his prescription. There wouldn't be one in Marty's name and one in Elvis' name. There's nothing wrong, or illegal, about doing that. I've checked the law.

"The problem was that when Elvis went to a doctor in a different city he didn't think to tell the doctor what he was taking, and the doctor might prescribe something else for him. It might be something which should not be taken with the first medication. That's a common error of doctors and patients.

"I knew three years before Elvis died that he had a heart disease, and I told him so. His hands were swollen when he was in the office and I could tell it came from a heart disease.

"Elvis' problems with drugs were like those of the president's wife, Mrs. Ford. Elvis wasn't an addict, he just became dependent on certain drugs from taking too many of them. He would never take anything which wasn't prescribed by a doctor, he would not take anything illegal.

"Elvis was a loyal person. He came from a small town where a doctor was considered to be absolutely dependable. Elvis had great confidence in all doctors and he would take whatever they told him to take, regardless of what it did to him.

"Elvis was best man at my wedding and Ginger was maid of honor. He insisted on having the wedding at his Palm Springs home. He arranged the whole thing, he called the jeweler and bought the rings, he did everything and the wedding was beautiful. Elvis was a very generous and good-hearted man. I don't mean just the automobiles and the jewelry he gave away. Things like that were just on the surface, but down deep he was a very kind and generous man.

"I can verify Ginger's story. Elvis told me he loved Ginger very much and that he had asked her to marry him. They were engaged. I did dental work for Ginger and for a singer Elvis had working for him. I never got paid for that work. There was a newspaper story that I was suing for the money but it wasn't true, I put in a claim against the estate, that's all. The court denied it because they wouldn't let the singer testify, there's some law that says you can't testify if you were the beneficiary of something. We are appealing the decision.

"When I went back to Memphis for that hearing, Vernon and I sat in the hall outside the courtroom and cried. We were on opposite sides then, but Vernon is just doing what the lawyers tell him to do, but we cried together and talked for a long time. He really looks awful, I feel so sorry for him.

"Elvis knew I had invented an artificial heart and the last

thing he ever said to me was, 'Max, please make one for me. Make one for Ginger and one for my daddy, but please make one for me as soon as you can.'

"I wish I had been there when he died."

When asked to elaborate on the amount and kinds of drugs which were used by Elvis Presley, Marty Lacker says, "Quantity is hard to talk about. You can't really tell, just like nobody knew how many I was taking. You learn to be very careful and take those things when nobody is looking. When we started with the uppers there was every kind imaginable, Dexadrene, Dexamill, Eskotrol, Desbutal, and I don't even remember how many others.

"There were some funny sides to all of it. This happened the first time we went to Vegas. We were in the suite getting ready to go to the Stardust to see a show and just before we left Elvis handed me a box. It looked like a box a watch would come in, and he said, 'Here, you hold on to this.'

"I said, 'Okay, but what's in it?'

"Elvis laughed and said, 'Open it.'

"I opened it and the damn thing was packed so full of pills I spilled some on the floor when I raised the lid. It was like giving a baby a box of candy to keep, I'd never seen so many in one place. It didn't even dawn on me that what I was doing was probably illegal because these were not in prescription bottles. Anyway, I put it in my coat pocket and we went to the show.

"The first part of the show was an act where a guy was billed as the world's greatest pickpocket. We were sitting on the side where there was easy access in and out but I was right on the aisle. Elvis was next to me and Joe was on the other side. The pickpocket began his act and he was good. He could take a guy's necktie off without the man even knowing it. He was walking around in the audience talking to people and then holding up something he had taken from them.

"I had never seen the guy before and I believed all of it. Well, I'm sitting there with this box of pills in my pocket and I begin to worry. What the hell would I do if he came over and managed to get the box?

"I really started to get worried as the guy got closer to where we were sitting. I slipped the box of pills out of my coat pocket and held it under the table. I tried to kick Joe to get his attention but he was watching the act and not concerned with me or the box. I finally leaned over to him and said, 'Joe, take this damn box, man, that son of a bitch is liable to pick my damn pocket.'

"Joe started to laugh and said, 'No, man, he's not going to come over here.'

"That was my first trip to Vegas but Joe knew the ways, so I laughed too, and relaxed and enjoyed the show. I later learned they don't do those things to people like Elvis, but it sure scared me for a few minutes.

"As time went by we got off the uppers and started things like Empirin Codeine, Percodan and Demerol but the only Demerol I had anything to do with were pills. I've seen some liquid around but I never used it and I don't know for a fact that Elvis did. I always believed the shots he was getting were B-12.

"As far as the sleeping pills were concerned there were Placidyl, Valmid and Dalmane. I wasn't there when the Quaalude started, but I used to hear Ricky Stanley, Dee's son, talking about 'ludes, which is the street name for it. It was always 'ludes this and 'ludes that, but I don't know for certain that Ricky was the one who was bringing them in.

"As far as quantity is concerned, I don't think Elvis took them like I did during the time when he was going to be out of bed. I sometimes took them during the day, just to get a buzz from them, but I don't think I've ever seen Elvis do that. He was pretty straight when he had something to do. Maybe he took a Demerol or a Percodan, a pain pill, but I don't think he used the sleeping pills when he was going to be awake.

"Now I'm talking mostly about sleeping pills which make you groggy and out of it. The pain pills may make you feel numb but the sleeping pills can really make you groggy and incoherent. There were times when he would stay upstairs in bed and we would go up to see him and could tell he was out of it.

"He was not sloppy out of it all the time, and I think that's important to emphasize. The man rode a motorcycle sometimes as fast as eighty or ninety miles an hour. There's no way he could have done that if he had been out of it. He may have had something in him, but he wasn't sloppy out of it, no way.

"He stayed straight when he had a challenge, like the

Satellite Show or some of the other things which he enjoyed. When thôse challenges were gone he tended to become bored and get back on the pills, but the man did great things and if anybody says he was out of it all the time they're exaggerating, and if they believe it they're mistaken."

Chapter Eight

The Doctor as Pusher

The medical doctor is the number one drug pusher in the United States, according to drug abuse authorities. It is not the street junkie, who is selling to maintain a habit, who does the lion's share of the damage, but rather the family physician in terms of his careless prescribing practices.

The doctor is overloaded with patients and often overworked. There are not enough doctors available, according to those in the profession who are concerned with the unethical practice of the minority and the careless practice of the majority. The conscientious segment of the medical profession, though opposed to the free and easy dispensation of drugs, explains the practice by pointing out that almost eighty percent of the patients who come to their office are affected with nothing more serious than hypochondria.

Doctors get very impressive printed material from the pharmaceutical companies, with promises of instant relief of pain and pressure for their patients, and they all too often fall to the temptation of solving an undiagnosed malady with a prescription for one of the magic drugs. Valium, for example, is the most-prescribed, and over-prescribed, drug in America.

There are more admissions to hospital emergency rooms for Valium complications than for any other drug. Not heroin, not alcohol, not cocaine. Valium is the drug of choice. It is the most abused drug in the country. Valium is meant to be, and is quite effective as, a muscular relaxant, but now it is being prescribed as a calmative agent for men, women, and children who are unable to define that which is bothering them. Valium is the doctor's friend, the pill which allows him to write a prescription. He knows the patient will not be satisfied unless he receives a prescription which must be filled by a pharmacy. But Valium is a self-elevating drug, if one is good, two is better and the Valium patient all too often ends by abusing the drug. The doctor who pushes pills will argue that the patient demands more than advice, and will not accept anything less than a drug prescription.

Unfortunately, even the most scrupulous doctors seem to fail to realize that the eighty percent whom they think of as hypochondriacs are seeking a cure for something. It may be an unnamed disease brought about by the stress of a family argument, a flat tire, or a broken refrigerator but it is nevertheless a very real disease to the sufferer and a prescription for addictive drugs is not the answer.

There is a cartoon showing a bewildered patient, standing before a doctor who is handing him a prescription and saying, "Take two a day until addicted."

It's funny to everyone except those who have lived through the terror of trying to get off a drug habit.

Pharmacists seem to tend to be more cautious than doctors. They often ask a patient if the doctor knows how many times a prescription has been refilled, but this, of course, is not the responsibility of the pharmacist. The cautious doctor will not write a prescription which may be refilled, although under the law he can usually allow up to five refills from one prescription. In the perfect world of sound medical practice, the doctor would require the patient to return for a consultation or physical check-up prior to allowing a prescription for an addictive drug to be refilled.

The temptation may be great for the doctor to write a prescription for Valium and get on to something more important. It may satisfy the doctor's need to do something and, in fact, it may make the patient feel better but it does not solve the problem, and may well create a new and far more serious problem by being the first step to an addiction. The physician should be honest with the patient. If he is unable to find a cause for the patient's distress he should say exactly that.

The people who do the most intensive research on the drugs are the pharmaceutical companies who are also the manufacturers. The profit motive is obviously the base line for these companies which are, of course, commercially oriented, and yet there exists a very incestuous relationship between the doctor and the pharmaceutical company. This relationship is fostered by the Bible of the medical profession, the *Physicians Desk Reference,* which contains the names and descriptions of every drug on the market. The drug descriptions are written by the manufacturing firms which, thereby, tell the doctor what to prescribe for the patient. To add to this love affair the pharmaceutical companies supply free samples to the doctors to use with their patients. Prescribing patterns, therefore, are not based on well-thought-out research and experience, but by the education brought to the doctor by the pharmaceutical companies. Promotional expenses for brand name drugs amounted to more than 350 million dollars last year.

There are thousands of prescription drugs, but only hundreds of formulas, so the difference comes in the packaging, the way they're put together. The companies bombard the doctors with so much promotional literature they can't possibly keep up with all the new information. The doctors, then, are dependent upon the pharmaceutical companies for what they prescribe for their patients.

The danger of abuse is ever-present. Mixing one drug with another can be deadly, and alcohol is included in the drug category. Perhaps the most dangerous is the mixture of alcohol and any drug in the depressant category like the barbituates, tranquilizers, opiates and narcotics. The mixture of any of these with alcohol can be lethal, especially alcohol and barbituates.

According to the Shelby County Medical Examiner, Dr. Jerry Francisco, the following drugs were found in therapeutic levels in the body of Elvis Presley during the autopsy performed at Baptist Memorial Hospital:

Ethinamate, trade name Valmid, is a sedative-hypnotic. The *Physicians Desk Reference* says, the concurrent ingestion with other central nervous system depressants, especially in overdosage, will increase the potential hazards of these agents.

Methaqualone, trade name Quaalude, is also a sedative-hypnotic. A hypnotic (sleep-inducing) dose should be taken only at bedtime, immediately before the patient retires, since

Quaalude may produce drowsiness within ten to twenty minutes. Care should be used during administration with other sedative, analgesic or psychotropic drugs because of possible addictive effects. Quaalude acts on a different central nervous system site than barbituates or glutethimide.

Large overdoses have been accompanied by cutaneous edema, bloating of the fluid in the skin, and renal insufficiency. Shock and respiratory arrest may occasionally occur.

Quaalude should not be used continuously for periods exceeding three months.

Barbituates are used as hypnotics for anxiety, and sedatives for anxiety and tension. They are central nervous system depressants, and are also used as anticonvulsants.

Codeine is a narcotic analgesic or pain killer. Patients receiving other sedative hypnotics or other central nervous system depressants concomitantly with codeine may exhibit an additive central nervous system depression. When such combined therapy is contemplated, the dose of one or both agents should be reduced. In severe overdose, circulatory collapse, cardiac arrest and death may occur.

The medical authorities with whom this case has been discussed state unequivocally that there is absolutely no medical reason for mixing the above drugs. No doctor, in other words, would prescribe Quaalude, Valmid, barbituates and codeine for use at the same time. There would simply be no medical reason for prescribing these drugs in combination.

The following drugs have been reported as being used by Elvis Presley in addition to those four found in therapeutic levels during the autopsy:

Hycodan is a cough tablet or syrup. It contains a codeine derivative.

Ritalin, methylphenidate hydrochloride, is used on children with minimal brain dysfunction.

Percodan, oxycodone hydrochloride, is a sedative and semisynthetic narcotic analgesic.

Demerol, meperidine hydrochloride, is a narcotic analgesic.

Dilaudid, narcotic analgesic.

Drug *abuse* means the taking of drugs beyond the amount necessary to effect the cure of, or alleviate the distress from, a physical or mental disorder. Drug *use* simply means the taking of prescribed drugs in the proper amounts.

A person may be a drug abuser without manifesting the visible signs of having a drug *problem.* A drug problem exists when the use of drugs interferes with the accepted normal social functions of an individual. A person who takes two Valium, or two martinis, or two Quaalude, or two shots of heroin a day may, or may not, have a drug problem. There are as many types of drug problems as there are people who abuse drugs.

There are thousands of people who have two or three alcoholic drinks with lunch and several more with dinner and, according to most authorities, these people are alcoholics. If, however, they are able to function properly they may not have a drug *problem,* for the time being anyway, as far as our society is concerned.

Tolerance means that a user of a given drug will need larger and larger amounts of that drug as time passes, to achieve the same effect once gained from a small quantity. *Toxicity* is the degree to which a drug is lethal. The toxic, or lethal, dose of a drug may remain constant while the tolerance level increases. For example, five milligrams of drug X may be lethal to a given individual who originally was able to achieve the desired *high* from one milligram. As tolerance increases the drug abuser may find he needs two, three, or four milligrams, to achieve the same euphoria. If, or when, tolerance increases to five milligrams, which is also the lethal dose, this individual will overdose and probably die as a result of so doing.

A *polydrug* user is a person who uses more than one type of drug. Usually these people are comfortable with everything from aspirin on up, and often mix drugs to achieve a desired sensation.

The sedative-hypnotic, or tranquilizer type drugs such as Placidyl, Quaalude, Valium, Valmid and Dalmane, are considered *psychoactive* or *mind altering* drugs. The *high* comes from resisting the intended effect of the drug. One forces himself to remain awake while the drug is trying to induce sleep. The high, or feeling of intoxication, is usually described in very sexual terms of tingling sensations, feelings of complete relaxation and the sensation of being asleep while actually being awake.

Drug experts say that approximately two per cent of the 500,000 doctors who are authorized to write prescriptions in the United States are involved in the practice of supplying drugs for other than medical needs. This means that there are 10,000 legal pushers plying their trade in this lucrative field of medical malpractice with virtual immunity.

The same experts feel that the illegal traffic in prescription drugs is now greater than the trade in the hard drugs, such as heroin and cocaine. During 1977, over two million doses of legal drugs were sold for improper use. The estimated income to the sellers for these painkillers, stimulants and sedatives was in the hundreds of millions of dollars. One Dilaudid tablet, for example, may cost only a few cents at the pharmacy but on the street it will bring as much as thirty to forty dollars.

Dilaudid has become known as drug-store heroin and others are blended, mixed and combined to produce heroin-like trips, at one-third the price of heroin, by knowledgeable addicts. Valium, Ritalin, Quaalude and Percodan are also popular on the street.

Prescription pads are stolen or copied and the unwary pharmacist becomes a link in the chain of illegal drug traffic. Addicts and pushers with some medical knowledge find it easy to feign a variety of diseases which respond to one of the many desired drugs, and the careless doctor writes a prescription for the sought after substance.

The less honest doctor finds the trade in legal drugs a very lucrative business. When a doctor teams up with a pharmacist, and they split the profits, it is almost impossible to prove any wrongdoing. Making a criminal case against a physician is a difficult and time-consuming task. Law enforcement officials generally prefer to direct their efforts against the pusher of hard drugs, who is more often a stereotype criminal, because the authorities have found that doctors are reluctant to testify against other doctors. Because of this, it is difficult to obtain a conviction in other than the most flagrant cases of abuse.

The mission of law enforcement officials is made even more difficult by the scarcity of complaining victims. Drug abusers seldom come forward and report cases of being given, or sold, excessive drug prescriptions. More often than not the doctor literally buries his mistake, or his greed, with the body of the overdosed abuser. For as long as he is alive, the abuser is in the clutches of the physician who has become his source of the needed drug, and when he is no longer alive his friends and relatives are reluctant to mention his drug habit. Society for many years has frowned upon the drug abuser as something dirty or less than human.

Such is the case with Elvis Presley. Had Elvis suffered from cancer, whether or not it was the cause of his death, those who knew and loved him would not hesitate to talk about the disease, if by so doing they could help prevent others from contracting it. Because the disease was drug abuse some now feel they would be soiling Elvis' image by talking about it.

There is a weakness in the human race which makes us seek heroes, and sometimes create them if they are not readily found. We try to make our heroes into beings which they are not. We seek advice on politics from famous artists and advice on art from politicians. We often fail to understand that it is possible to love and respect someone for what they can do without making them all-powerful. Our heroes become gods by our doing, and our making gods from heroes destroys, too often, those we claim to love, and who from the beginning were really only human, and subject to human frailties.

Tales told by doctors involved in the treatment of drug abuse are shocking. Men who actively seek arrest and enforced abstinence from heroin, to be able to feel again the thrill of the first fix when they are released, are commonplace. Children who make pill salads from their parents' uppers and downers, and anything else they find in the medicine chest, and wind up in the hospital, or the grave, are far more numerous than most of us know.

People jump from windows or off bridges, shoot themselves or shoot others, wreck their cars and the cars of others, murder strangers or their own families, steal, cheat and riot under the influence of drugs and alcohol. We die like flies from lung cancer, and fill the hospitals with addicts and alcoholics and there is little reason to believe that any major change of our national habits will take place in the foreseeable future. As a people we've mostly ignored the warnings against cigarette smoking, and we will undoubtedly ignore the warnings against drugs.

If, however, we can understand that even a man like Elvis Presley can become addicted to drugs, if we can understand how easily the disease can be acquired, and how difficult it is to cure, then perhaps there is a chance of preventing its continual spread. There is absolutely no chance if we hide from it and pretend it does not happen. Drug addiction is not a disgrace, it is a disease and should be recognized as such by all of us, including the most devoted fan of Elvis Presley.

We need education. We need to understand drugs and drug abuse. We need to learn to question the necessity of a drug prescription, and refuse it if the prescribing doctor can possibly provide an alternative. The medical profession also needs education. Those who simply err in their judgment concerning the dispensation of prescription drugs must be made to understand the potential danger which they dispense at the same time. Those who use drugs as a means for their own gain should be held responsible for their acts, and controls should be instituted to make the acquisition of prescription drugs more difficult.

None of this is anymore intended as a wholesale condemnation of the medical profession than it is a condemnation of the behavior of Elvis Presley. Those who are, or who know, sincere dedicated physicians are aware of their concern for the health and well-being of their patients. The vast majority of doctors are honest and seek only to help those who call upon them for assistance. To believe otherwise is as absurd as feeling that Elvis Presley was less talented, or less good, or less lovable, or less generous because he was afflicted with the all too common disease of drug addiction.

Elvis would have been a greater man had he been able to come out and say, "I have a drug problem."

Elvis would have been a greater man had he been able to do that, but the fact that he could not, or did not, does not make him less than he was. Any who love him less for the knowledge they now have, loved him little to begin. To love a brother, a father, a son or a friend less because he is ill speaks little for the person with that feeling.

If Elvis Presley was one tenth the man that those who claim to love and know him say he was, there is not one single doubt possible that he would now want the young people, about whom he cared so much, to profit from the knowledge of his misfortune. If Elvis Presley were able to say, "Look what it did to me, don't let it happen to you," he would say it.

If a forthright, honest admission of the drug problem, by the friends who now hold back, would prevent just one young man or woman from following the same path, then their silence and denials do Elvis no favor. If only one out of the millions who thought he was the greatest understands that if this horror could happen to Elvis Presley, then how easily it can happen to them, then, in fact, they were right, he was the greatest.

Epilogue

The story is finished. Elvis Presley died on the red-carpeted bathroom floor of his Memphis mansion, Graceland, on the afternoon of August 16, 1977. Elvis Presley, the young man who began his career with the Beale Street sounds of Memphis, was an American phenomenon. Living a rags to riches life in the strictest sense of the words, Elvis achieved more recognition and fame than most popes, presidents and kings combined. His charisma far exceeded that of our greatest leaders.

Within the world of music, Elvis' success was so extraordinary that his nearest competitors come off as amateurs. For more than a score of years he remained at the summit of popularity and remains there today, more than a year after his death. Every record in the music industry collapsed before the onslaught of his drive to success.

Few men in history have known the love and devotion of so many people.

His friends and fans continue to mourn his death and his grace is visited daily by thousands of admirers, tourists and curiosity seekers. Over twenty books have been written about his life, and death, and his name continues to be big business. There is talk of Elvis clones, and at least one man has undergone plastic surgery to make himself look like Elvis. There are a dozen or so imitators who entertain in Elvis-like costumes in places ranging from the local barroom to plush Las Vegas hotels.

The hucksters sell Elvis mementoes as near the grave as they can, and a bizarre scheme to kidnap his body was uncovered shortly after his funeral. Elvis Presley was big business in life and continues to be big business in death. Hardly a month goes by that one magazine or another does not have a new story about Elvis. The weekly sensational newspapers report *facts* about drugs, firearms, secret love affairs and exclusive interviews with relatives and friends in almost every issue. Most of the stories begin with the pen of a writer who finds a ready market for his daydreams. It's easy to do. Just make up a story and print it. A large segment of the public generally believes what it reads in a newspaper, regardless of the quality of the paper, and celebrities and public officials learned long ago that a denial is usually not worth the effort.

The *National Enquirer,* one of those most guilty of scandalizing, carried an article in the August 22, 1978, edition headlined, "Exclusive: Secret Autopsy Report." The article tells of an exclusive bombshell interview with Maurice Elliott, official spokesman for Baptist Memorial Hospital, and quotes him as saying things which he flatly denied having said. The same article quotes Tennessee State Senator Jim White as saying, "Under Tennessee law an autopsy report is public record."

If the senator made such a statement he doesn't know Tennessee law, but it's very doubtful he said it in the first place. The same issue carries a photograph of Elvis in his coffin, a photograph made by a cousin, without the knowledge of the family, and sold to the *Enquirer* reportedly for five thousand dollars.

There is also an exclusive interview with Priscilla, in the same issue, in which she tells the *Enquirer* all the secrets of her life with Elvis. Priscilla denies that she ever gave the *Enquirer* an interview about anything. It's pure and simply a made-up story to sell newspapers. And it does sell newspapers.

Unfortunately, even the most respected publications seem to fall prey to the affliction of exaggeration and make-believe when their use may bolster an otherwise weak story. The Memphis, Tennessee *Commercial Appeal,* for example, published a story in their issue of July 14, 1978, which they picked up from the Associated Press who, in turn, were releasing a report which appeared in the *Washington Post.* The article quotes an FBI memo which was written on

December 31, 1970, by M. A. Jones of the FBI crime records division to Thomas E. Bishop, then assistant director of the FBI.

The *Commercial Appeal* article says the *Washington Post* said the Jones memo quoted Elvis Presley, during his visit to the Bureau, as blaming the Beatles' "filthy unkempt appearance and suggestive music" for many problems facing young people.

According to the story, the FBI official said Presley "advised that the Smothers Brothers, Jane Fonda and other persons in the entertainment industry will have a lot to answer for in the hereafter for the way they have poisoned young minds by disparaging the United States in public statements and unsavory activities."

Elvis' associates confirm the quotations as far as their being a true reflection of Elvis' sentiments, but the FBI memo by Jones simply says no such thing. The Jones to Bishop memo is, if anything, a classic example of bureaucratic waste where an FBI official writes a two-page document to a superior to convey the following message which is the next to last paragraph of the memo, "Presley's sincerity and good intentions notwithstanding he is certainly not the type of individual whom the Director would wish to meet. It is noted at the present time he is wearing his hair down to his shoulders and indulges in the wearing of all sorts of exotic dress. A photograph of Presley clipped from today's *Washington Post* is attached and indicates Presley's personal appearance and manner of dress."

Hopefully, Jones was more observant when dealing with criminals because while his observations about the exotic dress were correct, Elvis never wore "his hair down to his shoulders."

Jones' memo is an interesting commentary on the times. The President of the United States welcomed Elvis Presley to his office and, in fact, awarded Elvis a Federal Narcotics Bureau badge during his visit to Washington when Jones was trying to keep J. Edgar Hoover from meeting the entertainer because of his hair and dress.

When questioned about the apparent double standard which existed with Elvis' desire to become involved in the fight against drug abuse and his own use of drugs, Marty

Lacker says, "Elvis sincerely felt he was a special person. He could do things which were not right for others to do. I can't explain it but that's the way he was. It wasn't phony or insincere or anything like that, Elvis simply felt certain things which were right for other people just didn't apply to him. He was also very much opposed to hard drugs like heroin and he didn't even like marijuana.

"I remember a time when we were at the movies in Memphis and he handed me a piece of paper with three names on it and said, 'You know these guys?'

"I told him I thought I recognized the names as being those of three well-known Memphis drug pushers. He said that was right and he wanted to be the one to bust those guys. According to Elvis the authorities were trying to find them but had been unsuccessful. Elvis was really in a rage about it and wanted me to help him find those guys so he could be the one to arrest them.

"I didn't want to play policeman, especially with three potentially dangerous men and I didn't want Elvis to do it, but I had to tell him I would see if I could find out anything. He kept after me for months about it. Everyday when I saw him he would ask if I had found out anything and I would tell him that I hadn't yet, but I had some guys working on it. Thank God he finally quit asking and, I guess, forgot about them."

NBC recently televised a news program concerning fraud in the coal industry. One item on the program dealt with a twenty million dollar coal tax scheme in which Elvis Presley had invested $500,000. Elvis was apparently bilked out of his half million but according to the program he, along with the other investors, didn't suffer very much because they were taking advantage of a tax loophole which allowed them to take income tax deductions of up to five times the amount invested. In Elvis' case that amounted to a two-and-a-half million dollar tax deduction.

Assuming the news report was accurate it means Elvis made two decisions not too long before his death which were completely out of character for him. One, he was not an investor. The inventory of his assets after his death show a few shares of Del Webb stock as being his only investment. His associates assume the Del Webb stock was part of a payment agreement for a Las Vegas appearance since the Del Webb Corporation is highly invested in that city. Two, Elvis never tried to avoid paying taxes. He often talked with his friends about what America had done for him and how he felt proud of being able to pay a high income tax.

There is no reason to doubt the truth of the NBC report except the inventory of Elvis' assets does not include an investment in any coal operation. It is possible, of course, that Elvis disposed of his holding in the coal fields prior to his death.

The sorting of the truth from the fantasy is difficult. There are a lot of stories, and a lot of facts concerning the life and death of Elvis Presley. Reasonable conclusions can be reached when proper patience is exercised and sufficient time is spent reviewing the facts and the opinions. A certain amount of speculation may be in order when that speculation is based on known facts and known behavior patterns. To begin, there is the story as told by Sonny West, Red West and Dave Hebler in their book, *Elvis, What Happened.*

We know that certain facts are true. Sonny, Dave and Red were close to Elvis, and in a position to know what was happening. They had been fired, were in difficult financial positions and were somewhat bitter. Their story was told to a writer who worked for a weekly newspaper known for its sensationalism. The facts of the story are corroborated by others who were near Elvis, but some insist these facts were exaggerated in the book.

The conclusion which may logically be reached from the above is that the facts of the book are true, but the story is told in a way to make events more dramatic and sensational than they actually were.

A comment may be necessary to clarify this conclusion. A story can be told in a bitter or a tender manner. The bad can be emphasized and the good left out, or the good can be emphasized and the bad left out. The resulting story may be true in facts, but it is more a reflection of the author's own feelings than a well-balanced report of the events.

There is the press release as issued by Shelby County Medical Examiner, J. T. Francisco, and reports of opposing opinions by the Staff of Baptist Memorial Hospital to be considered.

The facts we know to be true are as follows: Doctor Francisco is a well-respected member of the medical community. There is not a shred of evidence to indicate he reported anything other than the truth.

The law forbids Baptist Memorial Hospital to release the autopsy report without the consent of the nearest relative. Ethics prevent the staff of the hospital from openly discussing the results. The autopsy report is in the possession of Vernon Presley and could be released by him.

The conclusion is that there was an honest difference of opinion between Doctor Francisco and some of the staff of Baptist Memorial Hospital. Forensic pathology and toxicology are probably not as exact a science as we sometimes believe.

There are too many reports of a difference of opinion between the Medical Examiner and Baptist Memorial Hospital for there to be no truth in them. Were the hospital staff in complete agreement with the report as written by Doctor Francisco, a public statement to that effect would have silenced the controversy. Such a statement of agreement would neither have violated the law or their code of ethics.

If the autopsy report stated unequivocally that drugs were not a contributing factor to death, and were not present beyond a therapeutic level, Vernon Presley would have no reason to keep secret the report.

The nature of the drugs under consideration is such that doses above therapeutic levels could have been taken regularly without being found, had they not been taken within the twelve to twenty-four hour period prior to death.

There are quite a few facts to be considered before any conclusion can be reached concerning the abuse of prescription drugs, and the use of illicit or hard drugs.

There are statements by at least ten people who were close to Elvis that drugs were being *abused*. Most of these people have nothing to gain from the disclosure. There are also statements by others that drugs were not being *used*, except those prescribed by Elvis' physician. The Medical Examiner's report should be considered.

The conclusion has to be that too many people confirm the abuse of prescription drugs not to believe it is true. Most of the drugs used were prescribed by his physician. Probably some cocaine was used, but to no great extent or it would have been evident during the autopsy.

The Medical Examiner's report does not state that drugs were never used, only that they were not found beyond therapeutic levels, and that they did not significantly contribute to death.

Part of the conclusion, then, must be that no hard, or illicit drugs were used except the possible occasional use of cocaine, but there was definite abuse of prescription drugs.

Some comments here may be in order. Learning can be painful. It often demands a cleansing of preconceived thoughts, a rejection of long believed truths and an opening of the mind to ideas new and different from what has been a closely-held part of our lives. Learning can be painful and the price of examples, from which we learn, is often high. No man's life has a greater intrinsic value than that of another, but some, because of wealth, talent, intelligence or even terror are better known, and by being better known are more readily visible as examples from which we may all learn.

Learning from the life and death of Elvis Presley was painful for his associates, and it may be painful for those millions of fans to whom Elvis was a very special person, but for the sake of his memory and the growth of all of us an effort should be made to learn and to understand. It is important for those who would follow in Elvis' footsteps to know that he was neither good nor bad because of drugs. Drugs made no difference whatsoever as far as his talent was concerned, and only affected his ability to perform when their excessive use began to interfere with his memory and coherency. There was never a time when Elvis was a better artist because of the drugs, and those closest to him tell of his greatest performances being executed when he was free of the drug interference. It would be easy for a young man or woman to believe that Elvis Presley became the great entertainer he was with the help of drugs, but the facts are just the opposite. Elvis became great before he ever heard of narcotics and certainly not because of them.

It is also important to understand that it makes not one bit of difference whether illicit drugs or prescription drugs were being used. To argue that Elvis Presley was any less addicted to drugs because he used Quaaludes for a fix, rather than cocaine or heroin, is the height of absurdity. It would make as much sense to argue that an alcoholic is less an alcoholic because he gets drunk from a high-priced Scotch rather than bathtub gin.

Like it or not, our society is drug-oriented. Cocaine is the new fad and considered to be the rich man's toy. Abuse of prescription drugs is far more prevalent than generally known and many members of the medical profession find it easier to give a patient what the patient wants rather than what he should have.

Drugs, including alcohol, are part of our way of life. The United States government reports that seven per cent of the population has an alcohol abuse problem. The cost to society is estimated to be forty-three billion dollars a year for the problems caused by the ten million or so who abuse alcohol. The figures are staggering both financially and in the number of people whose lives are affected. When we add to this information the number of people who have prescription drug problems, and those who have illicit drug problems, the numbers become almost beyond comprehension, but it is a very real part of our everyday life and a situation with which we as a society must someday come to terms.

Perhaps the most important thing which we must understand is the simple fact that Elvis Presley was not the culprit, he was the victim. To discuss the drugs, to try to learn how they affected Elvis Presley's life and to try to understand what they can do to any of us does not imply that Elvis was any less great because of their use. He was an uncommonly talented entertainer who won the love and respect of millions of people around the world. His fans should understand that his ability to remain at the summit of popularity even after having fallen prey to the all-too-common disease of drug abuse speaks highly for his skill as a performer.

The conclusion must be that an overdose of drugs was not the immediate cause of Elvis' death. Had Elvis taken an overdose and fallen dead as a result of so doing, the drugs would have been easily found during the autopsy. There is no question, however, among medical authorities that the use of drugs to the extent that Marty Lacker, for example, used them for a ten-year period, will eventually lead to severe bodily damage and death. The amount of time, the quantity of drugs, their interaction, and the general physical condition of the individual involved are factors which determine the period over which the drug abuse may be continued.

Drugs did contribute to Elvis Presley's death either by affecting his heart, if reports attributed to Baptist Memorial Hospital are believed, or, at the very least, by keeping him from being sufficiently concerned about his diet and general health.